T0281423

Two- and Three-Dimensional Patterns of the Face

Two- and Three-Dimensional Patterns of the Face

Peter W. Hallinan

Gaile G. Gordon

A. L. Yuille

Peter Giblin

David Mumford

CRC Press
Taylor & Francis Group
Boca Raton London New York

CRC Press is an imprint of the
Taylor & Francis Group, an **informa** business
AN A K PETERS BOOK

First published 1999 by A K Peters, Ltd.

Published 2019 by CRC Press
Taylor & Francis Group
6000 Broken Sound Parkway NW, Suite 300
Boca Raton, FL 33487-2742

© 1999 by Taylor & Francis Group, LLC
CRC Press is an imprint of Taylor & Francis Group, an Informa business

First issued in paperback 2019

No claim to original U.S. Government works

ISBN 13: 978-0-367-44758-8 (pbk)
ISBN 13: 978-1-56881-087-4 (hbk)

Visit the Taylor & Francis Web site at
http://www.taylorandfrancis.com

and the CRC Press Web site at
http://www.crcpress.com

Library of Congress Cataloging-in-Publication Data

Two-and three-dimensional patterns of the face / Peter W. Hallinan ...
    [et al.].
        p.   cm.
    Includes bibliographical references and index.
    ISBN 1-56881-087-3
    1. Human face recognition (Computer science)   2. Face-
    -Mathematical models.   3. Computer vision. 4.   Geometry,
    Differential.   I. Hallinan, Peter W.
    TA1650.T86   1998
    006.3'7--dc21
                                                    98-37189
                                                    CIP

Contents

Preface

One of the beautiful features of the fields of applied mathematics, applied statistics and engineering is that often very general theories and concepts take on a vivid and intriguing life when they are applied to a very specific and familiar example. This book deals with exactly such a case: the elucidation of the intricate and detailed patterns of the human face using the tools of 'pattern theory', of statistical pattern recognition and of differential geometry. From an engineer's perspective, the book deals with a specific topic in computer vision, the recognition of faces in general and of individual faces. This problem has been studied for some 25 years and has become a hot topic recently, as better hardware and better software have become available. From a statistician's perspective, we specifically approach this problem using Grenander's ideas, which he calls pattern theory, an adaptation of Bayesian statistical inference to the analysis of patterns and the inference of hidden structure in all kinds of signals and events encountered in daily life. From a mathematician's perspective, we find tools from probability theory, elasticity theory and, above all, differential geometry to be highly relevant. The thread that ties these together is the characterization of the patterns found in two-dimensional images of faces and in the three-dimensional surface formed by a face.

This book grew out of the work at the Harvard Robotics Laboratory in the early 1990s. At that time, Mumford and Yuille were on the Harvard faculty and Gordon and Hallinan were writing their Ph.D. theses on the three-dimensional structure of the face and stochastic models for two-dimensional images of faces respectively. Subsequently, the entire group dissolved, and almost all the work presented here was never published. We came together again in 1998 to pull this material together into a coherent whole, including providing substantial background material both in vision and in differential geometry. We were most fortunate to add Giblin to our team, as he and his colleagues in Liverpool had worked out all the necessary theoretical aspects of the differential geometry of surfaces in three space.

Our hope is that this book can serve multiple purposes. For the specialist in computer vision, we give fully worked out examples of two approaches to face recognition. For the statistician, we hope to make clear what is distinctive about pattern theory and how powerful a tool it is. For the mathematician, we hope to demonstrate the interesting new mathematics suggested by the face, in both its two- and three-dimensional aspects.

David Mumford
March, 1999

Chapter 1

Faces from a Pattern-Theoretic Perspective

1.1 Pattern Theory

The term "pattern theory" was introduced by Ulf Grenander in the 1970s (Grenander 76-81) as a name for a field of applied mathematics which gave a theoretical setting for a large number of related ideas, techniques and results from fields such as computer vision (D. Geman 90), speech recognition (Rabiner 90, 93), statistical pattern recognition (Ripley 96), neural nets (Hertz 91) and parts of artificial intelligence (Pearl 88).[1] As these research fields have grown explosively, it is helpful to understand the common themes which unite them. Pattern theory proposes that the types of stochastic models used in one field will crop up in all the others. The underlying idea is to find stochastic models which capture all the patterns which we see in nature, so that random samples from these models have the same 'look and feel' as the samples from the world itself. Then the detection of patterns in noisy and ambiguous samples can be achieved by the use of Bayes's rule, a method which can be described as 'analysis by synthesis'.

The manifesto of pattern theory may be laid out as follows:

- *A wide variety of signals result from observing the world, all of which show patterns of many kinds, caused by objects, processes and laws present in the world. These patterns can be used to infer information about these unobserved factors.*

- *Observations are affected by many variables which are not conveniently modeled deterministically because they are too complex or too difficult to observe. To make inferences in real time, we must model our observations partly stochastically and partly deterministically.*

---

[1] This Chapter is a revision of the senior author's 1992 address to the European Congress of Mathematics (Mumford 92).

- *Accurate stochastic models which capture the patterns present in the signal, while respecting the natural structures, i.e. symmetries, independencies of parts, marginals on key statistics, are needed. These models should be learned from the data and validated by sampling. Inferences from them can be made using Bayes's rule, provided that samples from the models resemble real signals.*

These patterns may occur in the signals generated by one of the basic animal senses. *Hearing* refers to the analysis of the patterns present in the oscillations of 60-20,000 hertz in air pressure at a point in space as a function of time, both with and without human language. It contains patterns in local periodicity coming from sustained musical notes and vowels, in the sequence of intervals with differing spectra, in the sentences which we infer from these, etc. *Vision* refers to the analysis of patterns detected in the electromagnetic signals of wavelengths 400-700 nm. striking a lens from different directions. It has similar patterns: local textures, decomposition of the image into visible surfaces of different objects, placement of these objects in the scene, etc. Other classes of patterns are present, not directly in the senses, but in more complex measurements made by instruments. For instance, point processes such as neuronal spike trains, or discrete strings such as DNA all contain both local patterns and a decomposition into parts. Patterns may occur in the data presented to the higher processing stage of cognitive thought. For example, *medical expert systems* are concerned with the analysis of the patterns in the symptoms, history and tests presented by a patient: this is a higher level modality, but still one in which the world generates confusing but structured data from which a doctor seeks to infer hidden processes and events. Finally, these patterns may be temporal patterns occurring in a sequence of *motor actions and the resulting sensations*, e.g., a sequence of complex signals 'move-feel-move-feel' involving motor commands and the resulting tactile and proprioceptive sensations in either an animal or a robot. On a higher cognitive level, we can analyze the patterns present in complex time series, e.g. climatological, demographic or financial, possibly with interleaved causative events.

In this book, we shall study the patterns present in the human face as manifested in two types of signal: in optical images resulting from the reflection of visible light off a face, and in range images resulting from describing the surface of the face as the graph of a function in some coordinate system. Optical images are studied in Chapters 2 through 5. In this case, we have a well-developed stochastic model to which the full machinery of pattern theory can be applied. In Chapter 5, we describe how well this model works in identifying individual faces. Range images are studied in Chapters 6 through 9, using a description of the face in cylindrical coordinates as $r = f(\theta, z)$. In contrast, this study is still in the stage of identifying the key features which create the characteristic pattern of the face in a way which is independent of the coordinate system. Our study will focus on the so-called ridge curves on the face, but will give the results of one study of face recognition using these tools. We believe that a good stochastic model for range images will require the use of a second tool: the medial axes/surfaces of a three-dimensional shape.

To do pattern theory properly, it is essential to identify the patterns present in the signal correctly. Although we often have an intuitive idea of what are the important patterns, the human brain does many things unconsciously and takes many short-cuts to get things done quickly. Thus a careful analysis of the data to see what it is telling us is preferable to slapping together an 'off the shelf' Gaussian or log-linear model. Remarkably, there are strong similarities between the models encountered in different modalities, hence it has been possible to codify, to some extent, a taxonomy of basic pattern-theoretic models. We will describe this in the next section. To apply such a model, we use Bayesian probability theory implemented in a feedback architecture to make perceptual inferences. These elements will be introduced in the following sections.

1.2   Three Universal Classes of Stochastic Models

The first element of pattern theory concerns the nature of the patterns which arise in perceptual signals. These are, in principle, the result of applying the deterministic laws of physics to a full description of the world. But in most cases, this is a totally impractical and unhelpful way of computing signals. The world is both too complex and too difficult to observe in full detail. What we need are stochastic models whose random variables include the observed signal and the most significant, immediately relevant unobserved variables. For instance, if we are dealing with a face, the observed variables would be the pixel values (colors or grey levels). Significant unobserved variables would include orientation and lighting on the face, the individual identity, and variables describing the type of face (gender, age, proportions of features, etc.) and expression. Examples of variables which affect the signal but might not be included are minor facial details, the word being pronounced if the person is speaking, the person's state of mind, the precise reflectance characteristics of the skin, or minor shadows cast by other objects on the face. All the above might have a major impact on the appearance of the face and might be needed in some cases to explain the observed pattern, but often are too difficult to work out precisely and are not needed by most observers.

In Grenander's language (Grenander 93), there is a standard signal, which he calls the 'pure image': this might be an archetypal face or perhaps a set of standard views of each person you know well. Then the other variables act on this pure image to 'deform' it, giving the observed signal. These deformations are random variables which must be modeled. We may think of the observed signal as a coded version of the pure image which reveals clearly the full state of the world. A basic hypothesis of pattern theory is that the world does not have an infinite repertoire of different tricks which it uses to disguise what is going on. Consider the coding schemes used by engineers for the transmission of electrical signals: they use a small number of well-defined transformations such as AM and FM encoding, pulse coding, etc., to convert information into a signal which can be efficiently communicated. Analogously, the world produces sound to be heard, light to be seen, surfaces to be felt, etc., which are all, in various ways, reflections of its structure. We may think of these signals as the productions of a particularly perverse engineer, who sets us the problem of decoding this message, e.g. of recognizing a friend's face or estimating the trajectory of oncoming traffic. Pattern theory contends that such signals are derived from the world by a small set of transformations or deformations, which occur again and again in different guises. The bad news is that these transformations, when occuring simultaneously, produce much more complex effects than the coding schemes of engineers, hence the difficulty of decoding them by the standard tricks of electrical engineering. The good news is that these transformations are not arbitrary recursive operations which produce unlearnable complexity.

A very similar situation occurs in the study of the syntax of languages. In the formal study of the learnability of the syntax of language, Gold's theorem gives strong restrictions on what languages can be learned if their syntax is at all general (see Osherson-Weinstein 84 for an excellent exposition). In fact, Chomsky (65) has suggested that all languages have essentially the same syntax, with individual languages differing only by a small number of parameters. His transformational grammar has a structure similar to pattern theory: each sentence has an underlying deep structure, analogous to Grenander's pure images. It is subjected to a restricted set of transformations, analogous to Grenander's deformations. And finally one observes the spoken surface form of the sentence, analogous to Grenander's deformed image.

To describe each of these transformations, we need to (i) describe the unobserved random variables which must be present; (ii) describe the relationship between the unobserved variables and the observed ones; and (iii) put a probability model on all these variables. We want to describe *three* fundamental classes of stochastic models of this type, all of which have unobserved and observed variables and which occur in almost every application. These are:

1. *Linear superposition.* Perhaps the most standard sort of model creates the observed signal from the linear superposition of fixed or learned basis functions. We assume the observed signal has values in a real vector space: $s : X \longrightarrow V$ and that it is expanded in terms of auxiliary functions $s_\alpha : X \longrightarrow V$ as:

$$s = \Sigma_\alpha c_\alpha s_\alpha.$$

   In vision, X is the set of pixels and, for a greylevel image, V is the set of real numbers. Here the coefficients $\{c_\alpha\}$ are random variables while the

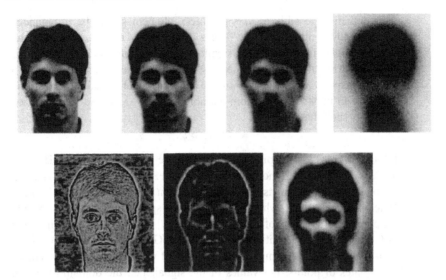

Figure 1.1. A face on four scales and the difference images. The original image (top-left) is the linear superposition of the three difference images (2nd row) and coarsest scale image (top-right). In this is an example each component carries different patterns: the overall shape of the face, the features and the precise edges and textures.

functions $\{s_\alpha\}$ may be either a universal basis like sines and cosines, or wavelets or some learned templates as in Karhunen-Loeve expansions. Or the $\{s_\alpha\}$ may be random: the simplest case is to allow one of them to be random and think of it as the residual, e.g., an additive noise term. The individual terms in the expansion of s correspond to looking at the signal at different scales and they may then all be random, i.e. simply be the components of s on scale α. See Figure 1.1 for an example where a face is expanded into three images representing its structure on fine, medium and coarse scales. Other variants are (i) AM modulation in which the low and high frequencies are combined by multiplication instead of addition; and (ii) the case where s is just a discrete sample from the full function $\Sigma c_\alpha s_\alpha$. Quite often, the goal of such an expansion from a statistical point of view is to make the coefficients $\{c_\alpha\}$ as independent as possible. In case the coefficients are Gaussian and independent, this is called PCA or a Karhunen-Loeve expansion; in the non-Gaussian but independent case, it is called ICA. We shall see how such expansions work very well to express the effects of lighting variation on face signals.

2. *Domain warping.* Two signals generated by the same object or event in different contexts typically differ because of expansions or contractions of

their domains, possibly at varying rates: phonemes may be pronounced faster or slower, the image of a face is distorted by varying expression and viewing angle. In speech, this is called 'time warping' and in vision, this is modeled by 'flexible templates'. Assume that the observed signal is a random map $s : X \longrightarrow V$ as above. Then our model includes the warping which is an unobserved random variable $\psi : X \longrightarrow X$ and a normalized signal s_0 such that:

$$s \approx s_0 \circ \psi.$$

In other words, the warping puts s in a more standard form s_0. Here s_0 might be a fixed (i.e., non-random) template, or might itself be random although one aspect of its variability has been eliminated by the warping. Note that in the case where X is a vector space, one can describe the warping ψ as a vector of displacements $\psi(\vec{x}) - \vec{x}$ of specific points, (as in Grenander's and Amit's work on hands (Grenander et al., 91), (Amit et al., 91)). But the components of this vector are numbers representing coordinates of points, not values of the signal, i.e., the domain of s, not the range of s as in the previous class of deformations. This is a frequent confusion in the literature. An example from the work of Amit just cited is given in Figure 1.2.

3. *Parsing the signal.* A fundamental fact about real world signals is that their statistics vary radically from point to point, i.e., they do not come from a so-called 'stationary process'. Instead, they result from the presence of multiple objects or processes which are combined in the observed signal. A central point is always to tease apart these pieces, so as to label explicitly the distinct parts present in the world. In speech, these distinct parts are the separate phonemes, words, phrases and sentences. In vision, they are the various objects present in the viewed scene. Note that in both cases, the objects or processes are usually embedded within each other, forming a hierarchy. The generic formalism for this is a grammar. Put in this general setting, if once again s is a map $X \longrightarrow V$, the basic unobserved random variable is a tree of subsets $X_a \subset X$ typically with labels l_a, such that for every node a with children b:

$$X_a = \bigcup_{a \to b} X_b.$$

Typically, the grammar also gives a stochastic model for an elementary signal $s_t : X_t \longrightarrow R$ for all leaves t of the tree and requires that $s|_{X_t} \approx s_t$. An example is given in Figure 1.3, for the parsing of a scene into overlapping parts. The most developed formalism for such grammars are the models called equivalently random branching processes or PCFG's

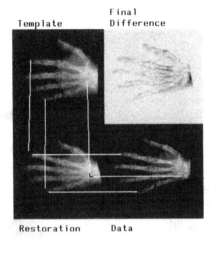

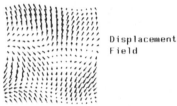

Figure 1.2. A particular X-ray of a hand is warped to the generic template X-ray of the hand. The warping vector field and the residual are shown (from Amit et al., 91).

(probabilistic context-free grammars). But most situations require context-sensitive grammars, i.e., the probability of a tree does not factor into terms, one for each node and its children. A parse tree of parts is natural for the face: the parts correspond to the usual facial features – the eyes, nose, mouth, ears, eyebrows, pupils and eyelids. However, we will not develop models of this type in this book.

Because all of the above models tend to coexist, the inference of the unobserved random variables in pattern theory becomes especially difficult. In fact, the full model of a signal may involve warping and superposition at many levels and a tree of parse trees may be needed to express the full hierarchy of parts. The world is not simple.

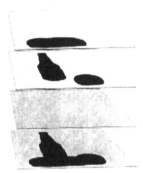

Figure 1.3. On the left, an image with three objects in front of a background cloth. On the right, this image 'parsed' into three distinct layers, with objects corresponding to the sets X_a in the text. (From Nitzberg et al., 93).

1.3   Bayes Probability Theory: Pattern Analysis and Pattern Synthesis

A second element of pattern theory is its use of Bayesian probability theory. An advantage of this Bayesian approach, compared with other vision theories, is that it separates the algorithms from the models. This also distinguishes pattern theory from neural network approaches such as multi-layer perceptrons (Hertz 91). From our perspective, these theories try to solve two difficult tasks — both modeling and computation — at once. In a Bayesian approach, as in Hidden Markov models and Bayes Nets, we first learn the models and verify them explicitly by stochastic sampling, and *then* determine algorithms for applying the models to practical problems. We believe that learning models and algorithms separately will lead to more tractable problems. Moreover, the explicit nature of the representations leads to a better understanding of the internal workings of an algorithm and its applications.

We now give a brief introduction to the techniques of Bayesian probability theory. In general, we wish to infer the state of the world **S** given some measurement **I**. Thus the variables **S** would correspond to the variables in our representations of the world, for example, the variables representing the shape of a face, while the measurement **I** would correspond to the observed images. Within the Bayesian framework, one infers **S** by considering $P(\mathbf{S} \mid \mathbf{I})$, the *a posteriori* probability of the state of world given the measurement. Note that by definition of conditional probabilities, we have

$$P(\mathbf{S} \mid \mathbf{I})P(\mathbf{I}) = P(\mathbf{S}, \mathbf{I}) = P(\mathbf{I} \mid \mathbf{S})P(\mathbf{S}).$$

Dividing by $P(\mathbf{I})$, we obtain Bayes' theorem

$$P(\mathbf{S} \mid \mathbf{I}) = \frac{P(\mathbf{I} \mid \mathbf{S})P(\mathbf{S})}{P(\mathbf{I})} = \frac{P(\mathbf{I} \mid \mathbf{S})P(\mathbf{S})}{\sum_{\mathbf{S}} P(\mathbf{I} \mid \mathbf{S})P(\mathbf{S})}. \qquad (1.1)$$

This simple theorem re-expresses $P(\mathbf{S} \mid \mathbf{I})$, the probability of the state given the measurement, in terms of $P(\mathbf{I} \mid \mathbf{S})$, the probability of observing the measurement given the state, and $P(\mathbf{S})$, the probability of the state. Each of the terms on the right-hand side (RHS) of the above equation has an intuitive interpretation.

The expression $P(\mathbf{I} \mid \mathbf{S})$, often termed the *likelihood function*, is a measure of how likely a measurement is given we know the state of the world. In this book, I is usually an image and this function is also called the *imaging model*. To see this, note that we are given the state of the world, e.g., the light sources, the objects, and the reflectance properties of the surfaces of the objects, then we can recreate, as an image, our particular view of the world. Yet, due to noise in our imaging system and imprecision of our models, this recreation will have an implicit degree of variability. Thus, $P(\mathbf{I} \mid \mathbf{S})$ probabilistically models this variability.

The expression $P(\mathbf{S})$, referred to as the *prior model*, models our prior knowledge about the world. In vision, one often says that the prior is necessary because the reconstruction of the 3-D world from a 2-D view is not "well-posed." A striking illustration is given by an image of a wire frame cube (called the Necker cube) as shown in the bottom right object of Figure 1.4. There are an infinite number of possible 3-D wire-frames which could produce this image such as the pyramid shaped wire frame on the left. But an observer only perceives one of the two cubes consistent with it (i.e., the object on the right or the result of reversing the internal vertices from front to back). Why is this so? In Bayesian terms, one explains this phenomenon by asserting that the prior probability for symmetric shapes such as cubes, which occur frequently in our world, is greater than for other irregular shapes. Thus, even though the values of the likelihood functions for a cube shaped wire-frame and an irregular shaped wire-frame may be equal, i.e., $P(I\mid$ cube-shaped wire-frame$) = P(I\mid$ irregular shaped wire-frame$)$, the prior term creates the observed bias toward cubes.

As with the Necker cube example, in general the image alone is not sufficient to determine the scene and, consequently, the choice of priors becomes critically important. They embody the knowledge of the patterns of the world that the visual system uses to make valid 3-D inferences. Some such assumptions have been proposed by workers in biological vision and include Gibson's *ecological constraints* and Marr's *natural constraints*. But more than general principles, we need probability models for all the important patterns of the world. It is

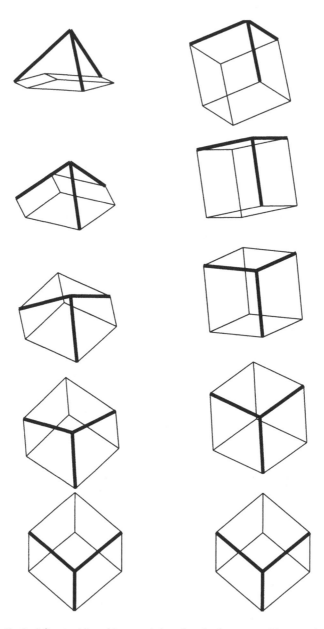

Figure 1.4. On the left, a tumbling object consisting of a wire frame pyramid over a planar hexagon; on the right, a similarly tumbling wire-frame cube. From one point of view they appear identical: but no observers of this common view would imagine they were seeing the pyramid wire-frame object.

becoming increasingly clear that fully non-parametric models need to be used to model virtually all non-trivial classes of patterns (as in Minimax Entropy learning theory (Zhu et al., 97)).

What can we do with a Bayesian model of the patterned signals in the world? On one hand, we can use it to perform probabilistic inference such as finding the most probable estimate of the state of the world contingent on having observed a particular signal. This is called the MAP or *maximum a posteriori* estimate of the state of the world. On the other hand, we can sample from the model, fixing some of the world variables **S**, and use this distribution to construct sample signals **I** generated by various classes of objects or events. A good test of whether the prior has captured all the patterns in some class of signals is to see if these samples are good imitations of life. From a pattern theory perspective, the analysis of the patterns in a signal and the synthesis of these signals are inseparable problems and use a common probabilistic model: computer vision should not be separated from computer graphics, nor speech recognition from speech generation.

It is helpful to consider the patterns in signals from the perspective of information theory (Cover-Thomas 91). This approach has its roots in work of Barlow (61) (see also Rissanen 89). The idea is that instead of writing out any particular perceptual signal **I** in raw form as a table of values, we seek a method of encoding **I** which minimizes its expected length in bits: we take advantage of the patterns possessed by most **I** to encode them in a compressed form. We consider coding schemes which involve choosing various auxiliary variables **S** and then encoding the particular **I** using these **S** (e.g., **S** might determine a specific typical signal I_S and we then need only to encode the deviation $I - I_S$). We write this:

$$\text{length}(\text{code}(\mathbf{I}, \mathbf{S})) = \text{length}(\text{code}(\mathbf{S})) + \text{length}(\text{code}(\mathbf{I} \text{ using } \mathbf{S})). \quad (1.2)$$

The mathematical problem, in the information theoretic setup, is, for a given **I**, to find the **S** leading to the shortest encoding of **I**, and moreover, to find the encoding *scheme* leading to the shortest expected coding of all **I**'s. This optimal choice of **S** is called the *minimum description length* or MDL estimate of **S**:

$$\text{MDL est. of } \mathbf{S} = \arg\min_{\mathbf{S}}[\text{length}(\text{code}(\mathbf{S})) + \text{length}(\text{code}(\mathbf{I} \text{ using } \mathbf{S}))]. \quad (1.3)$$

There is a close link between the Bayesian and the information-theoretic approaches which comes from Shannon's optimal coding theorem. This theorem states that given a class of signals **I**, the coding scheme for such signals for which a random signal has the smallest expected length satisfies:

$$\text{length}(\text{code}(\mathbf{I})) = -\log_2 p(\mathbf{I}) \quad (1.4)$$

(where fractional bit lengths are achieved by actually coding several **I**'s at once, and doing this the LHS gets asymptotically close to the RHS when longer and longer sequences of signals are encoded at once). We may apply Shannon's theorem both to encoding S and to encoding I, given S. For these encodings $\text{len}(\text{code}(S)) = -\log_2 p(S)$ and $\text{len}(\text{code}(I \text{ using } S)) = -\log_2 p(I|S)$. Therefore, taking $\log_2$ of equation (1.1), we get equation (1.4) and find that the most probable estimate of S is the same as the MDL estimate.

1.4 Pattern Theory Architectures

Finally, pattern theory also suggests a general framework for algorithms. Many of the early algorithms in pattern recognition were purely *bottom-up*. For example, one class of algorithms started with a signal, computed a vector of 'features', numerical quantities thought to be the essential attributes of the signal, and then compared these feature vectors with those expected for signals in various categories. This was used to classify images of alpha-numeric characters or phonemes. Such algorithms give no way of reversing the process, of generating typical signals. The problem these algorithms encountered was that they had no way of dealing with anything unexpected, such as a smudge on the paper partially obscuring a character, or a cough in the middle of speech. These algorithms did not say what signals were expected, only what distinguished typical signals in each category.

In contrast, a second class of algorithms works by actively reconstructing the signal being analyzed. In addition to the bottom-up stage, there is a *top-down* stage in which a signal with the detected properties is synthesized and compared to the present input signal (see Figure 1.5). What needs to be checked is whether the input signal agrees with the synthesized signal to within normal tolerances, or whether the residual is so great that the input has not been correctly or fully analyzed. This architecture is especially important for dealing with signals with parsed structure where one component of the signal partially obscures another. When this happens, the features of the two parts of the signal get confused. Only when the obscuring signal is explicitly labelled and removed, can the features of the background signal be computed. We may describe this top-down stage as 'pattern reconstruction' in distinction to the bottom-up purely pattern recognition stage.

This framework uses signal synthesis in an essential way and this requirement for feedback gives an intriguing relation to the known properties of mammalian cortical architecture (Mumford 91a). Note that, although stemming from similar ideas, 'analysis by synthesis' is logically separate from the Bayesian formulation and other aspects of pattern theory. Thus the Bayesian approach might be carried out with other algorithms and 'analysis by synthesis' might be used to implement other theories.

A variant of this architecture has been introduced in tracking algorithms (Isard-Blake 96) and is applicable whenever sources of information become available or are introduced in stages. Instead of seeking the most probable values of the world variables S in one step, suppose you *sample* from the posterior distribution

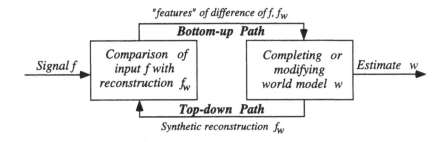

Figure 1.5. The fundamental feedback architecture of pattern theory.

$P(\mathbf{S}|\mathbf{I})$. The aim to sample sufficiently well so that no matter what later signal $\mathbf{I}'$ or later information on the world $\mathbf{S}'$ arrives, you can calculate an updated sample of $P(\mathbf{S}|\mathbf{I}, \mathbf{I}', \mathbf{S}')$ from the earlier sample.

1.5   And How About the Face?

The human face is a fascinating image, an endless inspiration for artists over thousands of years. Moreover, the ability to recognize faces and understand the emotions they convey is one of the most important human abilities. Babies can identify their mother's face within half an hour of birth, most of us are able to instantly recognize thousands of people, and it is claimed that Napoleon could recognize all the regular soldiers in his armies. A completely unscientific poll of various friends suggests that most people spend at least 50% of their waking moments with at least one face within their field of view.

As with many perceptual abilities, the ease with which humans can locate, recognize, and interpret faces disguises the difficulty of the problem. In fact, an important outcome of research on artificial vision systems has been an appreciation of the skill involved in performing these apparently simple tasks. This skill does not surprise biologists who have long known that over half of the cortex shows increased activity during visual processing (for monkeys, the proportion rises to sixty percent). It seems that the brain devotes more resources to vision than to apparently more demanding intellectual tasks such as pure mathematics.

Taking the perspective of pattern theory, the question is: can we describe accurately but stochastically the distinctive patterns of the face? Figure 1.6 shows four images represented in an unconventional way. Each of the four graphs shows an image I plotted as a landscape with intensity represented by height. Three of the plots are of a single person under different lighting conditions and expressions, while one is of a scene not containing a face. Though one plot is readily inter-

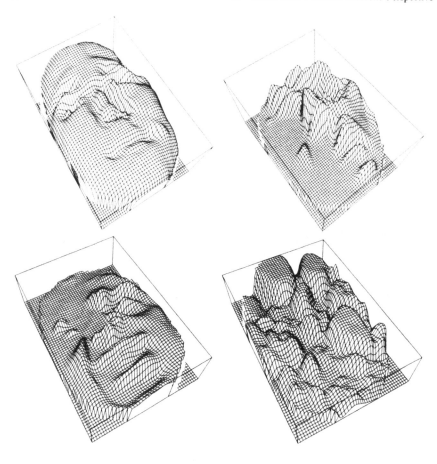

Figure 1.6. Four plots of images represented as the graphs $z = I(x, y)$ rather than by grey level intensity. One is a nonface image and three are images of the same person viewed when both lighting and expression are allowed to vary.

pretable, the others are much harder to decode. By contrast, Figure 1.7 shows the same images plotted using intensity. Although we can understand Figure 1.7 instantaneously (more precisely, within 150 milliseconds), this is merely because its representation allows us to summon the full power of the face recognition machinery of our visual cortex. Yet Figure 1.6 is a more realistic representation of the input to a vision system because it corresponds directly to the spatial pattern of light that reaches the receptors of a camera or an eye.

Another example, Figure 1.8, shows (on the left) two graphs of the light intensity $I(x, y)$ reflected by a human eye: it would be hard to recognize these as

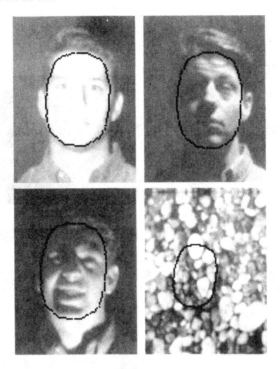

Figure 1.7. The same images as in the previous figure, now shown in the usual way as grey scale images. They are now readily interpretable by the reader's own vision system. Only the intensities lying within the dark boundaries were graphed.

eyes, but the black and white images defined by the same functions are shown on the right. How is it that we can look at these two eyes and see them as similar patterns? Note that from the point of view of overall brightness, they are different. The top eye is lit from the left, the bottom one from the right. Specular reflections occur at totally different places on the two eyes. Not only is the top eye bigger but its pupil is much bigger relative to the other parts of the eye. Finally the glasses and the specularity on them occlude the face, although blending in with the skin color at at least three spots.

How can we match these two images and find the common pattern? In terms of pattern theory, we have to compute all the deformations present and compensate for them. We can summarize the main ideas of the first part of this book by suggesting briefly the following answer: We need a warping ψ on the underlying domains; we need to label the part D of the domain where there is no occlusion or specularity; and we need basis functions ('eigeneyes') for the appearance of standard eyes lit from different places. Using all of this, we can say that an image

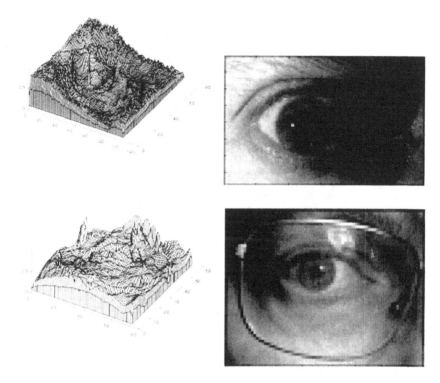

Figure 1.8. On the left are two graphs of spatial intensity patterns. On the right, we see that they correspond to the images of the same eye taken under different conditions. Observe how much the intensity patterns change simply by adding glasses and altering the lighting direction.

I represents an eye if:

$$I(x, y) \sim \sum_k c_k I_k(\psi(x, y)), \ \text{if} \ (x, y) \in D.$$

Here I_k are the 'eigeneyes', c_k are the lighting weights, D is the unoccluded, non-specular part of the image I and ψ is the warping. We also cannot say this makes the images identical: there is still variation of texture caused by hair, iris structure, skin blemishes, etc. Thus all of the deformations of pattern theory are strongly present. Excluding any of them would be dangerous.

Our final example is of the three-dimensional (3-D) geometry of a face. We have been discussing the two-dimensional (2-D) appearance of the face purely as a set of two-dimensional patterns. But, of course, the 2-D image results from the reflection of light off the surface of the face and we may seek to describe this surface directly. One line of research seeks to infer the 3-D structure of the face from one or more 2-D images of the same face. This is usually based upon the following approximation to the image intensity $I(x,y), (x,y) \in D$. Let $P(x,y) \in \mathbf{R}^3$ be the point in the surface of the face focused on (x,y), let $a(x,y)$ be the albedo of the face at $P(x,y)$, let $\mathbf{n}_{x,y}$ be the unit normal vector to the face at $P(x,y)$, let $C(x,y)$ be the set of unit vectors on rays joining $P(x,y)$ to a light source without being blocked by another part of the face or other object and let $s(\mathbf{u})$ be the brightness of the light source, if any, in direction $\mathbf{u}$. Then the brightness of the face at a point (x,y) is the sum of the light reflected off it from all sources. The simplest possible model expresses this in the formula:

$$I(x,y) \sim \int_{C(x,y)} s(\mathbf{u})a(x,y)\,(\mathbf{u}.\mathbf{n}_{x,y})\,d\mathbf{u}. \qquad (1.5)$$

Many papers have been written on approximately inverting this equation to find the 3-D structure of the face, given one or more images I.

Our concern in this book, however, is to study the 3-D patterns in the face, assuming its shape is known, e.g., by using a laser-range finder. Whereas with 2-D images, we sought to match intensities after warpings, a pure shape in 3-D has no obvious features and any head-like shape can be warped to any other or to the surface of a sphere. Moreover, although a surface can always be given, at least locally, as the graph of a function of two variables, this representation depends on choosing specific coordinates and the surface can be represented equally well in a wide variety of coordinate systems. The important patterns in such a shape should be things which are invariant under translation and rotation. Our approach is based on using the curvatures of the face to define its features and asking if these curvatures define the perceptually salient patterns that we see in faces. More specifically, the 3-D features which we are chiefly interested in are the parabolic lines and ridges.

It is easiest to explain these features by first considering the much more elementary case of shapes in the plane. The boundary of such a shape is a curve in the plane and it has three distinguished sets of points on it:

1. The points of inflection where the curvature is zero, hence it changes from convex to concave;

2. in the convex segments, points of locally maximum positive curvature, called convex vertices; and

3. in the concave segments, points of locally minimal negative curvature, called concave vertices.

If a curve is close to a polygon, we may expect one vertex as defined above near each vertex of the polygon, hence the reason for calling them vertices.

Figure 1.9. Attneave's cat, at left, is constructed by using straight line segments to join together the maximum curvature points of the silhouette of a real cat. Observe that Attneave's cat is easily recognizable but the maximum curvature points by themselves, on the right, are difficult to interpret.

Attneave (54) suggested, moreover, that many plane curves were well-approximated by the polygon obtained by joining their vertices with straight line segments. This is certainly true for his well-known cat (see Figure 1.9).

The right way to generalize this to surfaces in space is not obvious. We assume that the surface is closed or at least has an orientation, so one side can be designated as inside, the other as outside. Then the surface divides into three parts: the convex parts, the concave parts and the saddle-shaped parts. In differential geometric terms, these are the parts where both principal curvatures are positive, both negative or one of each sign. Separating these are the so-called parabolic curves, the analogs for surfaces of the points of inflection for curves. But what are the analogs for surfaces of the vertices of curves? If the surface is a polyhedron, it has 'edges', convex and concave, where two faces meet. We believe Koenderink was the first to propose a definition of curves on general surfaces which reduce to the edges for polyhedra. These are called *ridges*. The ridges which generalize the convex polyhedral edges are referred to as 'blue' (like the Blue Ridge Parkway) and the ridges which generalize the concave polyhedral edges as 'red' (like the Red River Valley). By definition, blue ridges are points where the larger of the two principal curvatures has a local maximum along its line of curvature. Similarly, red ridges are points where the smaller of the two principal curvatures has a minimum along its line of curvature. An example of the ridges on a face after some smoothing is shown in Figure 1.10.

In the second half of this book, we will study these ridges first in general and then specifically for the face. This theory is comparatively young and there is no stochastic theory yet. What we hope to make clear, however, is that the ridges do capture the basic patterns of the face in a way which is invariant under rotations

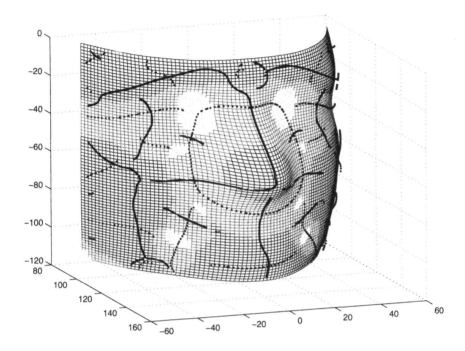

Figure 1.10. A 3-D view of a head after some smoothing, showing (i) its convex regions (dark mesh), saddle shaped regions (grey mesh) and concave regions (light mesh); and (ii) the ridges, blue ones solid, red ones dotted.

and can be used for face recognition based on 3-D data. We shall descibe briefly, in the last chapter, how we hope to build a structure including the ridges which is sufficiently rich to allow one to synthesize a shape using it. In the two-dimensional case, this has been made into a stochastic theory of shape (Zhu 99).

Chapter 2

Overview of Approaches to Face Recognition

2.1 Computer Vision Theories of Face Recognition

How do the concepts of pattern theory relate to existing computer vision theories of recognition? As we have seen, the image of an object depends on many imaging factors such as lighting conditions, viewpoint, geometric deformations of the object, albedo of the object, and whether it is partially occluded by other objects. In fact, one very careful study (Moses, Adini and Ullman 94) compared, using a number of different measures, the degree of variability of images of male faces (without glasses or beards and excluding hair) due to the three factors: (a) illumination, (b) viewpoint, and (c) different individuals. Their conclusion was that individual differences caused the least amount of change, viewpoint changes some 20% more, and illumination changes a whopping 150% more variability in the face image. Clearly, to recognize a particular face you must accomplish this in spite of a huge amount of variation from other factors. Existing theories of object recognition differ on how they deal with these factors. Do they follow the "analysis by synthesis approach" and invert the image formation process to determine what object(s) are most likely to have generated the image? How much use do they make of prior, or class specific, knowledge about particular objects? What types of transformations do they allow on the images?

The traditional approach to object recognition involves representing objects in terms of features. These features are extracted from the image and a decision function is then applied to classify them (Duda-Hart 73). This is the archetypal feed-forward architecture to which pattern theory is opposed, as discussed in Section 1.4. This school has been dominant historically and has been very popular in both computer vision (Grimson 90) and statistical pattern recognition (Ripley 96). Certain sophisticated versions of this approach (Lowe 85 and Ullman 96) however, use features extracted by low level processing to activate higher level hypotheses, such as explicit intensity models of objects, which are directly compared to the image. This final verification stage, by comparing object models to the input image, is similar to the synthesis strategy advocated by pattern theory. These techniques have been moderately successful when applied to man-made objects, e.g., printed words, tools, vehicles, buildings.

Can a feature-based theory be applied to faces? Let's look at the various classes of features that have been used in traditional object recognition:

1. One class of features which were popular early in the subject are global features. These are usually extracted by global filters applied either directly to the image (Fourier coefficients or moments) or to a thresholded image (so as to count the area or number of edge points). The problem with these features is their susceptibility to variations of illumination. At the least they require the object to have a planar face because curved faces will generate highly variable images as the light source varies. Even characters on a white page are notoriously hard to segment reliably because of slow intensity gradients of the white background across the page. (To convince yourself of this, take a digitized image of a white sheet of paper and examine the pixel values: unless you have a well-designed light table, you'll probably find that their values vary by more than 10% across the image.) Generally speaking, only man-made objects have planar faces. Thus these methods fail for faces.

2. To fight the variability due to illumination, researchers turned to edge-based features. Now 'edges' in an image, i.e., curves where there is an intensity discontinuity or high intensity gradient, arise from three main sources: (i) albedo discontinuities on the visible surface; (ii) '3-D edges' where the tangent plane to the surface is discontinuous; and (iii) object boundaries where a foreground object occludes the background as seen from the lens. Again, man-made objects are rich in 3-D edges which provide stable landmarks on their surface. These are weakly present on the face, in the sense that the nose ridge, brow ridge and chin are curves where the tangent plane to the face varies fast: but their location is not nearly as easy to extract from images. This will be a theme in the 3-D part of this book. The lesson is that there are only a small number of sharp edges in images of a face, mainly the albedo edges outlining the eyes, eyebrows and lips. Even these are easily obscured by lighting effects such as shadows. Most of the face has slowly varying intensity.

3. Even better than edges for object recognition are well-localized point features, e.g., corners on edges or 3-D vertices where more than two faces of an object meet. These are the bread and butter of most object recognition schemes, hence the intense focus on totally unnatural classes of objects

like oddly bent paperclips. There are a small number of consistent point features on the face, e.g., corners of the eyes and possibly the mouth.

4. Another class of features is based on using nearly parallel edges to locate cylindrical parts of the object. A large class of man-made objects have parts which are at least 'generalized cylinders' (cylinders which have been mildly deformed by twisting, turning, squeezing or changing their cross-section to something non-circular). The limbs of animal bodies are good examples. Sadly there are none on the face!

5. A final class of higher-level features has proved very useful in object recognition: bilateral or rotational symmetry of at least part of the object (cf. Mundy and Zisserman 92). Here is one 'feature' that the face shares with many man-made objects and which might even be significant in human ability to recognize faces seen at many angles. But note that even this is only approximately valid and deviations from bilateral symmetry of several percent are common.

It is clear from this discussion that the only reliable features on the face relate to the eyes, mouth, chin or ears. The importance of these was clear to the earliest workers (e.g., Goldstein-Harmon-Lesk 71). But detecting even these features in real images turned out to be a hard problem except under standard lighting and with fixed pose and expression. Otherwise the intensity patterns not only of the whole face but even of these features varies too much. A group at the Sarnoff Labs in Princeton under Peter Burt sought to develop a face recognition system in the late 80's for Nielson ratings: the aim was to mount TV cameras on the TV sets of their volunteers and count how many people were watching what as well as whether the TV was on. Their big problem was that faces varied too much in these typically bad lighting conditions and this product was not deployed. In our section below on facial features, we will illustrate some of the problems and outline one approach using deformable template models (Yuille, Hallinan and Cohen 88).

Assuming that some local features have been found, how does one proceed to check that these arise from a specific object? In the case of man-made objects a large body of work has been devoted to the special case of recognizing an object for which a geometrically precise model is given, e.g., an engine part machined to small tolerances. In this case, it is a tractable mathematical problem to check whether there is some imaging geometry under which the features of the known model in 3-D create the detected features in the 2-D image. Classical ideas from projective geometry such as cross-ratios are often helpful. Outside of a factory setting, however, such approaches are rarely applicable: the geometry of man-made objects such as cars or hammers varies over a wide range, just as the geometry of faces does. What we need to check is whether some 3-D model fits loosely and then the parameters of this loose fit can be used to seek the model of the car or the name of the person.

In 1973, two papers introduced techniques for matching images by stretching and shrinking their parts: Fischler and Elschlager (73) and Widrow (73). We believe these are the first places where the idea of a loose fit was explicitly introduced. Fischler and Elschlager described an elastic model of the frontal view of a face consisting of a set of local features joined together by springs to favour certain configurations. In their model the eyes, the mouth, the nose and the sides of the face were all explicitly represented and connected by these springs (see Figure 2.1 from their paper). This is an instance of a model incorporating what we called 'domain warping' in Chapter 1. These models in vision are called flexible or deformable templates. Note that Fischler and Elschlager's model does not explicitly introduce probabilities for various configurations: instead, they use a physical model with spring energy, so that more probable configurations correspond to lower energy and less probable ones to higher energy. One can create probabilities from energies by the Gibbsian formula $p(x) = \exp(-E(x))/Z$, where Z is just a normalizing constant.

Quite close to this was the work in Kanade's thesis (73) where he implemented a model that could extract local feature from faces, under controlled viewing conditions, and then used spatial relationships between the features to perform recognition. This thesis was arguably the first complete face recognition system which could take an image as input, extract features automatically, and classify the faces to reasonable accuracy. Kanade's model did not, however, consider the likely and unlikely values of these spatial relationships: instead, he used these relationships as higher order features. In this sense, he was not fitting a model by feedback, but extending the complexity of the features used in a purely feed-forward algorithm.

About this time, Haig (84) did psychophysical experiments in which he altered the relative positions of facial features. His results showed that observers were often extremely sensitive to the spatial relationships between these features. Small changes in the distance between the eyes, for example, were enough to affect recognition. This argues strongly that these spatial relationships are a large ingredient in human facial recognition ability.

Starting in the late eighties there has been an explosive growth in computer vision papers on face recognition. We will illustrate these schools by briefly reviewing in the rest of this Chapter some of the more influential computer vision theories of face recognition from a pattern theory perspective. There is no space here for an extended discussion and we refer the readers to some of the excellent review articles on the subject (e.g., Chellappa et al. 95 and Zhang et al. 97) which attempt comparisons between different algorithms. We should point out that it is always difficult to evaluate the relative success rates of the different face recognition algorithms. Small changes in implementation can sometimes greatly

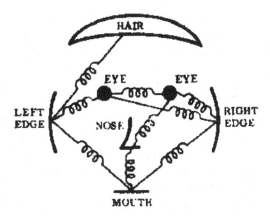

Figure 2.1. This figure from the paper of Fischler and Elschlager introduces a physical model with springs to match a standard face template with an observed face image.

affect the success rate of an algorithm. In addition, some algorithms perform best on certain data sets and under certain range of conditions. Mysteriously, even when the algorithms are implemented by their designers on ideal data sets with pre-specified evaluation criteria there are still conflicting reports about which algorithms performed best.

2.2 Facial Features via Filters

As we have seen, it is essential for face recognition to locate the features of the face — the eyes, lips, nose and ears. Two standard computer vision methods for this are: (i) apply a single matched filter and look for peaks in its response, or, (ii) apply a general purpose filterbank made up of Gabor filters or derivatives of Gaussians or other wavelets; the response of these filters to eyes, for instance, will cluster around a characteristic 'eye response', so that the vector of responses can be used as input into a statistical, or neural net, classifier.

In the case of a single matched filter, one creates an average eye image by normalizing many eyes with respect to size, orientation, mean and variance of their intensity. The resulting eye template $E(i, j)$, supported on a small set of 100 pixels (i, j) for example, can then be convolved with an unknown image at all scales and orientations:

$$r(T) \quad = \quad \sum_{i,j} I(T(i,j))E(i,j) \qquad (2.1)$$

Here the variable T is a composition of a translation, rotation and scaling. All local maxima of r define candidate eyes in the image.

In the second method, we choose a filterbank of filters $\{f_\mu(\vec{x}) : \mu = 1, ..., N\}$ which are tuned to different scales, directions, and possibly frequencies. These filters are convolved with the image to obtain a set of filtered images $\{F_\mu(\vec{x}) = f_\mu * I(\vec{x})\}$. At each point $\vec{x}$ in the image we have a vector $\vec{F}(\vec{x}) = (F_1(\vec{x}), ..., F_N(\vec{x}))$ of filter responses. These vectors of filter responses can then be matched to *prototype* responses $\vec{F}_{\text{eye}}$ for eyes (obtained by applying the filters to a set of sample eyes). One can, for example, define a test which specifies that there is an eye at position $\vec{x}$ provided $\left|\vec{F}_{\text{eye}} - \vec{F}(\vec{x})\right| < T$, where T is a threshold. More sophisticated criteria based on statistics can be used (see Ripley 96). Such approaches can function very quickly provided the number of filters is small, or if special purpose hardware is available to perform the convolutions.

Unfortunately, the performance of eye detectors of both types is rather disappointing. So far nobody has found the magical set of filters for which a simple test like this will work (except under controlled lighting situations). One can, of course (as in Perona 95), use tests of this type to determine possible candidate positions for eyes. This can be formulated probabilistically by defining probabilities $P_e(\vec{F}(\vec{x})|eye)$ and $P_{n-e}(\vec{F}(\vec{x})|no\ eye)$ which can be determined by statistics of training data. Bayes theorem can then be applied to determine $P(eye\ at\ \vec{x}|\vec{F}(\vec{x}))$. Candidates with high probabilities are then verified/rejected by the presence of other eye and mouth candidates in the appropriate spatial relationships (this uses prior knowledge about the likely geometical structure of the face, as in Fischler-Elschlager (73)). This approach has been used especially by von der Malsburg's group (see Section 2.5).

2.2.1   Logical-linear filters and AND/OR trees

A variant of this approach replaces the ordinary linear filter responses $F_k(\vec{x})$ by Boolean expressions in the signs of linear filter responses, i.e.,

$$P(\text{sign}(F_{k,1}(\vec{x})), \cdots, \text{sign}(F_{k,m}(\vec{x})).$$

These are called 'logical-linear' operators by Iverson and Zucker (95). Special local Boolean-valued filters of this type are used in a face recognition algorithm due to Y. Amit et al. (97), (98), which is very different from all other approaches. This algorithm addresses the detection of candidate faces in cluttered scenes (as opposed to registering a template with a face image or extracting features of identified faces), i.e., the initialization problem for what is done later in this book, and aims to be computationally efficient.

It is based on the statistical technique of decision trees (Breiman et al., 84). A standard decision tree is a binary tree with a Boolean test on the data assigned to each of its non-terminal nodes and an answer to the desired classification problem attached to each terminal node (or leaf). Then given some data, one starts at the root of the tree and proceeds down, applying each test that you come to and taking the left or right branch depending on the answer. When you reach a leaf of the tree, a decision is made using the label of that leaf. Their algorithm is a good bit more sophisticated in that multiple hierarchically arranged trees are used. Thus a single tree amounts to making an 'AND' of the Boolean tests encountered on going down the tree. Multiple trees can be combined and the classification results (assumed Boolean) ORed, giving an AND/OR tree. Secondly, instead of a simple test at a node of the tree, the test may refer to the outcome of an associated AND/OR tree attached to that node, making the whole structure hierarchical.

How does all of this apply to recognizing faces? First, the simplest trees in their structure are based on logical-linear tests of the form $|I(a) - I(b)| > |I(a) - I(c)|$, where a, b, c are pixels in a small neighborhood of each other. Small trees are built out of these, each using pixels from a single very small part of the image. These are *not* hand-constructed but are learned through training on discrimination tasks, and turn out to recognize local features such as edge fragments in a way which is robust to illumination changes. These are then combined in the next higher level of trees (again learned from data) which do an 'AND' on triples of such local features, but ones located further apart. A key point is that the exact location of the local features is not specified. Instead, the tree asks for the presence of these local features at some points with a rough geometric relationship, e.g., feature A above and to right of feature B. One can think of these higher order trees as being spiders, seeking to put down 3 legs on the right sort of structure and roughly in some pattern. These detect more complex local features, for instance eyes, etc. These are combined further in yet higher order trees to seek face-like structures suggested by an arrangement of these features on a reference grid. By an ingenious method of coding, the whole decision is made very efficiently and fast.

This is basically a feed-forward feature-based algorithm, although it can be followed by further processing in which you go back to the face candidates which have been identified and carry out more refined tests, registration of templates, etc. The key points are that it uses (i) logical-linear tests to resist the effects of variable illumination; and (ii) coarse geometric relationships to resist the effects of geometric warping. The authors report very good results on finding multiple faces in a cluttered scene. One way to understand this is that the various component tests are all trained by comparing their performance on faces to their performance on background, and these two classes of images seem to have very different statistics.

2.3 A Deformable Template Approach to Facial Features

An approach based on pattern theory was developed by two of the authors in the late 80's. By looking at eye images we see that the most salient intensity features are the dark central region surrounded by white blobs. Moreover, the geometry of these regions varies in a regular and systematic way for different examples of eyes (Yuille 88, Hallinan 91, Yuille et al. 91). We describe this in some detail.

2.3.1 The template geometry

We first describe the eye template geometry shown in Figure 2.2. It is represented by nine parameters $\vec{g} = (\vec{x}_t, \vec{x}_c, r, a, b, c, \theta)$. $\vec{x}_c$ and $\vec{x}_t$ correspond to the centers of the iris and the eye respectively. θ specifies the orientation of the eye and defines two directions $\vec{e}_1 = (\cos\theta, \sin\theta)$ and $\vec{e}_2 = (-\sin\theta, \cos\theta)$. The boundary of the eye is specified by two parabolas determined by the parameters a, b, c: they correspond to $\vec{x}(\alpha) = \vec{x}_t + \alpha\vec{e}_1 + \{a - \frac{a}{b^2}\alpha^2\}\vec{e}_2$ and $\vec{x}(\alpha) = \vec{x}_t + \alpha\vec{e}_1 - \{c - \frac{c}{b^2}\alpha^2\}\vec{e}_2$ for $-b \le \alpha \le b$.

Varying the parameters $\vec{g}$ will give rise to different eye configurations. Not all of them, however, are realistic. It was found empirically that the properties of realistic eyes could be approximated by a Gaussian model with

$$p(\vec{g}) = \frac{1}{Z} e^{\left(-k_1|\vec{x}+t-\vec{x}_c|^2 - k_2(b-2r)^2 - k_3\{(2c-a)^2 + (b-2a)^2\}\right)}. \qquad (2.2)$$

If we define the energy to be the negative logarithm of the probability, i.e., the expression in the exponent, then the smaller the energy of the configuration, the more realistic the eye. This prior model was adequate for the experiments reported in Yuille, Hallinan and Cohen 88 and Hallinan 91, but could be improved by more extensive training.

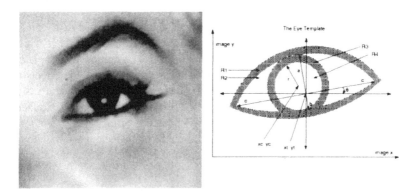

Figure 2.2. On the right is an "archetypal" eye. On the left is the human eye template as parameterized by $a, b, c, x_t, y_t, x_b, y_b, r_b, \theta$. R_1 and R_3 are edge regions bounding the whites and iris respectively. Intensity data within these regions is ignored. R_2 and R_4 are intensity regions containing the whites and center of the eye respectively. Both prefer the absence of edges. R_1 and R_2 are bounded by parabolic curves and R_3 and R_4 by circles.

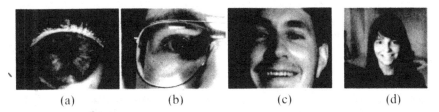

(a) (b) (c) (d)

Figure 2.3. The eye in image (a) would have to be smoothed before recognition could occur. Eyes in images (b) and (c) can be located by our system. Eyes in image (d) are at the minimal resolution required by the system.

2.3.2 The intensity model

We now consider the intensity patterns of the different regions of the eye. As described above, the most salient features are that the iris is an intensity valley and the whites of the eyes are intensity peaks. There will also tend to be intensity edges between the iris and the whites and at the boundaries of the eye. This is the basic pattern but it can have some significant exceptions. For example, there is often a specularity in the iris caused by the flash of the camera taking the photograph. The way we model the intensities must take into account such occurrences. Some of these variations may be described by standard additive white noise which can be filtered out by standard engineering techniques such as Wiener filters. But specularities in the iris are more difficult because their intensities are typically extremely different from those of the rest of the iris. They are better thought of as a superposition of a specularity signal on top of an iris signal. As we will show, one practical method for dealing with them involves robust statistics (Huber 81). We call these robust peak and valley detectors.

We illustrate this by a robust valley blob detector. The blob geometry is given in Figure 2.4 and is parameterized by location x, y and radius r. Since the surround of the blob could extend indefinitely, the outer radius is arbitrarily set to $2r$. For valley detectors, the region R_b preferring darker intensities is the center region R_2 and the region R_w preferring lighter intensities is region R_1. For peak detectors the pairing is reversed.

To define a robust measure of fit between the template and image data $I(x, y)$, let $\mu_{\alpha,i}, \sigma_{\alpha,i}^2, n_i$ be the α-trimmed mean, α-trimmed variance, and α-trimmed number of pixels in region i respectively. This means that we throw out a proportion α of the least well-fitting pixels (pixels in the region dark in the template which are brightest in I and pixels in the region light in the template which are darkest in I) and take the statistics on the remaining pixels. Let $\tilde{n}_i = n_i / \sum_j n_j$. Then the energy functional for a valley detector is given by a robust t-statistic:

$$E_V[\vec{g}; I(x, y), \alpha] = \frac{(\mu_{\alpha,b} - \mu_{\alpha,w})}{h + \gamma(\tilde{n}_w \sigma_{\alpha,w}^2 + \tilde{n}_b \sigma_{\alpha,b}^2)^{\frac{1}{2}}} \tag{2.3}$$

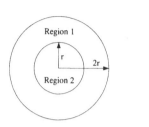
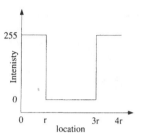

Figure 2.4. The blob geometry and a cross-section of the intensity model for an ideal valley.

where $\vec{g}$ is the parameter vector and h and γ are positive constants. The variance will not contribute significantly until γ is large, and letting $\gamma \to \infty$, we see that E_V solves a two-class, one feature discrimination problem in a way similar to that of Fisher's linear discriminant, which maximizes the ratio of between-class scatter to the within-class scatter. Thus E_V can be interpreted as favoring bimodality of the intensity histogram over the entire support of the template, or equivalently, unimodality within each disjoint region. The properties of E_V are that (i) it is bounded for all non-constant images I; and (ii) it is minimized by valleys and maximized by peaks (to obtain a detector minimized by peaks, just multiply the numerator by -1 and swap the assignments of R_w and R_b); and (iii) is invariant under linear transformations of I. If we define a probability distribution by $p(I) = \frac{1}{Z}e^{-E_V(I)}$, we get an improper probability on I but a well-defined exponential-like distibution on I after normalization of its mean and variance.

2.3.3   The Full Model

The full energy functional is the sum of data and prior terms,

$$E_{template}[\vec{g}] = E_{data}[\vec{g}] + E_{prior}[\vec{g}] \tag{2.4}$$

which correspond to log probabilities in a Bayesian interpretation. The data term is itself a sum of a region-based term and an edge-based term. The latter uses a field Φ_E gotten as follows: first threshold the gradient magnitude $||\nabla I||$ at the βth percentile of the histogram of $||\nabla I||$ over $\cup_{i=1}^{4}R_i$, where $\beta = \frac{n_1+n_3}{n_1+n_2+n_3+n_4}$ to get a set of strong edge pixels and then smooth (this is very important if the template doesn't fit precisely). The full data term is thus

$$E_{data}[\vec{g}; I(x,y), \Phi_E, \alpha] = k_1 \frac{(\mu_{\alpha,b} - \mu_{\alpha,w})}{h + \gamma(\tilde{n}_w \sigma_{\alpha,w}^2 + \tilde{n}_b \sigma_{\alpha,b}^2)^{\frac{1}{2}}}$$

$$+ k_2 \frac{(\mu_3^\alpha + \mu_5^\alpha) - (\mu_2^\alpha + \mu_4^\alpha)}{\sum_{i=2}^{5} \mu_i^\alpha} \tag{2.5}$$

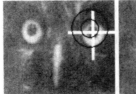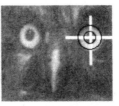

Figure 2.5. The valley template run on an owl's eye occluded by two bars. Left, the starting position of the template. Middle, the final fit when no trimming is performed. Right, the final fit when $\alpha = 49$. Note that the large size of the occluder, and its different intensity properties from the valley, require a large amount of trimming.

$h, \tilde{n}_i, \mu_{\alpha,i}, \sigma^2_{\alpha,i}$ are defined as in the blob template and μ_i^α is the α-trimmed mean of Φ_E over R_i. Again, the pixels trimmed depending on whether the intensity or edge strength is intended to be high or low. The intensity term has the familiar structure from before, while the edge term is even simpler—just desiring the mean edge strength to be highest in the edgy regions R_2 and R_4.

For precise details of the algorithm, see Hallinan (91). Overall performance is good (see table), and the approach is very robust. It can, for example, be used to detect an owl's eye even when there is a significant occluder (see Figure 2.5).

Deformable templates of this type, or the closely related deformable models based on snakes, are very suitable for tracking. A real time tracker is initialized by setting the deformable templates parameters to specific values. As the image sequence arrives it suffices to update these parameters. There are now a number of sophisticated tracking devices for eye and lips, such as Bregler (95) which learns the geometrical configurations from training data and is used to lipread mouths.

2.4 Gaussian Models of Whole Faces

The simplest approach to modeling the statistics of any class of real valued signals is to use a Gaussian approximation. To be precise, suppose $\{\vec{x}_\alpha\}$ is a set of data points in $\mathbf{R}^n$. Then one can form the mean and covariance matrix of this sample and there is a unique Gaussian distribution on $\mathbf{R}^n$ with the same mean and covariance matrix. If one diagonalizes the covariance matrix, the resulting basis is called the Karhunen-Loeve basis for this set of signals. In particular, images I are vectors of intensity values, i.e., we have one coordinate for each pixel and form the vector $\vec{I} = (I(1, 1), \cdots, I(N, M)$.

Sirovich and Kirby (87) were the first people who applied this direct approach to faces. For this to make any sense, we need all our faces to have the same number of pixels. The natural idea is to translate, rotate (if needed) and scale all our face images to standard size. It is often more natural to put the eyes and mouth in fixed positions and to crop the hair (which is very variable) by restricting the image to some oval. Notice, however, that because of the variety of face shapes there is no guarantee that simple affine warping will be able to align the physical features of the face sufficiently accurately (imagine trying to scale Mike Tyson's face to allign it with Kim Bassinger's). The standard face images might live in an ellipse included in a 90×50 rectangle (as in the Sirovich study), creating an image vector in about 3,500 dimensional space. The set of possible patterns in this space is immense and hard to grasp.

Given a set of images $\mathbf{I}(x)_\mu : \mu \in \Omega$, we first subtract the mean image $\bar{\mathbf{I}}(x) = (1/|\Omega|) \sum_{\mu \in \Omega} \mathbf{I}(x)_\mu$. Then we compute the covariance matrix:

$$\mathbf{K} = \frac{1}{|\Omega|} \sum_{\mu=1}^{|\Omega|} (\mathbf{I}_\mu - \bar{\mathbf{I}})(\mathbf{I}_\mu - \bar{\mathbf{I}})^T \qquad (2.6)$$

We can compute the eigenvectors $\mathbf{e}$ and eigenvalues λ of $\mathbf{K}$. Any image can then be expressed as an expansion:

$$\mathbf{I}(x) = \bar{\mathbf{I}}(x) + \sum_{i=1}^{N} \{(\mathbf{I} - \bar{\mathbf{I}}) \cdot \mathbf{e}_i\} \mathbf{e}_i(x) \qquad (2.7)$$

where N is the number of eigenvectors in the representation, i.e. the minimum of the number of pixels and the number of samples. In many cases, however, this expansion can be truncated at some smaller N by omitting the eignenvectors with small eigenvalues. Kirby and Sirovich demonstrated that only a limited number of eigenvectors were needed to achieve good reconstruction. In fact, using only 50 terms, their face images were reconstructed with a 3.6% mean square error. It is interesting to compare this with a related approach using neural networks. Cottrell and Fleming (90) used an autoassociative net to extract nonlinear features for representing and classifying faces (in such a net, the data is squeezed through a small number of hidden units and the receptive fields of these hidden units determine the non-linear features.)

In order to appreciate the strengths and weaknesses of using principal component analysis (PCA) for images, it is useful to look at a toy example used in Mumford (91b) in a commentary on Turk and Pentland's paper (91) on this method. Imagine that we are dealing with images of a single gray dot on a uniform black background. If we pixelize the image into N pixels, hence representing the image by a vector $\vec{I} = (I(1), \cdots, I(N))$, then the sample images of this elementary object will be just a positive constant times a delta function $a\delta_k = (0, \cdots, 0, a, 0, \cdots, 0)$, where the a is in the kth slot. We assume that all values of k are equally likely and that the grey value a has an arbitrary distribution. Then it is easy to see that the covariance matrix C of the components of the signal $\vec{I}$ is just $C_{i,j} = \lambda + \mu \delta_{i,j}$ for some λ and μ. It follows that $(1, \cdots, 1)$

is one eigenvector corresponding to the mean intensity, and the entire orthogonal complement of vectors $\vec{x}$ with $\Sigma_k x_k = 0$ is an eigenspace with a single eigenvalue. In other words, except for the mean gray level, the PCA tells us *nothing* about the pattern of the signal, e.g., it does not tell us that it is always localized. (If one allows the dot to fall between pixels, then one will have signals $(0, \cdots, 0, s, t, 0, \cdots, 0)$ where $s, t > 0$ and the PCA will be almost the same—all eigenvalues in the subspace of zero sum signals will be nearly equal.) What does this tell us? It says clearly that deformations which are represented by warpings, or by flexible templates are not captured at all well by Gaussian models applied to the signal vector. Some aspects of the variation may be well captured, as we will see below, but warpings, esp. large scale warpings, are not.

The principal component approach to face recognition was further developed in a series of papers by Turk and Pentland (cf. Turk and Pentland 91, Turk 91). Perhaps the most successful adaption of these ideas is the method called *appearance based models* due to Murase and Nayar (Murase and Nayar 95). They argue that even if projecting images onto a low dimensional eigenspace has substantial error, this projection can be very informative for object recognition by avoiding the 'curse of dimensionality'. Thus if one has a moderate sized data set, e.g., a few thousands of images, these are hopelessly sparse in 10,000-dimensional space. But if one projects them to a 20-dimensional eigenspace, it is quite possible to see their full 'shape' and, for instance, interpolate them with splines into a non-linear submanifold which describes their distribution closely. Note that in the presence of many sharp well-localized features with variable proportions, the error in the projection will become large and these methods will be less reliable exactly when the more traditional feature-based methods of Section 2.1 become more reliable. It was appreciated that the alignment of faces was critically important and that it was necessary, for example, to get features such as the eyes and mouths to allign correctly. This typically required geometrically scaling the image by an affine transformation. The authors claimed high accuracy results on large databases for these techniques though it has also been reported that this approach breaks down under illumination variations different from those used to construct the eigenvectors (Zhang et al. 97).

It can also be argued (Belhumeur et al. 96, Etemad and Chellappa 97) that if the goal is discrimination between objects, rather than representation, then better linear filters can be used based on Fisher's linear discriminant. PCA projects into the subspace which captures the most overall variance. By contrast, Fisher's linear discriminant (Fisher 36) projects into the subspace which maximizes the variation between different classes of objects while minimizing the variation between different objects in the same class. This can be illustrated by considering applying both techniques to a set of faces in which a small subclass of people have glasses. The PCA approach would tend to project onto a subspace which ignores the glasses (because they appear in too few samples to significantly affect the variance). By contrast, Fisher's linear discriminant would project into a subspace which included the glasses because they would be powerful cues for distinguishing between people (see Belhumeur et al. 96 for detailed comparisons between Fisher and PCA for face discrimination). PCA, FisherFaces, and their neural network variants can be thought of as extracting global features from faces. The face can then be represented by the projection onto these features. The resulting features, however, rarely have simple interpretations, though it is interesting to observe in Fisherfaces how the features tend to pick up aspects of faces which are relatively invariant to lighting changes (Belhumeur et al. 96).

2.4.1 Lighting Variations and PCA

One aspect of the physics of images which is accurately modeled by linear super-position is lighting variation. If the geometry of the objects in a scene and of the camera are held fixed but the light sources are varied, the resulting set of images are all linear superpositions of the images resulting from single point sources. This is the basic idea behind ray tracing: the image which one records at each pixel comes from light rays which have bounced back and forth some number of times and ultimately came from a light source in the scene. When two light sources are present, they create an image which is the sum of the images created by each light source acting alone. This is true even if the objects cast shadows and reflect on each other. The story gets even simpler if we ignore shadows and mutual reflectance and assume that each body reflects light according to the Lambertian Law. This law says that the brightness of a surface is independent of viewpoint and, for each light source, this brightness is given by the product of the surface albedo, the cosine of the angle between the surface normal and the light source and the strength of the light source. The result is the equation (1.5) in Section 1.5. The link with PCA is given if we rewrite this equation:

$$I(x,y) \quad \sim \quad \left(\int_{\mathbf{R}^2} s(\mathbf{u})\mathbf{u}d\mathbf{u} \right) . (a(x,y)\mathbf{n}_{x,y}) \tag{2.8}$$

$$-\int_{\mathbf{R}^2-C(x,y)} s(\mathbf{u})a(x,y)\left(\mathbf{u}.\mathbf{n}_{x,y}\right)d\mathbf{u} \tag{2.9}$$

If most light sources fall within the visibility come $C(x,y)$ of most surface points, then the second term in the above equation will be relatively small and the first term will dominate. This means that the image satisfies:

$$I(x,y) \quad \sim \quad a(x,y)\bar{\mathbf{s}}.\mathbf{n}_{x,y} \tag{2.10}$$

where

$$\bar{\mathbf{s}} \quad = \quad \left(\int_{\mathbf{R}^2} s(\mathbf{u})\mathbf{u}d\mathbf{u} \right) \tag{2.11}$$

Thus, as the lighting varies, the resulting I's will all be very nearly in the three-dimensional subspace spanned by the three components of $\mathbf{n}$:

$$I^{(k)}(x,y) \;=\; a(x,y)\mathbf{n}^{(k)}_{x,y}, \qquad k = 1,2,3 \qquad (2.12)$$

What this means is that the eigenobject approach is very good at capturing in a low-dimensional approximation the variation due to lighting; but it does not lead in any obvious way to a method for removing the variation due to lighting. Thus, if you are seeking invariants which distinguish objects, eigenobjects are not easy to use; but if you follow a pattern theory approach and want to explicitly describe image variability, eigenobjects are very effective for variability due to illumination. From the standpoint of pattern theory, eigenfaces are prime candidates for synthesizing faces under complex illumination conditions. As we will describe in a later chapter, we have performed extensive studies of face images taken under a range of lighting conditions. These results show that while there is an enormous variation in facial appearance, it can also be modelled by a low dimensional linear model. Moreover, the dimensions of the model are roughly in agreement with those that a simple Lambertian model would predict.

2.5 Face Warps

The PCA approach ideally would assume that face images can be aligned pixel by pixel by performing an affine transformation. Given the enormous variety of human faces this can only be considered a first order approximation. In addition, the patterns of face images often change geometrically as the facial expression changes or as the viewpoint changes. So it is important to model as explicit random variables the spatial warps present in the 2-D image. The model must be "elastic" to allow for these variations. A variety of systems (starting from Fischler and Elschlager 73) have allowed spatial warping of isolated features. To the best of our knowledge, after a gap of 8 years, this work was next developed by (a) Burr (81), (b) in a PhD thesis under R.Bajcsy (Broit 81), and (c) from a biological perspective by von der Malsburg (81).

The work in Bajcsy's school introduced the explicit use of elasticity theory (see Chapter 4 below for details) and a cost functional based on the strain energy. After Broit (81), these ideas were applied by Bajcsy's school to two and three dimensional medical images, matching CT scans against templates (Bajcsy et al. 83, Schwartz and Bajcsy 85, and Bajcsy and Kovacic 89).

We will describe at some length the work of von der Malsburg and his school, which has been pursuing this approach since 1981. Their research was not originally motivated by the engineering challenge of recognizing faces, but by modeling how neurons can carry out the sort of computations needed for perception and cognition. Von der Malsburg's theory, originally published in a preprint (von der

Malsburg 81),[1] was that the brain must use *dynamic links*, in the form either of precise spike timing or fast modifications of synaptic weights, to represent some aspects of thought such as the warpings and the parse tree which we discussed in Chapter 1.2. In particular, warping variables are interpreted as a set of dynamic links between two arrays of neurons. The application to shape recognition was developed by his collaborators, Bienenstock and Doursat (89, 91, 94). Like Broit (81), they used a quadratic elasticity-based energy expression expressing the strain in a match $\vec{\phi} : S \rightarrow S$:

$$E(\vec{\phi}) \quad = \quad \iint_S ||J(\vec{\phi}(\vec{x})) - I_2||^2 dx_1 dx_2 \tag{2.13}$$

where $J(\vec{\phi})$ is the 2×2 Jacobian matrix of the map $\vec{\phi}$. In discrete form, this energy is:

$$E(\vec{\phi}) \quad = \quad \Sigma_{i_1, i_2} ||(\vec{\phi}(i_1) - \vec{\phi}(i_2)) - (i_1 - i_2)||^2 \tag{2.14}$$

where the sum ranges over adjacent pixels (i_1, i_2). This can be viewed as defining a generic Gaussian prior on warpings $\vec{\phi}$.

This line of research was further developed in Lades et al. (93) which explicitly addresses the general problem of object recognition using their techniques. To mitigate the problem of image variation due to changes in illumination, they replace the grey-scale image I by a a vector valued image obtained by applying a local filter bank of responses as in Section 2.2. Roughly speaking, these responses are smoothed directional derivatives of the image at different orientations and scales and describe the local 'edginess' of the image. Gabor filters are chosen because of their well known ability to give rich local representations of images, but other filters are believed to work equally well. This gives a feature vector representation $\{\vec{I^i} : i = 1, ..., N\}$ of the original grey-scale image I. Because of the properties of Gabor filters, the feature vector representation has some degree of invariance to illumination changes. N is 40 in one of their implementations.

When two images I_1 and I_2 are input, dynamic link matching seeks a mapping $\vec{\phi}$ between the pixels in the two images which minimizes both the amount of warping and the difference between the two feature vector images. This is done by minimizing an energy which is a weighted sum:

$$\lambda \iint ||J(\vec{\phi}(\vec{x})) - I_2||^2 dx_1 dx_2 - \iint \frac{\vec{I_1}(\vec{\phi}(\vec{x})) \cdot \vec{I_2}(\vec{x})}{||\vec{I_1}(\vec{\phi}(\vec{x}))|| \cdot ||\vec{I_2}(\vec{x})||} dx_1 dx_2$$

These ideas were applied specifically to faces by Wiskott (95). See also Buhmann et al. (89). The approach is reported to be very effective and able to deal with some lighting variations and geometric deformations.

---

[1] Widely circulated by Samizdat and eventually made publicly available in von der Malsburg (94)

2.5.1   Generic priors on the warping

Bajcsy and von der Malsburg's groups proposed the use of a general warping defined on a dense set of points in the image domain, and a quadratic energy functional to evaluate how well the warp satisfies all the constraints. However, they did not introduce explicitly a probabilistic model or a Bayesian framework. This interpretation was introduced independently by Grenander and his school in Amit, Grenander & Piccioni (91) and by Durbin, Szeliski and Yuille (89). In the paper by Amit et al., they introduce a Gaussian prior on the space of continuous maps $\vec{\phi}$ from the unit square in $\mathbf{R}^2$ to itself, and assume that the measured image I is given by the sum of a deformed template image $I_T \circ \vec{\phi}$ and white noise. They then pose the problem of finding the most probable $\vec{\phi}$ if an image I has been observed. Like Bajcsy, they used medical images rather than faces, esp. X-ray images of hands, where variation due to illumination does not exist (cf. Figure 1.2). In terms of log probabilities, this is almost the same as the problem posed above and works out to correspond to minimizing:

$$\lambda \iint ||\triangle I||^2 dx_1 dx_2 + \iint (I - I(\vec{\phi}))^2 dx_1 dx_2$$

Note that the first term now involves second derivatives, not first: this has the effect that samples from this distribution are almost surely continuous. These ideas were developed in Amit (94) using a wavelet expansion of the deformation $\vec{\phi}$, and in Dupuis, Grenander and Miller (98) where the constraint is added that $\vec{\phi}$ should be a homeomorphism, i.e., injective. A recent survey of the work of this school is contained in Miller et al. (97).

2.5.2   Specific priors on face warpings

All of the above work has used generic priors or penalty terms on the warping which do not take into account the application domain. It is clear that these priors will not reproduce the true distribution of warps in any particular case, but that the correct prior should be learned from data. The first work in this direction seems to be that of the group of Cootes and Taylor (Cootes and Taylor 92, Cootes et al. 93). Their approach was to model the face with a small number of polygonal curves on which they were able to find a substantial number of fairly well-defined feature points P_k: 169 in one implementation. They were energetic enough to locate these points by hand on a database of faces: call these $P_k^{(f)}$ on the fth face. This gives them the 'correct' homeomorphism ϕ between any pair of these faces, at least on the 169 points, but one can interpolate to an everywhere defined ϕ. They can then compute the mean configuration of points $\bar{P}_k = \frac{1}{N} \Sigma_f P_k^{(f)}$ over all N faces: this describes their mean face. And they compute the covariance matrix for this configuration of points (considered as a vector in $\mathbf{R}^{2*169}$). They use these to define a Gaussian model on the set of all face-like configurations $\{P_k : k = 1, ..169\}$ which makes explicit the most common ways in which faces vary and the ways the individual points covary as a face changes. If we use PCA and diagonalize the covariance matrix, then we get an expansion:

$$P_k = \bar{P}_k + \Sigma_\ell c_\ell Q_k^\ell \qquad (2.15)$$

where the coefficients c_ℓ are independent with variances σ_ℓ given by the eigenvalues of the covariance matrix. In particular, most of these coefficients are very likely small and we can truncate this expansion to a small number of terms, e.g., 40, and find that almost all faces can be written as above with a small number of c's.

An equivalent way of expressing this is to define the warp $\vec{\phi}^{(f)}$ from the mean face to the fth face by:

$$\vec{\phi}^{(f)}(\bar{P}_k) = P_k^{(f)} \qquad (2.16)$$

on the basic points, and linearly interpolated via a triangulation on the rest of the face if desired. Then the Gaussian model above defines a probability distribution on set of all possible ϕ:

$$\vec{\phi}(\vec{x}) = \vec{x} + \Sigma_\ell c_\ell \vec{\psi}_\ell(\vec{x}) \qquad (2.17)$$

where $\vec{\psi}_\ell$ is the linear interpolation of the map which takes $\bar{P}_k$ to Q_k^ℓ. The $\vec{\psi}_\ell$ with the largest eigenvalues determine the directions of maximal variation of facial geometry, just as with eigenfaces. We can call these *eigenwarps*. It is important to realize that this is a totally different PCA however from that used in the theory of 'eigenfaces'. In the calculation done by Sirovich and Kirby, they write a general face *image I* as a sum of eigenfaces; here they write a general face *warp ϕ* as a sum of eigenwarps. The numbers now are coordinates, not intensity values. This is a powerful tool in determining the probable face configurations and dependencies between different variations in geometry. It has been followed up extensively, e.g. in analyzing the changes in facial expression.

We can now place the research in the 2-D section of this book in context. Based on the research of the first author (Hallinan 94, 95), it puts together the ideas of eigenfaces with warpings, based on the idea that illumination changes are well captured by very small eigenface expansions (e.g., with 5 terms), but that variation due to viewpoint change, expression change and differing facial types are best expressed by warping. As we will see below, we believe that combining these two gives a remarkably accurate generative model for 2-D images of faces. The first paper, to our knowledge, in which these were combined is Choi et al. (90) and the same approach has been developed by Poggio and his collaborators (Beymer and Poggio 96, Jones and Poggio 98). This work is closely related to the work of their group on the issue of 2-D vs. 3-D object recognition strategies to be discussed in Section 2.6.

Finally, we briefly mention another use of facial warping for the problem of face interpretation. The task here is to track the facial features and identify expressions. A variety of approaches are promising. For example, Hager and Belhumeur (96) have succesfully tracked faces by representing the face by its intensity image and allowing for small spatial deformations and lighting changes between different images. Another very different approach is the work of Black and Yacoob (95) who model and track isolated physical facial features.

2.6 Three-Dimensional Face Models

Finally we want to consider models based on explicit representation of the face as a surface in three dimensions. The image of a face is made by light reflecting off this surface and being sampled from a specific point, the lens of the imaging system. We may ask whether the shape of this surface can be inferred from the resulting image. This is the so-called 'shape from shading' problem. But, as described earlier, even if we assume the simple Lambertian reflectance model, this problem is underconstrained and it is impossible, in general, to solve it for the shape of the viewed object. Two approaches have been investigated to develop methods of inferring 3-D structure: one is to use multiple images of a face under varying lighting conditions and the other is to use one image but add to it prior knowledge of the expected shape and albedo of the face. The former dates back to the work of Hayakawa (94) and has been developed by Epstein, Yuille and Belhumeur (96). We will discuss this work in Section 3.5.

A powerful approach is to use knowledge about the likely geometric structure of the head. Such knowledge can be obtained, for example, by using laser range data images as we shall describe in the 3-D section of this book. Workers in computer graphics have made three-dimensional models of faces complete with muscles. Facial expressions can be quantified and related to the actions of certain muscle groups (Ekman 72). By specifying muscle activations they can synthesize highly realistic expressions (Waters and Terzopoulos, 90, 92). Ifran Essa (95) described a solution to the inverse problem: given an image sequence of a facial expression, determine what muscle activities caused the motion and thereby deduce the expression. He uses prior knowledge about likely facial expressions and the image pattern motion that they cause. The use of analysis and synthesis makes this work very much in the spirit of pattern theory.

From a sufficient number of range images of heads, it should be possible in principal to learn a probability distribution for head shapes. At once, however, one runs into several problems: how are these surfaces described, i.e., do we choose a coordinate system so that faces are graphs and, if so, do we align specific features and how do we locate these? The most appealing coordinate system to use is given by cylindrical coordinates (r, θ, z). Then describe the face via a function $r = f(\theta, z)$, and give it discretely by a set of three-dimensional data points $\{r_k, \theta_k, z_k)\}$. How can we align this data with that from another head? As for eigenfaces, we can try to align the data so that salient structures like the nose and mouth occur at corresponding positions for all heads. But, as again for eigenfaces, the variations in heads are so big that any simple alignment scheme must be at best a first approximation. In the second 3-D part of this book, we will explore the three-dimensional geometry of faces. Based on the research of the second author (Gordon 91), we first develop rotation invariant features on the face. These are then used both to define numerical invariants of a face and to define canonical coordinates in terms of which the face does have a fixed representation as a graph. Both these procedures lead to face recognition algorithms.

2.6.1   Eigenheads

In this section we want to complete the picture of current research by describing the work of Atick, Griffin and Redlich (96) which applies once again the idea of PCA and a Gaussian model this time in the simplest possible way to three-dimensional heads. Their approach is based on the assumption that the set of heads is approximately a linear subset of the vector space of functions $r = f(\theta, z)$, which they will learn from data by PCA obtaining what they call *eigenheads*. The eigenhead approach can be viewed as constructing an explicit prior model for heads in the spirit of pattern theory. A generative model is used to model image formation which assumes a simple Lambertian lighting model. However, Atick et al. do not use this probabilistic formulation.

The eigenheads are obtained by doing principal component analysis on a dataset of heads which, presumably, are aligned with each other. This gives a *mean head* $r = f_0(\theta, z)$ and a set of principal components which are called *eigenheads* $\{\psi_i(\theta, z)\}$. A specific head $r = f(\theta, z)$ can then be represented by an expansion:

$$r = f(\theta, z) = f_0(\theta, z) + \sum_i \alpha_i \psi_i(\theta, z) \qquad (2.18)$$

where the $\{\alpha_i\}$ are the coefficients representing the specific face.

How do they use this model? Assume the image plane has coordinates $(r \sin(\theta), z)$ and that the face is Lambertian with constant albedo and no self-shadowing. Then the observed image I satisfies:

$$I(r \sin(\theta), z) \quad \approx \quad \vec{L} \cdot \vec{n}(\theta, z) \qquad (2.19)$$

where $\vec{L}$ is the light source direction and $\vec{n}(\theta, z)$ is the surface normal. These seem to be reasonable initial assumptions because the strong geometric knowledge embodied by PCA overides errors caused by the non-uniformity of the albedo,

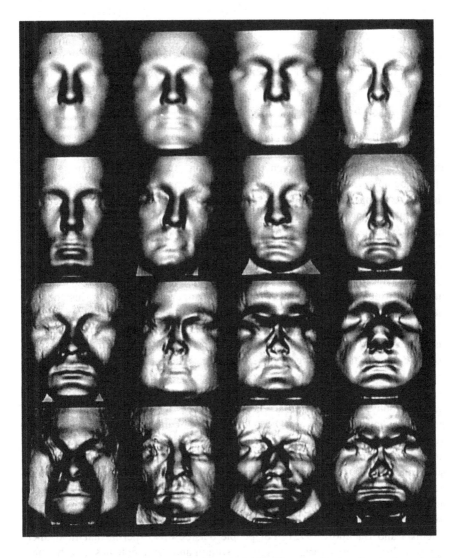

Figure 2.6. Eigenheads (figure courtesy of Joseph Atick): The mean-head surface is shown in the upper left corner. The remaining frames show the top 15 eigenheads. To display them, each eigenhead (principal component) is added to the mean-head and then rendered assuming front-on lighting.

self-shadowing, etc. A goodness of fit energy is defined to be

$$E[\alpha, \vec{L}] = \iint \left(I(r\sin(\theta), z) - \vec{L} \cdot \vec{n}_\alpha(\theta, z) \right)^2 d\theta dz \qquad (2.20)$$

where the shape, given by α and light source direction $\vec{L}$ are the unknowns to be solved for. Atick et al. give an iterative algorithm for minimizing this function in $\vec{L}$ and α. Results are reported to be good: the three-dimensional prior allows them to estimate the shape of the head, hence the surface normals, from a single image.

2.6.2 2-D vs. 3-D approaches

It is interesting to compare the approach of modeling the patterns in face images by warping as in Section 2.5 with that of modeling them as derivative from the three-dimensional patterns, given in this section. Clearly, more accurate results should be obtained from a full three-dimensional approach which "explains" why the image changes the way it does. So why should one try to model directly the effect on the image by a warping in the image plane? This choice is an example of a far-reaching split between two schools in computer vision. The argument for using the 2-D approach is this: the 2-D images are the ones we measure with cameras and eyes, which are directly available to computers and to animals. If we can model these signals directly to a reasonable degree of accuracy by applying universal principles, accurately enough to recognize known faces for instance, we have a more elementary and general explanation of perception. The argument for the 3-D approach is that it explains the patterns of faces much more accurately, using the correct physics of the world. In some special cases, it may be possible to relate directly the warping in the 2-D image to the 3-D geometry, although this is hard in general (see Yuille, Ferraro and Zhang 98).

The distinction between 2-D and 3-D models has been vigorously debated in the psychophysics and cognitive science literatures. Marr and Nishihara (1978) proposed what they called a 3-D model for recognizing objects in terms of basic geometric parts such as generalized cylinders. Biederman (1987) proposed a related theory using what he called 'geon' primitives and reports experimental data supporting the 3-D approach (Biederman and Gerhadstein 1993). By contrast, another school argues that 2-D models should be used (Ullman, Basri 1991, Poggio and Edelman 1990) and many experiments have been performed which appear to support this viewpoint (Tarr and Pinker 1989, Buelthoff and Edelman 1992, Edelman and Buelthoff 1992). For people outside this experimental field, there appear to be distinctive differences in the stimuli and methodologies used by these various schools, hence it is hard to reach a clear conclusion.

Some recent results indicate ways that these different results might be reconciled. The work of Tjan and Legge (98) suggests that some of the confusion lies in the lack of a metric for assessing the representational requirements of a recognition task. When recognizing a member of a set of 3-D objects, how much detail is required to achieve a specific accuracy criterion? For certain classes of objects, very little detail may be needed, and it may be very easy to recognize them from novel views. In related work, Liu and Kersten (98) argued that ideal observer studies demonstrated that human observers use at least some 3-D information for some recognition tasks. Another interesting result is the finding of Gauthier and Tarr (1997) that learning to be expert for a class of objects (they use an artificial class they call 'Greebles'), makes it easier to to recognize a specific Greeble from an unusual viewpoint. These three lines of work seem very promising and are very much in keeping with our pattern theory perspective. We expect that the development of metrics for performance, including class specific knowledge, and the resulting quantitative experiments will succeed in clarifying these issues.

Chapter 3

Modeling Variations in Illumination

3.1 Linear Models for Lighting Variation

As we remarked in the previous chapter, when recognizing a fixed object from a fixed viewpoint, the dominant source of variation in image intensity is lighting changes. In this chapter, we propose a low-dimensional model for human faces that can both synthesize a realistic face image when given lighting conditions and estimate lighting conditions when given a face image. The methods and results given here were sketched in Hallinan (94). The most important feature of this model is that it does not make any assumptions about either the surface geometry or the bidirectional reflectance function of the object being modeled. Thus non-Lambertian, specular and self-shadowing non-convex surfaces such as faces can be modeled. Other characteristics of the model are that it can be updated to handle any arbitrary lighting condition, it is easily extended to any other viewpoint or to any other object and it is designed for use by recognition or scene analysis algorithms that employ sets of two dimensional viewpoint specific models instead of three dimensional models.

Our motivating assumption is that successful recognition algorithms must be able to compare synthesized images or feature maps of hypothesized objects with the actual input data or feature maps in order to overcome problems of lighting, geometric deformations, occlusions, and noise (see Chapter 1 for a full discussion). In this chapter we focus exclusively on lighting, and do not deal with problems of occlusion and noise, of differing viewpoints, or of deformations in the object itself (e.g., the closing or opening of an eye).

The key idea underlying our model is the fact that any given set of lighting conditions can be exactly decomposed as a sum of point light sources. For any fixed object and fixed viewpoint, there is, up to a scale factor, just one image associated with each direction of light source. Linear combinations of these directional images generate the entire set of physically realizable images of the object, and, importantly, completely capture all shading effects, including self-shadowing and specularities.

As sketched in Chapter 2, most of the research in object recognition has handled lighting variation by employing features which are relatively lighting-invariant, such as edges, allowing lighting to be estimated by a subsequent analysis. Under small to moderate changes in illumination, it is very plausible that certain intensity-based features will not vary in their strength and geometry. On cylindrical Lambertian surfaces, Koenderink and Van Doorn (82) have argued that intensity extrema are in fact very good features since there will be an intensity minimum at each point of inflection of the one dimensional cross-section and intensity maxima will be drawn to the curvature maxima of this cross-section. However, larger changes in lighting (e.g., on the order of 90 degrees) can obviously erase entire features, and in general, for a fixed viewpoint of any object, one can find a lighting condition that alters the geometry, strength, and/or existence of any given intensity-based feature. (For a critique of the lack of lighting-invariance of several local operators such as Gabor filters and edge detectors see Moses et al. (94).

Perhaps the most striking example of human recognition abilities for objects, most of whose features have been erased by extreme lighting, are given by the famous Mooney images. These are starkly lit faces in which all points are either in shadow and black or illuminated and white (see Figure 3.1). Note that the boundaries between black and white, the apparent edges in the image, are of three types: (a) outer contours of the solid head against the background; (b) cast shadows of parts of the head seen on other parts of the head; and (c) 'attached shadows' where an illuminated part of the face curves away from the light and becomes black. Only edges (a) don't change when the direction of the light changes. Edges (b) and (c) are highly variable and, for most objects, confusing and misleading. For faces, we have a remarkable ability to reconstruct the shape and lighting creating these extreme images. Cavanagh (91) shows that we can in principle compute these three types of edges if the illuminant direction is known, and there are no contours due to highlights or to albedo changes (conditions not met in face images). But Moore and Cavanagh (98) shows that experimental subjects cannot label contours in Mooney-like images of non-face objects *even if they are shown the direction of lighting.* Despite this, people have no difficulty recognizing the Mooney images of faces such as the ones in Figure 3.1. We suggest that the methods developed in this chapter might be a basis for this ability.

Other algorithms have been proposed which use 'shape-from-shading', estimating the lighting direction and the surface shape simultaneously (e.g., Pentland 92, Horn and Brooks 89, Zheng and Chellapa 91 and Nayar et al. 91). These methods usually impose very restrictive assumptions, e.g., convexity and Lambertian surfaces.

Our approach is to use principal components analysis to find a low-dimensional approximation to a carefully selected set of directional images. The approximation

Figure 3.1. Humans have an extraordinary ability to recognize faces even when the lighting is so extreme as to make the entire face and background saturate at white with totally black shadows. Left: a stylized Mooney face. Centre: a Mooney face obtained by thresholding a real photograph. Right: the edge map of the centre figure. Observe that the black and white images are easier to interpret than the edge map.

forms a basis for a space of images that is close in an L^2 sense to the space of images of arbitrarily illuminated faces. In this respect, the model is closely related to the eigenfaces of Sirovich and Kirby (87). But we are using linear methods here specifically to *model* illumination effects, not to discount illumination, nor to model geometric distortions. The model is evaluated not by a recognition rate for a set of faces, as is the case for previous eigenimage-based systems, but by its success in the synthesis and analysis of face images under different lighting conditions.

Our work is also related to that of Shashua (92) who independently proposed that lighting effects could be discounted using a three-dimensional basis for face space with basis vectors that were actual images. The justification for this approach is straightforward. Letting $\{\vec{e}_j\}$ be a basis for R^3, $\vec{n}$ be a surface normal, and $\vec{l}_i$ be the direction of the ith point light source, Shashua re-expresses an arbitrary input image I by

$$I = \sum_i \max(0, \vec{n} \cdot \vec{l}_i) \approx \vec{n} \cdot \sum_i \vec{l}_i = \vec{n} \cdot \sum_{j=1}^{3} \alpha_j \vec{e}_j \approx \sum_{j=1}^{3} \max(0, \alpha_j (\vec{n} \cdot \vec{e}_j)) = \sum_{j=1}^{3} \alpha_j I_j$$

(3.1)

To find the coefficients $\{\alpha_j\}$, one can select any set of 3 or more pixels and find the least squares solution of the resulting system of equations. Shashua selects 8 such points that are less likely to lie in an area of highlight or shadow, and finds that the resulting reconstructions are good for several test images.

We will present results showing that five lighting basis vectors suffice to both analyze and synthesize images under a wide range of lighting conditions, and that the eigenimage model performs much more successfully than a model that uses the directional images themselves as basis vectors. These results hold both for models of individual faces and for a model of a generic male face.

3.2   Constructing the Lighting Model

In this section we give the details of our construction of the lighting model. The method we will use, principal components analysis, can be used to construct both generic face models and models for individual people, though the underlying assumptions in each case are different. Throughout, we will treat images with d pixels as elements of a d-dimensional linear vector space. No particular ordering of the pixels is required; we concatenate image rows.

Since any given set of lighting conditions can be exactly decomposed as a sum of point light sources (or approximately represented as a sum of small but still highly-directional area light sources), then a surface patch's radiance when illuminated by two light sources is the sum of the radiances for the light sources applied separately. Thus for any given object and viewing projection, there is (up to a scale factor $c(\theta, \phi)$) just one image $J(\theta, \phi)$ associated with each point light source $L(\theta, \phi)$; of course, more than one illumination condition may give rise to the same image. It must be emphasized that the images $J(\theta, \phi)$ by definition are exactly physically correct in every detail including self-shadowing. So to synthesize a scene lit with any number of these lights, we just need to add the images corresponding to each directional light source weighted by the intensity of each source. Except for sensor effects, all the nonlinearities inherent in the synthesis process occur in the generation of the image corresponding to each direction, and not in the combination of effects from different sources. If a new surface is introduced into the scene, the concomitant mutual illumination effects are handled simply as additional light sources. Now if we limit the total irradiance of the scene to be C, then the set $\mathcal{P}$ of all possible images of the object is compact and convex, with the boundary of the set consisting of the maximally bright directional images $\{CJ(\theta, \phi)\}$. By sampling this boundary with a finite set of images $\{CJ(\theta_i, \phi_j)\}$, where θ_i and ϕ_j are uniformly spaced in the interval $\pm 90°$ around the frontal direction,[1] we get an approximation to the shape of the set $\mathcal{P}$.

---

[1] This method overemphasizes the 'north pole' and 'south pole' directions, where the sampling becomes denser. Possibly, one should weight these samples in the principal component analysis below with the factor $\cos(\phi)$ (from the spherical coordinate jacobian), but, in nature, light from the sky or overhead lights is more frequent than horizontally projected light. It might also be preferable to have included images with light from *behind* which illuminates one edge of the face. The present method was chosen as the simplest.

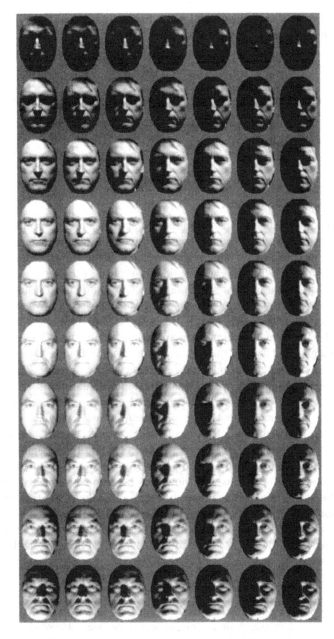

Figure 3.2. The training set $\mathcal{T}$ of input images for the subject m0. The direction of lighting varies in increments of 15 degrees between 0 degrees and 90 degrees longitude and -60 degrees to 75 degrees latitude.

We use principal components analysis to find an orthogonal basis $\{J_k\}$ for this finite sample of boundary images, such that

$$CJ(\theta_i, \phi_j) \approx \sum_k \alpha_{ijk} J_k \tag{3.2}$$

Then an arbitrary image $I = \sum_{ij} c(\theta_i, \phi_j) J(\theta_i, \phi_j)$ can be approximated as

$$I \approx \sum_k s_k J_k \tag{3.3}$$

where

$$s_k = \sum_{ij} \frac{c(\theta_i, \phi_j)}{C} \alpha_{ijk} \tag{3.4}$$

Principal component analysis is often used to approximate a probability distribution in d-dimensional space by a Gaussian distribution supported on a much lower dimensional space by taking only the eigenvectors of the covariance matrix with largest eigenvalues. Here, however, we do not want to assume that we know the probability distribution on light source directions. We are instead using principal component analysis to estimate the *shape* of the convex set $\mathcal{P}$. We are taking a sample of points $\{CJ(\theta_i, \phi_j)\}$ on the boundary of this convex set and approximating this sample by an ellipsoid in some linear subspace. The problem of finding the significant axes of this set is not statistical in nature, but geometrical; *no* assumption need be made about the distribution of face images. This gives us a simple model of the nature of the variation due to illumination.

In practice, there will be small experimental errors in the placement of the images along the boundary, but these perturbations are negligible with respect to the spacing of the images. However, in the case of boundary images for n individuals, we are computing one set of axes for n convex surfaces, and we rely on the assumption that the geometric variation between faces is less than the variation due to illumination. Our results will show that this assumption is reasonable.

While the use of principal components yields a low-dimensional model of the lighting conditions, it also complicates the connection between the weights of the basis images S_k and the direction from which a given input image is lit. If we denote the sets of all boundary image coefficients and eigenimage coefficients by $\vec{c}$ and $\vec{s}$ respectively, then we obtain a linear system

$$A\vec{c} = \vec{s} \tag{3.5}$$

Synthesizing novel lighting conditions is straightforward using this equation; the closest $\vec{c}$ is found to the desired lighting condition via interpolation and then plugged in. Analyzing lighting conditions involves inverting the mapping from the lighting coefficients $\{c(\theta_i, \phi_j)\}$ to the lighting basis vector coefficients, and is discussed below.

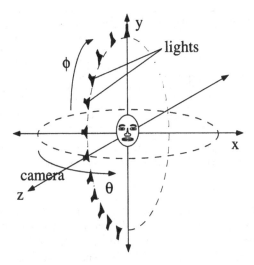

Figure 3.3. The experimental setup: lights placed on a large goniometer are varied in position while the camera and person remain fixed in position.

3.3 The Experiment

3.3.1 Data

The most critical step in constructing the approximation is the collection of a suitable set of boundary images. Figure 3.3 shows the experimental setup.

The data set should capture as wide a range of lighting conditions as is possible, given the extent of the solid angle subtended by the area light sources actually used. Accordingly, each subject was seated on a stool so that his/her head formed the center of a hemisphere 4.5 feet in radius, and was instructed to look in the direction $(0, 0)$ (straight ahead) at the camera without moving his/her head, though slight movements were unavoidable. A floodlight was then moved by increments of fifteen degrees to each position (θ_i, ϕ_j), and a picture was taken of the person with a serious expression and eyes open. Because of occlusions, images with $\phi <= -75$ or $\phi > 75$ proved difficult to capture, so data sets were unbalanced in their treatment of vertical lighting.

Because it is crucial to check the effect that the choice of sampling scheme has on the resulting lighting basis vectors, we experimented with each of the four different sampling schemes shown in Table 3.1.

Each different set of images is denoted by $\mathcal{T}_b^i$ where the superscript i indicates the subject (or set of subjects) and the subscript b indicates the sampling scheme. Each training set generates a corresponding eigenimage model $\mathcal{M}_b^i$. The set $\mathcal{T}_{\text{add}}$

Data Set	# images	sampling in θ	sampling in ϕ	note
T_{rss}^i	20	sparse	sparse	right side only
T_{rds}^i	35	dense	sparse	right side only
T_{rsd}^i	40	sparse	dense	right side only
T_{rdd}^i	70	dense	dense	right side only
T_{add}^i	130	dense	dense	both sides

Table 3.1. The different training sets T_b^i where i indicates the subject (or set of subjects) and b indicates the sampling rate. Each training set generates a corresponding eigenface model $\mathcal{M}_b^i$.

was collected for just one subject due to the considerable patience required to sit for 130 pictures. The set T_{rdd} was collected for the remaining subjects. The complements of the subsets are taken to be test sets. Figure 3.2 shows the training set $T_{\mathrm{rdd}}^{\mathrm{m0}}$. Also, the training sets T_b^{men} for the generic male face model are unions of the all corresponding individual training sets.

3.3.2   Geometric Normalization

Inherent in our use of principal components analysis is the assumption that face images are elements of a linear vector space. Clearly though, the linear combination $aI^i + bI^j$ of two arbitrary face images I^i and I^j will not be a face at all if the faces are offset even a little, i.e. $aI^i + bI^j$ will have 2 noses, 4 eyes, etc. We need to first normalize the positions of the feature points on the face by a geometric transformation ψ of the image plane. Craw and Cameron (91, 92) compute ψ for an image by locating some 70 feature points on the face, and then warping each point to a standard position via bilinear interpolation within the triangular patches defined by the feature points. This procedure depends critically on accurate manual identification of the feature points, and assumes that the geometry varies enough from image to image to render such a warping necessary. In our database, lighting varies dramatically, so the only feature points that can be reasonably estimated from image to image are the centers of the eyes. Most other features, such as the corners of the mouth or nostrils, are much harder to locate when shadowed without a very good estimate of the midline of the face. Additionally, geometric variations within images for a fixed person are minimal. Therefore, we use the eye centers alone to find a non-shearing affine transformation (i.e., rotation and scaling) within the image plane that aligns images in a standard position with a fixed interoccular distance. Variations in head orientation are typically too minimal to warrant estimating the affine transformation within R^3 and then projecting. Finally, each image is masked so that everything outside the domain of the face (including ears, hair, and neck) is set to zero.

3.3.3 Computing Eigenimages

After geometrically normalizing the images, we are in position to find the axes of a data set $\{I^i\}$ using principal components analysis. The first step in identifying the principal components is to center the set of boundary images by subtracting the mean image μ from each image, so that the input images, completely processed and ready to go, are

$$J^i(x,y) = I^i(\psi(x,y)) - \mu(x,y) \tag{3.6}$$

As expected, this last step does in fact enhance the lighting effects present in the images, because $\mu(x,y)$, as the average intensity radiated from a particular patch, can be interpreted as an albedo map except in regions that are strongly self-shadowed. More accurately, we expect the mean face image at a point P to be the product of the albedo of the face at P times the area of the solid angle subtended by the cone of rays starting at P and not meeting the face. This second factor models the amount of self-shadowing.

Second, we double the size of the database from $n/2$ to n by adding the mirror image of each input face, i.e., adding $J^i(x,y) = J^{i-n/2}(-x,y)$ for $i = n/2 + 1, \ldots, n$. This will cause the resulting eigenimages to be bilaterally symmetric or anti-symmetric and will simplify their interpretation. Though these mirror images will be used in generating the different eigenimage models, they will *not* be used in the training and test sets of the results section unless otherwise indicated.

Thirdly, we compute the principal components of the matrix $L \in R^{d \times n}$ with column i equal to J^i. Recall that principal components of a matrix such as L can be computed in several different ways. We can compute the singular value decomposition (SVD) of L:

$$L = UDV'$$

where U is a $d \times d$ orthogonal matrix, V is a $n \times n$ orthogonal matrix and D is a diagonal matrix whose entries are the singular values of L. Equivalently, we can diagonalize LL':

$$LL' = UD^2U^{-1}$$

or finally we can diagonalize $L'L$:

$$L'L = V^{-1}D^2V.$$

Thus the non-zero eigenvalues of LL' and of $L'L$ are the same and are equal to the squares of the singular values of L; the eigenvectors of LL' are the columns of U and the eigenvectors of $L'L$ are the rows of V. In our case, d is much too large (e.g., 512^2) for LL' to be diagonalized with available computer resources. But $L'L$ is $n \times n$, which, for our samples, is not too large to compute its eigenvectors. Or the SVD can be computed by an SVD routine, e.g., in MatLab.

3.4 Results

In this section, we will present results demonstrating that

- the first five eigenimages span a very stable subspace,

- the eigenimages are robust across individuals,

- the eigenimages can be interpreted in terms of lighting directions,

- the linear operators for synthesis and analysis work well, and

- the eigenimage model is extensible to other objects.

Throughout this section we will provide examples drawn largely from one subject to provide coherency. All results apply equally well to any face though.

3.4.1 Selecting Basis Vectors

To build the face model we need to know how many of the basis vectors, i.e., the eigenfaces, to use. The performance of the model will ultimately be judged by the quality of the recognition rates and scene analysis it admits, and by the cost of the computation incurred, but in the interim, some ad hoc method is required. Therefore we choose as basis vectors those components that:

- account for some large percentage of the variance of the sample of face images,

- lead to large goodness of fit values for each individual face image, and

- account for significant lighting effects.

Evaluating the eigenimages is complicated by the possible dependence of the face space dimension on the initial sampling of lighting positions. A priori, one might well expect to find that a denser sampling yields more accurate lighting basis vectors.

Figures 3.4 and 3.5 contain the most significant eigenimages for several subjects of varying sex and skin albedo. The changes in sign of some of the eigenimages occur because eigenvectors are unique only up to a scale factor. The changes in order of the eigenvalues are significant only in the extent to which they are limited; only eigenvectors having eigenvalues of comparable magnitude will swap. In practice, the first two eigenvectors form one subspace and the next three another. Although the first 7 or so eigenimages are extremely similar (up to a change in order and sign) across all sets, what is most striking is that the first five form an extremely stable subspace – they only exchange places with one another. Moreover, the generic model shows the same behavior with the same eigenimages, despite considerable geometric variation between the five men used as subjects.

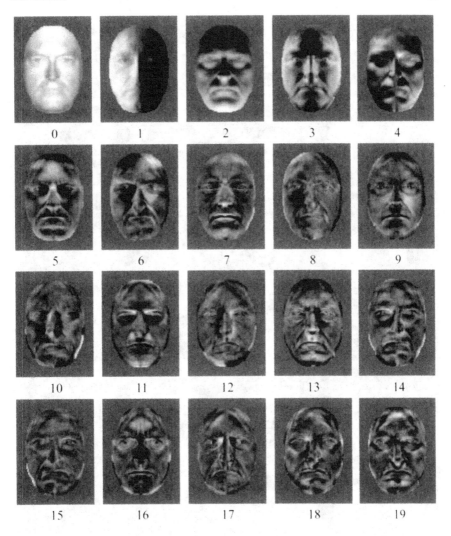

Figure 3.4. Subject m0, light-skinned male: The first 20 eigenfaces from data set $T_{\mathrm{rsxsy}}^{\mathrm{m0}}$ ordered by eigenvalues.

3.4.1.1 VARIANCE ACCOUNTED FOR The variance accounted for (VAF) by the top ten eigenimages of several models is shown in Table 3.2.

Profiles of plots of variance vs. eigenvalue index remain qualitatively identical to those in Table 3.2, even in cases where eigenimages swap positions. The slower decay in the generic case arises simply because of the greater geometric variation in the faces. These results show that three eigenimages suffice to explain 85-90

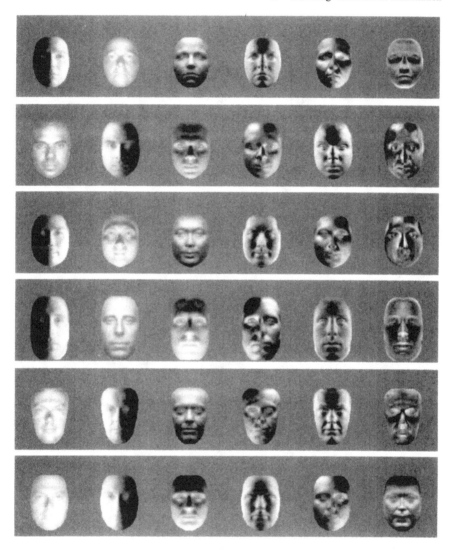

Figure 3.5. The first six eigenfaces from (a) 5 subjects who vary in sex, age, and skin color; and (b) the set of all males in the data set.

percent of the variance due to lighting and five suffice to explain 90-95 percent. On strict numerical grounds, three might then be considered enough. However, on perceptual grounds, three are not enough; as will be shown below, the fourth and fifth eigenimages contribute significantly to images lit from more extreme latitudes and longitudes. Thus the VAF statistic should be evaluated carefully.

$\mathcal{M}_{add}^{f0}$	%Variance	50	24	16	2	2	1	1	1	0	0
	Cumulative	50	74	90	92	94	95	96	96	96	97
$\mathcal{M}_{rss}^{m4}$	%Variance	42	35	13	2	2	1	1	1	0	0
	Cumulative	42	77	90	92	93	94	95	95	96	96
$\mathcal{M}_{rss}^{m0}$	%Variance	37	35	16	3	2	1	1	0	0	0
	Cumulative	37	73	89	92	94	95	95	96	96	96
$\mathcal{M}_{rdd}^{men}$	%Variance	36	35	13	2	2	2	1	1	1	1
	Cumulative	36	71	84	86	88	90	91	92	92	93

Table 3.2. The percent of total variance explained by each eigenvector, and the running total, for 3 individuals and the generic set. These percentages have typical orders of magnitude. In the generic case, we expect and find a less concentrated distribution because there is greater geometric variability to account for.

3.4.1.2 GOODNESS-OF-FIT In this section, we compare the four different bases to see which performs best at reconstructing individual boundary images from both the training and test images defined above. Boundary images are more difficult to reconstruct than images on the interior of the convex set because interior images are less sensitive to the exact value of $\vec{c}$. This follows because shading effects are most pronounced when lighting is bright and unidirectional.

First define the reconstruction of a preprocessed input image J^i as

$$R_{k,b}^i = \sum_{l=1}^{k} < J^i, S_{l,b} > S_{l,b} \tag{3.7}$$

where b indexes the different bases corresponding to different sample sets. Then the quality of the reconstruction can be measured by the goodness of fit function

$$\epsilon(i,k,b) = 1 - \frac{||R_{k,b}^i - J^i||^2}{||J^i||^2} \tag{3.8}$$

Since both $R_{k,b}^i$ and J^i have already had the mean image subtracted from them, and since $|| \cdot ||$ is an L^2 norm, criterion severely penalize mismatches. It also provides us with a clearcut method to trade model accuracy for fit. Our goal is to choose k and b such that $\min_i \epsilon(i,k,b)$ is acceptably low. Particular choices of k and b need to be evaluated across entire data sets. Figure 3.6 contains graphs showing the mean and minimum goodness of fits across both training and test data sets. Though the graphs stop at $k = 20$, all curves would reach the limiting value of 1 if k were continued out to its limit. These graphs show clearly why taking $k \approx 3$ does not suffice; there are simply too many images that are poorly reconstructed. At about $k = 5$ for each basis, we find that the increases in ϵ from k to $k + 1$ begin to taper off quite rapidly.

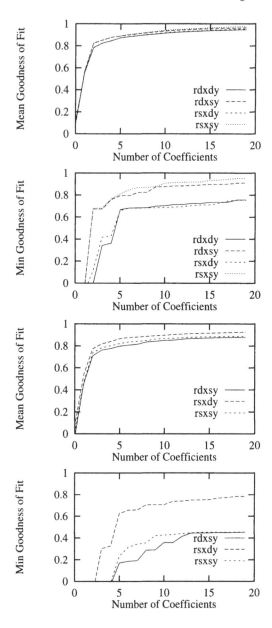

Figure 3.6. Subject m0: Plot of the mean and minimum goodness of fits $\epsilon(i, k, b)$ vs. number k of eigenfaces used in the fit. The top two have mean and minimum plots for the training sets, while the second two have mean and minimum plots for the test sets.

Common Position	Lighting Contribution	Symmetry
0	frontal/ambient lighting	symmetric
1	side lighting	anti-symmetric
2	lighting from above/below	symmetric
3	lighting from two corners	anti-symmetric
4	extreme side lighting	symmetric
5	extreme lighting from above/below	symmetric

Table 3.3. The interpretation of the eigenfaces in terms of lighting contributions. These interpretations hold across all data sets. Symmetry is measured with respect to the midline of the face. The exact order may vary. The eigenface representing the extreme side lighting is very unstable in position.

Note also that the graphs show two groups of reconstruction curves. This is due to asymmetry in the sampling of latitude. $T_{\text{rss}}^{\text{m0}}$ and $T_{\text{rds}}^{\text{m0}}$ have $\phi \in [-60, +60]$ while $T_{\text{rsd}}^{\text{m0}}$ and $T_{\text{rdd}}^{\text{m0}}$ have $\phi \in [-60, +75]$. Images lit from the more extreme latitudes are much more difficult to represent as combinations from the more tropical latitudes, particularly since the face is asymmetric vertically. Thus models $\mathcal{M}_{\text{rss}}^{\text{m0}}$ and $\mathcal{M}_{\text{rds}}^{\text{m0}}$ perform better on their training sets than on their test sets, while $\mathcal{M}_{\text{rsd}}^{\text{m0}}$ performs best on its test set ($\mathcal{M}_{\text{rdd}}^{\text{m0}}$ can only be measured against its training set.) Note though that extreme longitudes are difficult to capture perfectly as well, though the errors are not so pronounced. The underlying source of these errors is that under extreme lighting (particularly in latitude), most of the faces are in shadow, and those parts that are not shaded are captured by a relatively large number of eigenimages scattered throughout the set of unused eigenimages. The conclusion is clear; the optimal sampling rate for getting equally good performance under both central and extreme lighting has both types of images represented equally in the training set. In other words, the central and extreme lighting conditions are represented by distinct subspaces, and one must trade off accuracy in one against the other to maintain a low-dimensional model. The fact that the eigenvectors are virtually identical across all sample sets means that all sample sets will (as was found) perform equally poorly on the extreme cases. Thus for lighting conditions constrained to have directions within -60 and 60 degrees latitude and -75 and +75 degrees longitude, five eigenvectors from the model with the coarsest sampling suffice to raise the minimum goodness of fit to an acceptable level. These observations in no way preclude a more expansive training set from generating a model with a wider range of competency.

3.4.1.3 INTERPETING THE EIGENIMAGES   It is clear from inspection that the first five eigenimages of both the individual and generic models can consistently be interpreted as representing five very different lighting situations. If we include a common form of the sixth eigenimage, we get the nicely balanced interpretation of Table 3.3.

The interpretations can be cross-checked using several methods. One is to plot the coefficient value as a function of the latitude and longitude of the lighting direction illuminating the face; see Figure 3.7. Specifically, we set the intensity at pixel (i, j) of the kth plot to be the projection of the boundary image $J(\theta_i, \phi_j)$ onto the kth eigenimage.

Inspection of these plots yields the interpretations in Table 3.3 (modulo swaps in position). Note that beginning with eigenimage 10 the plots become much more difficult to interpret. This is because the eigenimages are correcting for geometrical distortions, artifacts of the masking process, and other minor effects.

A second way to interpret the eigenimages follows from considerations of their symmetry. Consider an intensity image as a function $I(\phi, \theta)$ of latitude ϕ and longitude θ. Then we can approximate $I(\phi, \theta)$ about $(0, 0)$ by

$$I(\phi, \theta) \approx I + \frac{\partial I}{\partial \theta}\theta + \frac{\partial I}{\partial \phi}\phi + \frac{\partial^2 I}{\partial \theta^2}\frac{\theta^2}{2} + \frac{\partial^2 I}{\partial \theta \partial \phi}\theta\phi + \frac{\partial^2 I}{\partial \phi^2}\frac{\phi^2}{2}$$

as long as $I(\phi, \theta)$ is thrice-differentiable over the domain of (ϕ, θ). Now observe that frontal lighting corresponds to $I(0, 0)$ while moderate side and above/below lighting corresponds to first derivatives and extreme side and above/below lighting corresponds to second derivatives.

$$I(\phi, \theta) \approx S_0 + S_1\theta + S_2\phi + S_3\theta\phi + S_4\frac{\theta^2}{2} + S_5\frac{\phi^2}{2}.$$

Thus the eigenimages can be interpreted as derivatives in a Taylor expansion. We emphasize that this interpretation is only qualitative, since numerical approximations of the derivatives would involve small perturbations about $(0, 0)$, not changes on the order of fifteen degrees, and since eigenimage S_5 cannot be consistently interpreted as suggested by the above equation.

3.4.2 Synthesizing Images

In Figure 3.8, we present the results of reconstructing $\mathcal{T}_{\text{rss}}^{\text{m0}}$ using five eigenimages from model $\mathcal{M}_{\text{rss}}^{\text{m0}}$. These reconstructions represent the best performance

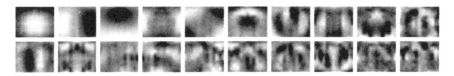

Figure 3.7. Coefficients of eigenfaces as a function of lighting direction. Images $1, \cdots, 20$ are in scanline order. The intensity at pixel (i, j) of image k corresponds to the projection of the face image lit from direction (θ_i, ϕ_j) onto the kth eigenface. Thus the bottom of the images corresponds to lighting from below, the left to lighting from the left, etc. Black is negative.

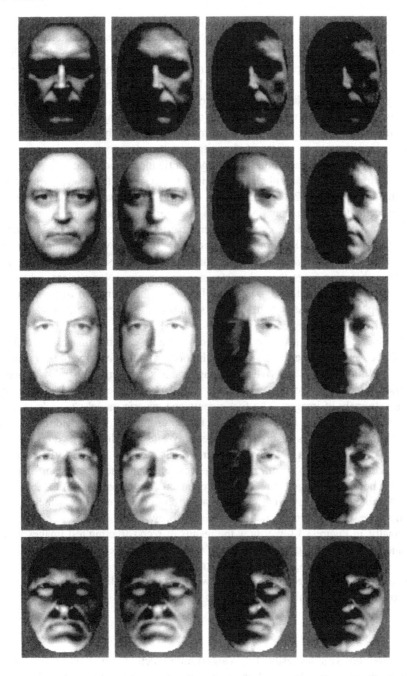

Figure 3.8. Reconstruction of 20 views of face m0 using 5 eigenfaces from the model rsxsy

of the model since (a) the training images are being reconstructed; and (b) the training set is the smallest and thus encompasses the least variation. Though the reconstructed images are not photo-realistic, they clearly capture global shading accurately. Examination of the reconstruction using five eigenimages from the generic face model $\mathcal{M}_{\text{rss}}^{\text{men}}$ yields analogous results. Though the geometry is wrong, the global shading is close. To consider the types of errors made more closely we present the reconstruction of one image in complete detail. The major difficulty with goodness-of-fit measures such as ϵ is that they weight errors equally, irrespective of their spatial position; salt and pepper noise is not as serious or as interesting a residue as a large contiguous region that fails to match the true image. For example, inspection of the residues (pixel with intensities in error by more than 20 out of 256) in Figure 3.10 shows that good values of ϵ can occur despite perceptually obvious errors in the shading around the nose, and in the coloration of the eyes. Another error is that face images reconstructed from just five or fewer eigenimages appear "dull"; they show insufficient contrast. This is because the higher order eigenimages capture the smaller highlights and shadows that give faces their characteristic appearance. Nonetheless, when we use the synthesis operator A to generate images in the interior of the convex set, it is not possible to distinguish between synthesized images for interpolated and non-interpolated lighting conditions.

In Figure 3.11, we show reconstruction of some extreme images from $\mathcal{T}_{\text{rss}}^{\text{m0}}$ using three and five eigenimage individual models and the five eigenimage generic model. While the three and five eigenimage models perform comparably on more centrally lit images, the five eigenimage model performs considerably better on more extremely lit images. The five eigenimage generic model succeeds as well as the five eigenimage individual model in capturing the global shading pattern, though the geometry is of course different. We also include for comparison a version of the Shashua (92) algorithm in which the face is reconstructed from its projection, not onto a sum of eigenspaces, but onto the linear span of three specific boundary images, namely the frontal one and those lit from (0,60) and (60,0). Note that this gives perfect reconstruction in the second row, which is part of the basis, but bad reconstruction in the third row.

Finally, in Figure 3.12, we show the results of reconstructing test images taken in uncontrolled lighting situations with direct and indirect sunlight as well as overhead fluorescent lights all contributing at once. Note that except for one image, in which strong direct sunlight was partially blocked (creating a strong shadow line), the global shading matches quite well.

3.4.3 Analyzing Illumination

In this section, we show results for an algorithm for determining lighting conditions from a given image. As posed above, the issue is one of recovering $\vec{c}$ from the

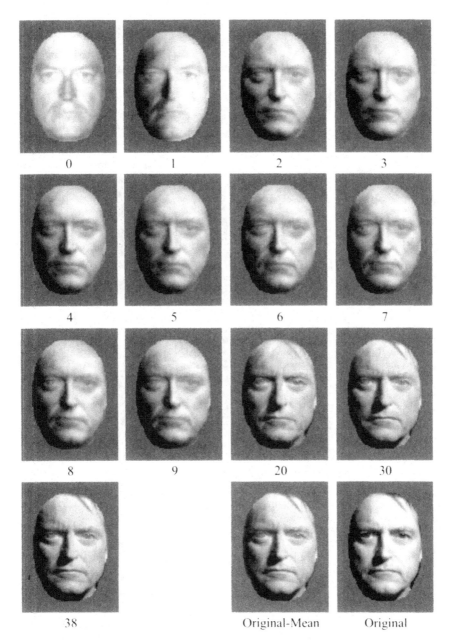

Figure 3.9. Reconstruction of face m0 lit from +30 longitude, +30 latitude with progressively more eigenfaces. Image n shows the synthesized image reconstructed using $n + 1$ eigenfaces. Each image should be compared with the second to last image, which is the original less the mean.

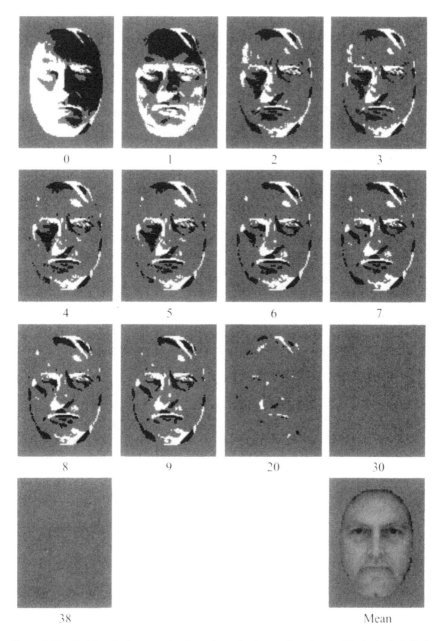

Figure 3.10. Residues in the reconstructions shown in the previous figure. Black pixels indicate synthesized pixel values that are at least 20 pixels too dark, while white pixels indicate pixels that are at least 20 pixels too light. Grey pixels indicate values that are within 20 pixels of the input intensity.

Original 3 Eigenfaces 5 Eigenfaces BI Model 1 5 Generic

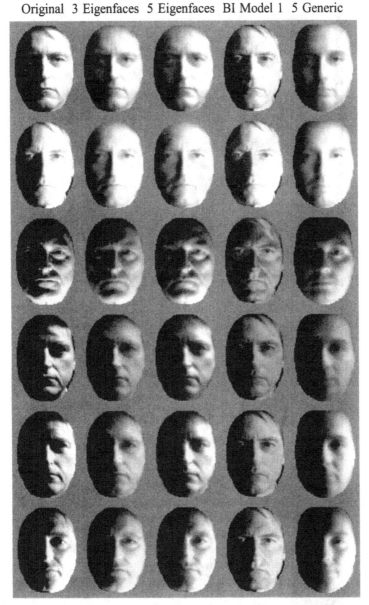

Figure 3.11. Reconstructions of images taken from subject m0 under extreme lighting conditions: From top to bottom the directions of lighting are (60,30), (60,00), (60,-60), (75,45), (90,30), and (90,-15). Col. 1 contains the original images. Col. 2-3 contain recontructions using 3 and 5 eigenfaces. Col. 4 contains reconstructions using the first boundary model. Col. 5 contains reconstructions using 5 generic eigenfaces.

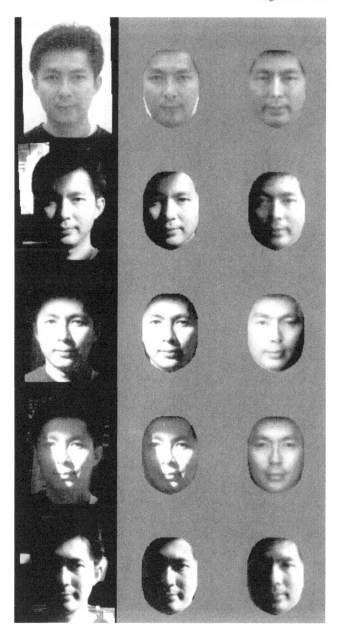

Figure 3.12. Reconstructions using 5 eigenfaces of subject m1 lit with multiple sources (overhead flourescent lights and strong sunlight). Left: original images; Center: masked images; Right: reconstructions. In row 4, the sunlight is partially occluded, creating a strong shadow configuration not present in any boundary image.

equation $A\vec{c} = \vec{s}$. Since $\vec{c}$ has 130 coefficients and $\vec{s}$ has 5, this equation has many solutions. The simplest approach is to choose the solution for which $||\vec{c}||^2$ is least, but note that the coefficients in $\vec{c}$ are restricted both to lie in $[0, C]$ and to have a sum less than C. Technically, this is a quadratic programming problem. Another solution to the problem can be found by minimizing the cost function

$$E[\vec{c}] = ||A\vec{c} - \vec{s}||^2 + \epsilon||\vec{c}||^2 + \gamma \left(g(\sum_i c_i; 0, C) + \sum_i g(c_i; 0, C) \right) \quad (3.9)$$

where $0 < \epsilon << 1$ and $1 << \gamma$. Here $g(x; 0, C)$ is a symmetric, convex, twice-differentiable function that is zero on the interval $[0, C]$ and increases exponentially on either side of $[0, C]$. When γ is zero, the minimum of E as $\epsilon \to 0$ approaches the pseudoinverse solution: the $\vec{c}$ of least norm satisfying $A(\vec{c}) = \vec{s}$, which is given by:

$$A^+(\vec{s}) = A'(AA')^{-1}\vec{s}.$$

If just the predominant direction of lighting $\vec{d} = [\theta_{max}, \phi_{max}]'$ is desired, a solution is

$$\vec{d} = \sum_{ij} \left(\frac{c_{ij}}{\sum_{ij} c_{ij}} \right) [\theta_i, \phi_j]' \quad (3.10)$$

In situations where there really is a predominant direction of lighting, one can compose the operator A^+ mapping $\vec{s} \to \vec{c}$ with this mapping $\vec{c} \to \vec{d}$ to get a new operator B mapping the projection coefficients directly to $\vec{d}$:

$$B\vec{s} = \vec{d} \quad (3.11)$$

The results of applying this operator constructed from $\mathcal{M}_{rdd}^{m0}$ to the set $\mathcal{T}_{rdd}^{m0}$ are shown in Figure 3.13. The approximate mean and standard deviation of the magnitude of the errors using five eigenimages is 19 and 18; for six eigenimages it is 16 and 10; and for ten eigenimages it is 12 and 7.

Pentland (92) found that humans performed with a mean error of 6 degrees and a standard deviation of about 12 degrees on a test in which they were asked to estimate the direction from which a Lambertian sphere was illuminated.

3.4.4 Basis Vectors for Other Objects

The apparatus and methodology given above have also been used to identify the dominant eigenvectors for a variety of objects that have more significant specular lobes and spikes and surface geometries generating more shadows than faces. Full details are reported in Epstein et al. (95), but the results demonstrate that, as long as the pose, surface properties (e.g., texture), and surface geometry of an object are held constant, then:

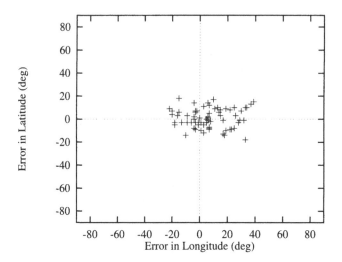

Figure 3.13. Errors made in estimating the predominant lighting direction for images in the training set for subject m0.

- the first few eigenvectors describe the lambertian component,

- the next few eigenvectors encode diffuse specularities and major shadows,

- the remaining eigenvectors encode specular spikes, small scale-cast shadows and other irregularities.

As a result, we conclude that for many objects:

- 5 ± 2 eigenvectors will suffice to model the lambertian and diffuse specular effects,

- specular spikes, small shadows and irregularities can be treated as residuals and eliminated by projecting the original image onto the low dimensional eigenvector model,

- the sampling of lighting directions required in the training set increases with both the specularity and the complexity of the surface geometry

Figures 3.15 and 3.16 contain graphs showing the mean and minimum goodness of fits across both training and test data sets for bases constructed from the sparse samples only. Though the graphs stop at $k = 17$, all curves would reach the limiting value of 1 if k were continued out to its limit. These graphs show clearly that, with the exception of highly specular objects, improvements in both average and worst-case performance begin to taper off at around $k = 5$. The results for bases constructed from denser sample sets were comparable.

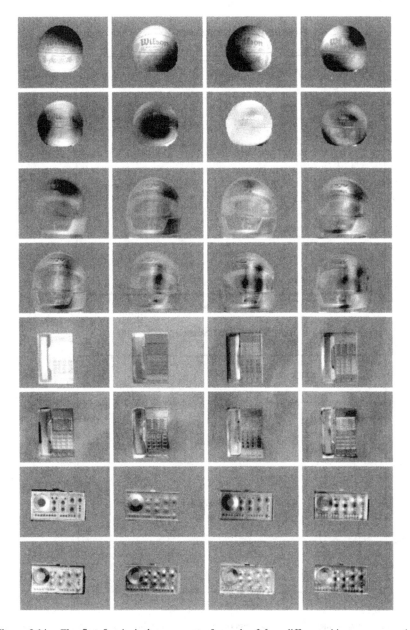

Figure 3.14. The first 8 principal components for each of four different objects: an essentially Lambertian basketball, a highly specular motorcycle helmet, a phone with specular lobes but a simple geometry, and a voltmeter with mostly diffuse reflection but a more complicated surface geometry that generates many small shadows

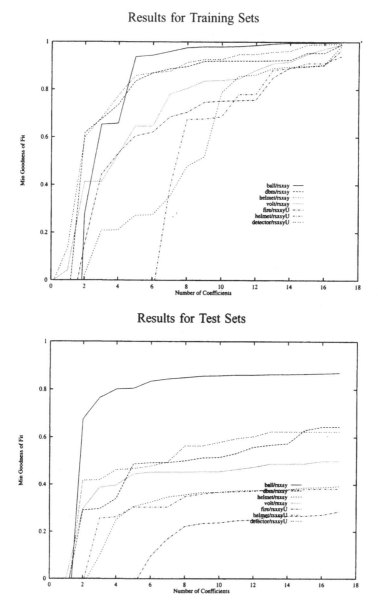

Figure 3.15. Plots of the minimum goodness-of-fit versus the number of eigenvectors for training and test sets of several different objects. All models were constructed using a sparse data set. The letter 'U' appended to an object's name indicates the background was unmasked. ball=basketball, dbm=face, helmet=motorcycle helmet, volt=voltmeter, fire=fire extinguisher, detector=infrared detector

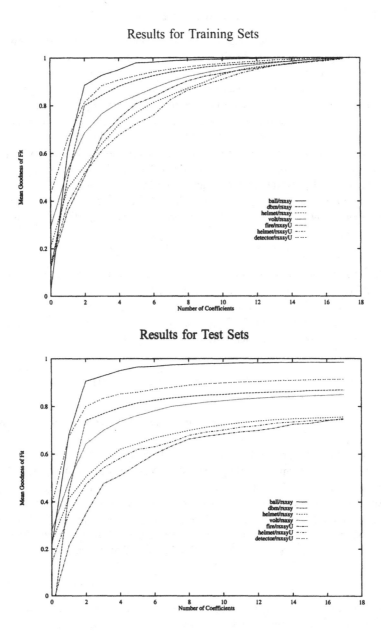

Figure 3.16. Plots of the mean goodness of fit versus the number of eigenvectors for training and test sets of the same objects used in the previous figure.

3.5   Generating 3-D Face Models from Illumination Variation

It is possible, given multiple images of the same object from the same viewpoint but under varying conditions of illumination, to estimate the three-dimensional structure of the object. This approach is known as "photometric stereo" and was studied by Hayakawa (94) for the case of unknown lighting. It has been extensively developed by one of the authors with his associates, esp. R. Epstein, P. Belhumeur and D. Kriegman, in recent years (see Epstein et al. 96, Yuille and Snow 97, Belhumeur et al. 97, Georghiades et al. 98, Kriegman and Belhumeur 98).

Suppose we have a set of images of the same object from the same viewpoint generated by a Lambertian reflectance model where the lighting conditions vary. We use $\mathbf{x}$ to label positions in the image plane Ω and let $|\Omega|$ be the number of these positions (we assume a finite grid). The light source directions are *unknown* and are labeled by $\mu = 1, ..., M$. *If we ignore all shadowing*, this gives us a set of M images:

$$I(\mathbf{x}, \mu) = a(\mathbf{x})\mathbf{n}(\mathbf{x}) \cdot \mathbf{s}(\mu) \equiv \mathbf{b}(\mathbf{x}) \cdot \mathbf{s}(\mu) \qquad (3.12)$$

where $a(\mathbf{x})$ is the albedo of the object, $\mathbf{n}(\mathbf{x})$ is its surface normal, $\mathbf{b}(\mathbf{x}) \equiv a(\mathbf{x})\mathbf{n}(\mathbf{x})$ (observe that $a(\mathbf{x}) = |\mathbf{b}(\mathbf{x})|$ and $\mathbf{n}(\mathbf{x}) = \hat{\mathbf{b}}(\mathbf{x})$), and $\mathbf{s}(\mu)$ is the light source direction. We will typically work with $\mathbf{b}(\mathbf{x})$ instead of $a(\mathbf{x})$ and $\mathbf{n}(\mathbf{x})$.

We wish to solve equation (3.12) for the albedo, shape, and light source directions. To do this, we define a least squares cost function:

$$E[\mathbf{b}, \mathbf{s}] = \sum_{\mu, \mathbf{x}} \{I(\mathbf{x}, \mu) - \sum_{i=1}^{3} b_i(\mathbf{x})s_i(\mu)\}^2 \qquad (3.13)$$

where the subscripts i denote the cartesian components of the vectors (i.e. $\mathbf{b} = (b_1, b_2, b_3)$).

It is possible to minimize this cost function to solve for $\mathbf{b}(\mathbf{x})$ and $\mathbf{s}(\mu)$ up to a constant linear transform using Singular Value Decomposition (SVD) (Hayakawa 94), (Epstein et al. 96, Yuille and Snow 97). To see this, observe that the intensities $\{I(\mathbf{x}, \mu)\}$ can be expressed as an $M \times |\Omega|$ matrix $\mathbf{J}$ where M is the number of images (light sources) and $|\Omega|$ is the number of points $\mathbf{x}$. Similarly we can express the surface properties $\{b_i(\mathbf{x})\}$ as a $|\Omega| \times 3$ matrix $\mathbf{B}$ and the light sources $\{s_i(\mu)\}$ as a $3 \times M$ matrix $\mathbf{S}$. SVD implies that we can write $\mathbf{J}$ as:

$$\mathbf{J} = \mathbf{UDV}^T \qquad (3.14)$$

where $\mathbf{D}$ is a diagonal matrix whose elements are the square roots of the eigenvalues of $\mathbf{JJ}^T$. The columns of $\mathbf{U}$ correspond to the normalized eigenvectors of the matrix $\mathbf{J}^T\mathbf{J}$. The ordering of these columns corresponds to the ordering of the eigenvalues in $\mathbf{D}$. Similarly, the columns of $\mathbf{V}$ correspond to the eigenvectors of $\mathbf{J}\ \mathbf{J}^T$.

Observe that $(1/M)\mathbf{J}^T\mathbf{J}$ is the $|\Omega| \times |\Omega|$ the autocorrelation of the set of input images where $|\Omega|$ is the image size (Observe that the mean image is not subtracted – if it was, we would obtain the covariance, or Karhunen-Loeve matrix used earlier in this chapter to compute the principal components of an image data set). There is a direct relationship between the eigenvectors and eigenvalues of the two matrices $\mathbf{J}^T\mathbf{J}$ and $\mathbf{J}\mathbf{J}^T$. This relationship was exploited earlier in this chapter to calculate the principal components in situations where the matrix $(1/M)\mathbf{J}^T\mathbf{J}$ is too large to calculate its eigenvectors directly.

If the Lambertian image formation model is correct then there will only be three nonzero eigenvalues of $\mathbf{J}\mathbf{J}^T$ and so $\mathbf{D}$ will have only three nonzero elements (this, of course, has long been known in the photometric stereo and vision literature (Shashua 92, Silver 80, Woodham 81)). We do not expect this to be true for our data set because of shadows, ambient background, specularities, and noise. But SVD is guaranteed to give us the best least squares solution in any case. Thus the biggest three eigenvalues of Σ, and the corresponding columns of $\mathbf{U}$ and $\mathbf{V}$ represent the Lambertian part of the reflectance function of these objects. We define the vectors $\{\mathbf{f}(\mu) : \mu = 1, ..., M\}$ to be the first three columns of $\mathbf{U}$ and the $\{\mathbf{e}(\mathbf{x})\}$ to be the first three columns of $\mathbf{V}$.

This assumption enables us to use SVD to solve for $\mathbf{b}$ and $\mathbf{s}$ up to a linear transformation. The solution is:

$$\mathbf{b}(\mathbf{x}) = \mathbf{P}_3\mathbf{e}(\mathbf{x}), \ \forall \ \mathbf{x}$$
$$\mathbf{s}(\mu) = \mathbf{Q}_3\mathbf{f}(\mu), \ \forall \ \mu \tag{3.15}$$

where $\mathbf{P}_3$ and $\mathbf{Q}_3$ are 3×3 matrices which are constrained to satisfy $\mathbf{P}_3^T\mathbf{Q}_3 = \mathbf{D}_3$, where $\mathbf{D}_3$ is the 3×3 diagonal matrix containing the square roots of the biggest three eigenvalues of $\mathbf{J}\mathbf{J}^T$. There is an ambiguity $\mathbf{P}_3 \mapsto \mathbf{A}\mathbf{P}_3, \ \mathbf{Q}_3 \mapsto \mathbf{A}^{-1\ T}\mathbf{Q}_3$ where $\mathbf{A}$ is an arbitrary invertible matrix which we will discuss below.

So far this approach has assumed a simple Lambertian model without any shadows. It is, however, fairly straightforward to modify this approach and treat shadows as outliers (Yuille and Snow 97, Georghiades et al. 98). We introduce a binary indicator variable $\mathbf{V}(\mathbf{x}, \mu)$ which can be used to indicate whether a point $\mathbf{x}$ is in shadow when the illuminant is $\mathbf{s}(\mu)$. This variable $\mathbf{V}(\mathbf{x}, \mu)$ must be estimated. To do so, we can use our current estimates of $\mathbf{b}(\mathbf{x})$ and $\mathbf{s}(\mu)$ to determine whether $\mathbf{x}$ is likely to be in shadow from light source $\mathbf{s}(\mu)$. This will be determined by setting $\mathbf{V}(\mathbf{x}, \mu) = 0$ if $\mathbf{n}(\mathbf{x}) \cdot \mathbf{s}(\mu) \leq T$, where T is a threshold. We then re-estimate $\mathbf{b}(\mathbf{x})$ and $\mathbf{s}(\mu)$ and repeat. $\mathbf{V}$ can also be used to remove areas where the image is very bright, either because the imaging setup is saturated or because these pixels are part of a bright specularity.

More precisely, we define a modified energy function:

$$E[\mathbf{V}, \mathbf{b}, \mathbf{s}] = \sum_{\mathbf{x},\mu} \mathbf{V}(\mathbf{x}, \mu)\{\mathbf{I}(\mathbf{x}, \mu) - \mathbf{b}(\mathbf{x}) \cdot \mathbf{s}\}^2 \tag{3.16}$$

For the removal of shadows alone, we may set

$$\mathbf{V}(\mathbf{x}, \mu) = \mathbf{0} \text{ if } \mathbf{b}(\mathbf{x}) \cdot \mathbf{s}(\mu) \leq \mathbf{T}$$
$$\mathbf{V}(\mathbf{x}, \mu) = \mathbf{1} \text{ if } \mathbf{b}(\mathbf{x}) \cdot \mathbf{s}(\mu) > \mathbf{T} \tag{3.17}$$

Then we minimize with respect to the variables $\mathbf{b}(\mathbf{x})$, $\mathbf{s}(\mu)$, in an iterative fashion. Initially we reconstruct the face assuming no shadows. Then, as we iterate, shadows get removed and the resulting reconstruction gets better (see Figures 3.17 and 3.18).

Once we have estimated $\mathbf{b}(\mathbf{x})$, hence $a(\mathbf{x})$ and $\mathbf{n}(\mathbf{x})$, we can try to solve for the 3-D shape of the object. Suppose the distance from the image to the object is given by $z(\mathbf{x})$. Then:

$$\frac{\partial z}{\partial x_1} = \frac{b_1}{b_3}$$
$$\frac{\partial z}{\partial x_2} = \frac{b_2}{b_3} \tag{3.18}$$

To solve these equations, $\mathbf{b}$ must satisfy the integrability constraints $\partial/\partial x_1 (b_2/b_3) = \partial/\partial x_2(b_1/b_3)$. We can add this constraint into our energy and minimize

$$E[\mathbf{V}, \mathbf{b}, \mathbf{s}] = \sum_{\mathbf{x}, \mu} \mathbf{V}(\mathbf{x}, \mu)\{\mathbf{I}(\mathbf{x}, \mu) - \mathbf{b}(\mathbf{x}) \cdot \mathbf{s}\}^2$$
$$+ \quad c_1 \sum_{\bar{x}} \{(b_3 \frac{\partial b_1}{\partial y} - b_1 \frac{\partial b_3}{\partial y}) - (b_3 \frac{\partial b_2}{\partial x} - b_2 \frac{\partial b_3}{\partial x})\}^2 \tag{3.19}$$

This extra requirement restricts the possible ambiguity $\mathbf{A}$ in the solution. It is straightforward to verify (Epstein et al. 96, Belhumeur et al. 97) that the only linear transformations which preserve surface integrability are the so-called "Generalized Bas-Relief Ambiguities":

$$z(x_1, x_2) \mapsto \lambda z(x_1, x_2) + \nu x_1 + \mu x_2 \tag{3.20}$$

where $z(x_1, x_2)$ is the distance to the surface of the viewed object, as above. This ambiguity corresponds to a scaling in depth and the addition of a plane. Such ambiguities occur in renaissance art and can frequently be seen in Italian cathedrals and churches. In fact, it can be shown (Belhumeur et al. 97) that such transformations leave unaffected the totality of images of a fixed object under varying illumination (called the *illumination cone* of the object), even when all shadows are included. Moreover, the GBR are the only transformations that leave the illumination cone invariant (see Figure 3.19).

From a pattern-theoretic perspective, one way to resolve the GBR ambiguity is by the use of prior knowledge. For face recognition such knowledge is almost always available. The work by Atick et al., described in Chapter 2, used such strong prior knowledge about the shape of heads that the effect of the GBR was, presumably, negligible. It can, however, cause significant biases in situations where the necessary prior knowledge is lacking. On the other hand, it helps justify the use of bas-relief sculptures with subjects for which the observers have strong perceptual priors. The sculpturers can save material by relying on the GBR and the observers' strong priors.

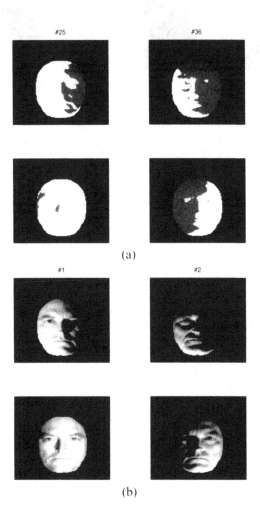

(a)

(b)

Figure 3.17. The top four images show the shadows extracted by our approach for the corresponding four input images at the bottom.

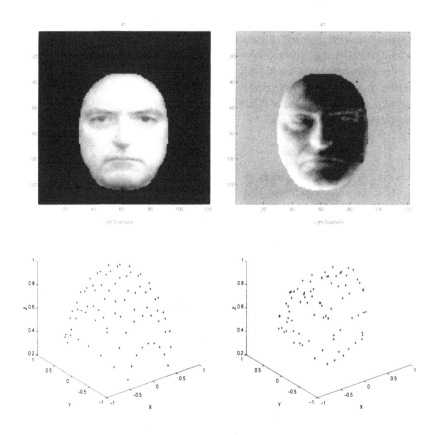

Figure 3.18. Top row: The albedo $\mathbf{a(x)}$ and an ambient lighting factor in $\mathbf{n(x).s}$ of a face image are obtained using the shadow rejection technique. Bottom: Tne bottom row shows the true lighting (left) and the estimated lighting (right) for 60 faces.

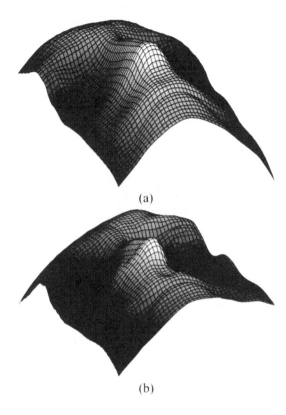

(a)

(b)

Figure 3.19. Figure (a) shows the face reconstructed using integrability. Observe that the reconstruction is remarkably accurate. In figure (b) we introduced a GBR by hand to demonstrate the type of deformations which might arise.

Chapter 4

Modeling Variations in Geometry

In this chapter, we propose methods for automatically warping the domain of a model image onto some subdomain of the input image. We will not consider illumination changes but assume that, after a suitable warp, the model or template matches closely the input image. Such warpings will be used to match two faces (i) when seen from a different viewpoints; (ii) when seen with different expressions; and (iii) of two different individuals. Specifically, for both rigid and plastic deformations, we will discuss the properties of and optimization methods for energy functions whose global minima are solutions to the warping problem. The sought-for match cannot be perfect if some features are visible in one image but not in the other, e.g., because some part of the face rotates into view in one image but not the other, the expression change opens or closes an eye or mouth or one individual has features such as hair or glasses absent in the other. However, we will show that the performance can be quite good even when the topographies of template and model do not match.

4.1 Global and Local Warps

We would like to find a warp $\phi(\mathbf{x})$ that minimizes the cost functional

$$
\begin{aligned}
E[\phi] \;=\; & \underbrace{|\mathcal{D}|^{-1} \int_{\mathcal{D}} \psi\{I(\phi(\mathbf{x})) - M(\mathbf{x}))\} d\mathbf{x}}_{\text{intensity matching term}} \\[2ex]
+ \; & \underbrace{\beta |\mathcal{D}|^{-1} \int_{\mathcal{D}} \psi\{\Phi_e(I(\phi(\mathbf{x})); \sigma) - \Phi_e(M(\mathbf{x}); \sigma)\} d\mathbf{x}}_{\text{edge matching term}} \\[2ex]
+ \; & \underbrace{E_{prior}[\phi]}_{\text{prior term}} \qquad\qquad\qquad (4.1)
\end{aligned}
$$

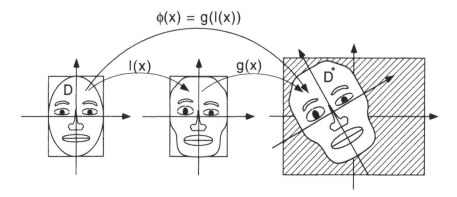

Figure 4.1. Global and local warping operating on the entire face

Here $\Phi_e(\cdot, \sigma)$ is an edge operator of scale σ. The simplest example would be:

$$\Phi_e(I, \sigma) \;=\; ||\nabla(I * G_\sigma)||^2 \tag{4.2}$$

where G_σ is a gaussian kernel of size σ, but other more sophisticated edge detectors can be used. The point of the edge term is to make explicit edge features in I and M and ask that they match (compare the eye algorithm in Section 2.3). In general, any set of dense feature maps computed from the input and model images can be used in the data term.

We assume that low-level processes can provide an adequate initial estimate of scale and location of the input face, so we are generally interested in the question of finding a warp $\phi(\mathbf{x})$ which is near an initial guess. Nonetheless, to find the correct $\phi(\mathbf{x})$ using a local optimization method like gradient descent with respect to the functional E, corresponding intensity peaks and valleys in the model and data images must overlap, so we are forced to explicitly define $\phi(\mathbf{x})$ as the composition of a global (affine) transformation $g(\mathbf{x})$ used to adjust the position, scale, and rotation of the face and a local transformation $\ell(\mathbf{x})$ used to adjust the precise boundaries and internal features of the face. By finding the best affine transformation first, we considerably raise the probability that the local warping will correctly perform fine-scale tuning. Similar ideas are developed in the thesis by Matevic (97).

As in Figure 4.1, the entire warp can then be written as the composition

$$\phi(x, y) \;=\; (g \circ \ell)(x, y) \tag{4.3}$$

The global warp will be given by

$$g(\mathbf{x}) \;=\; R_\theta S_\sigma (\mathbf{x} - \mathbf{a}) + \mathbf{t} \tag{4.4}$$

where R_θ is the rotation matrix defined by θ, S_σ is a diagonal scaling matrix diag$\{\sigma_x, \sigma_y\}$, $\mathbf{a}$ is the center of rotation (typically the center of the model domain), and $\mathbf{t}$ is a translation $(t_x, t_y)'$. $g(\mathbf{x})$ is constructed so that the model face can be scaled vertically and horizontally and then rotated, but not sheared, since shears play no role in weak perspective projection or individual variation. Mathematically, g can be characterized as the most general affine transformation such that there exists a reflection s_1 about some line such that $s_1 \circ g = g \circ s_0$, where s_0 is reflection about the vertical line through $\mathbf{a}$. In other words, g carries an object symmetric about a vertical line into an object symmetric about some other line.

The local warp is written as

$$\ell(\mathbf{x}) \quad = \quad \mathbf{x} + u(\mathbf{x}) \tag{4.5}$$

$\ell(\mathbf{x})$ will capture the different local compressions, expansions, shears, rotations, and shifts occuring on the interior of the domain being warped, e.g., how much thinner the nose bridge in the input image is than the nose bridge in the model. ℓ is allowed to be any diffeomorphism: recall that a homeomorphism is a one-to-one, onto, continuous function while a diffeomorphism is simply a homeomorphism that is differentiable over its entire domain and has a differentiable inverse. The continuity property of ℓ is important because it implies that the topology of the image is preserved. The one-to-one and onto properties insure that ℓ is invertible.

While the global warp is well-motivated physically and has obvious interpretations over both continuous and discrete domains, the local warp is not so obviously well-defined. In three dimensions, we can imagine that there exists some homeomorphism taking the face of one individual to the face of another, and that furthermore, after projection of the faces onto the image planes, there exist homeomorphisms warping the image domain of the first face to that of the second. However, this conception has three problems computationally.

First, it will not be possible to find a homeomorphism ϕ such that $I(\phi(\mathbf{x}))$ exactly equals $M(\mathbf{x})$ for several reasons: There are a variety of geometric changes that can cause topological changes in the intensity landscape, e.g., the skin can be heavily furrowed in one face, smooth in the other, the base of the nose can be differently tilted so the nostrils are more or less visible, the expression can change, and the direction of gaze can shift. Also, there will be errors in the intensities of the model image, so that the correspondence will be inexact at best. One way around this problem is to assume that there will be some coarse-enough resolution at which the input and model intensity landscapes are close enough that it does makes sense to look for a continuous warp, and then at higher resolutions to insist that the warp stay smooth in spite of intensity differences.

The second problem is that in fact we work with discretely sampled image domains and only compute the warp ψ on the lattice points of a grid. But the set of homeomorphisms yielding any given map between input and model lattice points

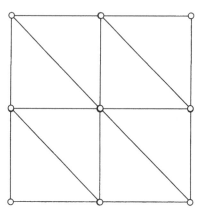

Figure 4.2. A section of the continuous domain $\mathcal{D}$ partitioned into triangular regions whose vertices are the lattice points $\{\mathbf{x}_{ij}\}$.

is infinite. However, the set of discrete warps defined on the image lattice can be put into one-to-one correspondence with a suitable set of piecewise bilinear homeomorphisms on the continuous image domain: imagine each two by two block of lattice points as defining two triangular regions that are each mapped bilinearly (see Figure 4.2). This gives us a canonical way to extend the warp from the lattice points to the whole domain. In the continuous setting, it is an easy result that a function is a diffeomorphism if (a) the boundary of the domain maps to the boundary of the range; and that (b) the determinant of the Jacobian at each point is positive. In the discrete setting, we get the result that if the map on lattice points maps each of these triangular regions into a triangle of the same orientation, then this bilinear extension is a homeomorphism. In this way, sufficiently smooth diffeomorphisms can be effectively described on the computer by their values on a lattice. This fails for diffeomeorphisms with complex local structure finer than the lattice.

A third problem, which effects both global and local warps, relates to what happens when the derivative of ϕ is very big or very small. To evaluate the integral E, we have to make it into a finite sum and there are three possibilities depending on whether we match using ϕ, ϕ^{-1} or a combination of both:

$$E_{forwards}[\phi] = |\mathcal{V}|^{-1} \sum_{\mathbf{x}_{ij} \in \mathcal{V}} \psi(I(\phi(\mathbf{x}_{ij})) - M(\mathbf{x}_{ij})) \qquad (4.6)$$

$$E_{backwards}[\phi] = |\mathcal{V}^*|^{-1} \sum_{\mathbf{x}_{kl}^* \in \mathcal{V}^*} \psi(I(\mathbf{x}_{kl}^*) - M(\phi^{-1}(\mathbf{x}_{kl}^*))) \qquad (4.7)$$

$$E_{both}[\phi] = \frac{1}{2}E_{forwards}[\phi] + \frac{1}{2}E_{backwards}[\phi] \qquad (4.8)$$

The problem is that for both $E_{forwards}[\phi]$ and $E_{backwards}[\phi]$ if the derivative of ϕ is too large (respectively, too small), then when computing this sum, one can skip lattice points in the range (respectively, the domain) of ϕ (see Figure 4.6) and I and M may match very badly at these skipped points. Using functional E_{both} avoids this problem, but then requires one to compute ϕ^{-1} from ϕ at each gradient descent step, which involves considerable computation. We will opt to use $E_{forward}$ since then the domain of integration is constant, so the cost per evaluation does not vary, and the derivatives with respect to the global parameters are simpler than if the domain varied. This will require the smoothness constraints to be more heavily weighted than they would be ideally, but will allow computation to proceed in a more timely fashion.

To summarize, the key restrictions we need to place on ϕ in order to do our minimization algorithm will work are that (i) it is reasonably smooth and locally orientation-preserving; and (ii) that its derivative be small enough, so that almost all template and all data points can be matched.

4.2 A Robust Treatment of Intensity Differences

Driving the domain warpings are the differences in intensities (or other features) of model and input images. Past approaches in the computer vision literature have always assumed that when two images are to be matched, the residual difference between them is Gaussian noise. For example, Horn and Schunck (81) assume that the changes in brightness between two frames in a motion sequence are due to small motions plus the additive Gaussian noise normally generated by an optical imaging system. This is equivalent in our problem to assuming $\delta = I(\phi(\mathbf{x})) - M(\mathbf{x})$ is distributed like gaussian noise (or, equivalently, to solving for ϕ by a least squares fit). This model is not at all accurate and the issue of noise needs to handled differently. Typically both the model and input images will have pixels whose intensity values are outliers, e.g., occlusions from glasses and facial hair, shadows from wrinkles, errors in the model intensity. For this reason we want to use a matching norm that forgives heavier tails than those of the normal distribution. This is the idea behind robust statistics.

One of the simplest robust models for errors is given by:

$$\Pr(\delta < a; h) = \frac{1}{Z} \int_{-\infty}^{a} e^{-\psi(x;h)} dx \qquad (4.9)$$

where

$$\psi(\delta; h) = \begin{cases} 2h|\delta| - h^2 & \text{if } \delta < -h \\ \delta^2 & \text{if } |\delta| \leq h \\ 2h\delta - h^2 & \text{if } \delta > h \end{cases} \qquad (4.10)$$

$$Z = \text{erf}(h) + \frac{1}{e^{-h^2}} \qquad (4.11)$$

In the application to warping, we will assume that the conditional probability of a particular input image $I(\mathbf{x}_{ij})$ given $\phi(\mathbf{x}_{ij})$ is

$$\Pr(I|\phi) \quad = \quad \Pi_{ij} e^{-\psi(I(\phi(\mathbf{x}_{ij}))-M(\mathbf{x}_{ij}))-\beta\psi(\Phi_e(I(\phi(\mathbf{x})))-\Phi_e(M(\mathbf{x})))} \quad (4.12)$$

where $I(\phi(\mathbf{x}_{ij}))$ and $\Phi_e(I(\phi(\mathbf{x})))$ are, in the discrete case, understood to depend on the interpolation method since I and $\Phi_e(I)$ are defined only for lattice points. If we only included the first term, this would assume that errors were independently and identically distributed between pixels. The presumption of independence is patently wrong when noise is actually due to physical objects or distortions and the independence assumption should be replaced by modeling regions as mixture distributions of the kinds of confounding signals most commonly expected (e.g., highlights on the eyes). The second term goes some way towards a more accurate model, though certainly not the really correct one. Note that the data term of the energy functional in equation (4.1) is obtained by composing equation (4.12) with $-\log(\cdot)$ so that the solutions to the minimization of the data term of equation (4.1) alone are the same as those to the maximization of equation (4.12). Figure 4.3 compares graphs of ψ and its derivative with the L^1 and L^2 norms associated with the exponential and normal distributions respectively.

As will be shown below, robustness can contribute significantly to expanding the range of model-input pairs for which a given cost functional will work. However, one potential drawback is that, as with any maximum likelihood type estimator for location, $\psi(x; h)$ is not scale equivariant (since h is fixed independently of the range of intensity differences) and so technically one needs to co-estimate a scale γ and optimize using $\psi(x/\gamma; h)$. However, intensities are scaled by the imaging system to always lie in $[0, 255]$ so this problem can be disregarded for our purposes. (If not, then later the coefficients of the lighting basis vectors used will effectively provide a scale estimate.)

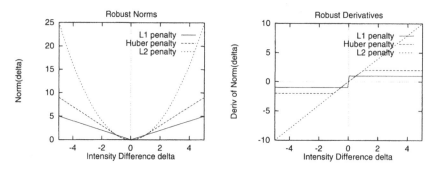

Figure 4.3. Robust norms (left) and their derivatives (right). The Huber norm has $h = 1$ for illustrative purposes. In practice, h is usually 50 or 100.

4.3 The Global Warp

The global warping is straightforward to locate in concept, but difficult in practice both because the space of transformations is non-Euclidean and because there are many local minima. Prior work on this problem has centered on computing the optic flow of moving rigid objects and has taken four tacks: brute force search (e.g., Fuh 92), linearization of the image intensities or filter outputs with respect to image coordinates (e.g., Horn and Schunck 81), matching corresponding sparse image structures such as lines (e.g., Cipolla and Blake 92) and linearization about the global parameters coupled with gradient descent from multiple starting points (e.g., Manmatha 94)). Since we assume above that there already exist reasonable estimates of scale, rotation, and translation, and since the global warps we might expect are not necessarily small (changes in scale of twenty percent or rotations of 15-20 degrees will not be unusual), we pursue a fifth approach, which is to solve for the global warp directly using gradient descent.

The continuous cost functional that we will use for finding the best affine transformation warping $\mathcal{D}$ to $\mathcal{D}I$ is

$$
E[g] \;=\; \underbrace{\alpha |\mathcal{D}|^{-1} \int_{\mathcal{D}} \psi(I(g(\mathbf{x})) - M(\mathbf{x})) d\mathbf{x}}_{\text{intensity matching term}}
$$

$$
+ \;\; \underbrace{k_1(\sigma_x - 1)^2 + k_2(\sigma_y - 1)^2 + k_3 \left(\frac{\sigma_x}{\sigma_y} - 1 \right)^2}_{\text{prior term}} \tag{4.13}
$$

The energy landscape is not convex, and is only as differentiable as the model and input image functions. Further, there is not necessarily just one local minimum. Also, it should be realized that the data term by itself can sometimes have minima in which the area of domain $\mathcal{D}^*$ shrinks to near zero, for example, when a very dark model latches on to a small intensity valley with a large surround in the input image. The latter possibility is of lesser consequence when the model image is fixed, but requires more consideration later when the model image intensities are themselves parameterized and subject to variation. In any case, the priors discussed below serve to excise such minima from the landscape.

The prior distributions on the global rotation and translation parameters are uniform. However, the distributions on the scale parameters are not. First, when we match input data against the model for a particular individual, we expect that $\sigma_x = \sigma_y$ under weak perspective projection. This is enforced as a hard constraint during the matching scheme (i.e., we search over a restricted space of transforms.) When comparing input data to a generic face model, we approximate the distribution of the ratio σ_x/σ_y by a normal distribution with unit mean and variance $1/(2k_3)$. This is clearly both arbitrary and incorrect since we could just as well choose σ_y/σ_x and since $\sigma_x, \sigma_y > 0$ (i.e., no flips are allowed), but it empirically proves to be an adequate constraint.

One further prior proves useful in practice. We will solve for g by a multiresolution method: i.e., we form a pyramid of progressively more and more coarsely smoothed and resampled images and carry out the matching starting at the coarsest image and refine it step by step. This means that we can assume we have a reasonable initial condition for gradient descent at each step.

4.3.1 Design Issues

To find g, we need to establish appropriate discretization, interpolation, quadrature, and pyramid schemes. Two approaches can be followed: (1) find an approximate solution to the set of partial-differential equations (the Euler-Lagrange equations) obtained using the variational calculus; or (2) discretize the original problem and find an exact solution to it. Both approaches depend on the premise that the underlying image is continuous, because in either case, it will be necessary to interpolate between known pixel values, particularly if the quadrature step size is less than one pixel. We follow approach two, for which the corresponding discrete data energy function is

$$E[g] = N^{-1} \sum_{ij} \psi(I(g(\mathbf{x}_{ij})) - M(\mathbf{x}_{ij})) \tag{4.14}$$

where $\mathbf{x}_{ij} = (x_0 + i\Delta x, y_0 + j\Delta y)$ and N depends on Δx and Δy. The derivative of E with respect to a parameter p (one of t_x, t_y, σ_x, σ_y or θ) is

$$\frac{\partial E}{\partial p} = N^{-1} \sum_{ij} \psi'\left(I(g(\mathbf{x}_{ij})) - M(\mathbf{x}_{ij})\right)\left(\nabla I(g(\mathbf{x}_{ij})) \cdot \left(\frac{\partial x'}{\partial p}, \frac{\partial y'}{\partial p}\right)\right) \tag{4.15}$$

where

$$\left(\frac{\partial x'}{\partial x_t}, \frac{\partial y'}{\partial x_t}\right) = (1, 0) \tag{4.16}$$

$$\left(\frac{\partial x'}{\partial y_t}, \frac{\partial y'}{\partial y_t}\right) = (0, 1) \tag{4.17}$$

$$\left(\frac{\partial x'}{\partial \sigma_x}, \frac{\partial y'}{\partial \sigma_x}\right) = x\hat{i} \tag{4.18}$$

$$\left(\frac{\partial x'}{\partial \sigma_y}, \frac{\partial y'}{\partial \sigma_y}\right) = y\hat{j} \tag{4.19}$$

$$\left(\frac{\partial x'}{\partial \theta}, \frac{\partial y'}{\partial \theta}\right) = \sigma_x x\hat{j} - \sigma_y y\hat{i} \tag{4.20}$$

where $\hat{i} = (\cos(\theta), \sin(\theta))$ and $\hat{j} = (-\sin(\theta), \cos(\theta))$. Derivatives at locations x_{ij} are obtained using centered differences. To insure differentiability, the interpolation method should in principle be at least cubic. However, cubic interpolation has the side effect of making the intensity landscape more bumpy that it would otherwise be, which in turn can increase the number of local minima. We compared both bilinear and bicubic Hermite methods, and found that bilinear interpolation seems slightly better for this reason, as well as being much faster computationally.

A parameter p would thus normally be updated according to

$$p^{t+1} = p^t - \delta \frac{\partial E}{\partial p} \tag{4.21}$$

where δ controls the step size. However, we cannot perform gradient descent directly because of three serious problems: local minima caused by misregistered features within the input and model faces, local minima corresponding to incorrect registration of model features and features exterior to the correct image subdomain, and the difference in physical units between the scale, rotation, and translation parameters. Each of these problems requires a distinct modification of the simple gradient descent algorithm.

4.3.1.1 COARSE-TO-FINE MATCHING First, consider an example in which input and model images are of the same face but are misaligned so that the open eye of the input initially matches to a point above the dark eyebrow of the model. If we then try to slide the input into alignment with the model image, we will find that if the eye and eyebrows of the model are resolvable then the input eye will lock onto the eyebrow. This problem can only be resolved by defining a Gaussian pyramid of model and input images, and registering each pair first at a coarse level and then at successively higher resolutions. In our implementation, pyramid levels are separated by a full octave, i.e., coarser resolutions are obtained from finer resolutions by smoothing two times with a 3×3 binomial kernel and then subsampling every other pixel. Because the input image background will influence smoothed versions of the face input at the boundaries of the face domain, pixels at a given level without full support at the next highest resolution are deleted, i.e., boundaries are eroded as the resolution decreases. Note though that such erosion can change the topology of the input intensity landscape to be quite different. For example, a small intensity peak between the boundary and a larger intensity valley can be totally eroded at a coarse-enough resolution.

4.3.1.2 ORDERED SEARCH OF PARAMETER SUBSPACES Second, both scale and rotation parameters are more easily found when the centers of expansion, contraction, and rotation of the input and model images are first aligned by estimating the translation parameters. This is again because of local minima. Similarly, rotations are best performed after the scale estimate has been found since then the features required to rotate a model face onto an input face are more likely to overlap. These observations give rise to a strategy that divides the minimization process into distinct epochs in which only some of the parameters are estimated and the remaining ones are held constant at values provided at the end of the proceeding epoch. Similar optimization schedules have been used in Yuille et al. (92) for more complicated parameter spaces.

4.3.1.3 PARAMETER WEIGHTS   Third, since the physical units of the parameters of the global warp are not comparable (e.g., radians for θ vs. pixels for $\mathbf{t}$), the step size for each parameter p needs to be rescaled by a factor c_p before a gradient descent step can be sensibly made, i.e.,

$$p^{t+1} = p^t - \delta \frac{\partial E}{\partial p} c_p \tag{4.22}$$

Two methods of determining the weights c_p were compared. One uses a sets of weights that were determined by trial and error. Another computes a "natural" metric

$$\|g\|^2_{nat} = \frac{1}{N} \sum_{ij} \|(R_\theta S_\sigma \mathbf{x}_{ij} + \mathbf{t}) - \mathbf{x}_{ij}\|^2 \tag{4.23}$$

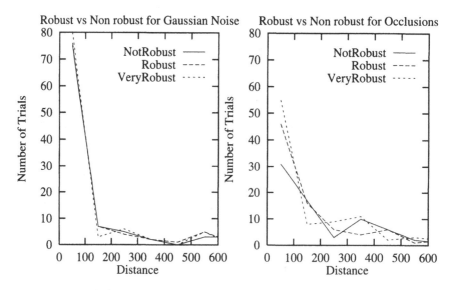

Figure 4.4. For both graphs, *robust* implies $h = 50$ while *very robust* implies $h = 20$. Left: Comparison of robust and non-robust optimization when the model has been corrupted by Gaussian noise of zero mean and standard deviation 20 (values outside [0,255] are clipped). The robust norm works almost as well as the least squares as expected. Right: Comparison the model has been corrupted by 5 randomly distributed black or white patches simulating partial occlusions of up to 17 percent of the image area. The robust norm works considerably better.

on the space of global warps, approximates this and uses it to rescale the individual components of the gradient so that their units are comparable. The heuristic method worked as well as the "natural" one and was used in all subsequent experiments.

4.3.2   Results

To test out different optimization strategies and implementation details, a set of experiments was run on twenty 256 x 256 greyscale images of different scenes, some natural, some artificial, and some containing people. A 90 x 90 patch of each image was defined as the model image so that a perfect match was known to exist. Then, five times for each model/input pair, a randomly generated five-parameter global warp was applied to the model, and then recovered by using one of the matching strategies described above.

The results can be summarized as follows:

- Ordered subspace search is required to overcome local minima.

- Subpixel quadrature step sizes yield no benefit.

- The interpolation method is relatively unimportant, though bilinear seems to have a slight advantage.

- Robust matching is very useful for partial occlusions and similar speckle noise, and is only mildly less effective for Gaussian noise situations than is least squares.

For example, Figure 4.4 shows histograms of $\|g\|_{nat}^2$ for the experiments comparing non-robust, robust, and very-robust matching terms.

We conclude with some examples of cases illuminating typical problems caused by local minima. In the leftmost pair of Figure 4.5 the white shirts of the running girls get matched against the white sand in the background behind the dark skirts. In the rightmost pair, there is a local minima at a coarser resolution where the lighter area of stone steps and columns and darker area of foliage stand in rough correspondence, but then at a higher resolution the edges of the columns cannot be slid across the lighter areas without incurring a penalty in energy.

4.4   Homogeneous Local Warping

Define the flow fields $\mathbf{u}(\mathbf{x}) = (u_x(x,y), u_y(x,y))$ and $\mathbf{v}(\mathbf{x}) = (v_x(x,y), v_y(x,y))$ induced by the forward and inverse local warpings respectively by

$$\ell(\mathbf{x}) \;=\; \mathbf{x} + \mathbf{u}(\mathbf{x}) \tag{4.24}$$

$$\ell^{-1}(\mathbf{x}) \;=\; \mathbf{x} + \mathbf{v}(\mathbf{x}) \tag{4.25}$$

Figure 4.5. Typical errors in the global warping process. The top row shows the images $M(\mathbf{x})$, while the second row shows the corresponding images $I(g(\mathbf{x}))$. See text for discussion

We will consider four issues that effect the design of the warping algorithm:

- the choice of data distributions, i.e., the use of robustness

- the choice of prior distributions, including any weighting parameters

- whether to use edge data as well as intensity data when matching

- the choice of boundary conditions

Relevant implementation issues such as choice of interpolation method, pyramid scheme, and direction of warping are resolved in the same fashion as for global warping, and so will not be discussed.

For a discretized local flow, the two most important issues are the density of the flow vectors and the spatial variation of the smoothness constraint (the prior distribution). In this section, we consider only dense flows under uniform (spatially non-varying) priors. Without the priors, this problem is ill-posed since with one displacement vector for each pixel there are $2N$ unknowns but N data points.

Figure 4.6 shows the type of warping problem we will commonly confront, i.e., we would like to be able to close the more widely opened input eye $I(\mathbf{x})$ just enough to match the model eye $M(\mathbf{x})$. However, the input eye has highlights that are not found in the model eye, and it also has an almost discontinuous change in topology at the bottom of the iris. In the reconstructed image $I(\ell(\mathbf{x}))$, however, the highlight has disappeared, a victim of the skipping phenomena caused by the determinant of the Jacobian getting too large. This skipping results in a final energy that is appears low but should be high. The bottom of the iris seems correctly handled, but in reality the color of the bottom eyelid is sufficiently close to the color of the whites that the skin can absorb some of the white without too high a penalty as is seen in $M(\ell^{-1}(\mathbf{x}))$, where the skin is pulled up to "create" more white area. If the skin was much darker than the white the distortion in that area would be considerably higher.

4.4.1 Prior Distributions

The choice of prior on general diffeomorphisms ℓ is a very interesting issue. As mentioned in Chapter 2, Bajscy and her students first introduced the elasticity theory for this purpose. We first recall some of the basic definitions of elasticity theory (see Gurtin 81, Marsden and Hughes 83). The setup of elasticity theory is very similar to that of warping a model image to an input image. In elasticity theory a body is given which has a reference configuration, call it $\mathcal{D} \subset \mathbf{R}^n$ and points $\mathbf{x} \in \mathcal{D}$ are called material points. Then one considers deforming the body by some diffeomorphism $\ell : \mathcal{D} \hookrightarrow \mathbf{R}^n$, and points $\mathbf{y} = \ell(\mathbf{x})$ are called spatial points. The subject is notationally complex because almost everything can be done both in material and in spatial coordinates. Here n may be any positive number, though $n = 3$ is relevant to the world and $n = 2$ is relevant to our image processing analogy. This deformation creates internal forces in the body, the stresses which one computes as a function of the deformation via the so-called constitutive equation. At each point $\mathbf{x} \in \mathcal{D}$ of the reference body, let the matrix of derivatives of ℓ be $D\ell(\mathbf{x})$. $D\ell' D\ell$ and $D\ell D\ell'$ are both called the *strain* matrix,

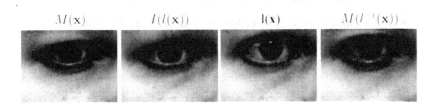

Figure 4.6. An example of locally warping the template to look like the input. The warp looks good, but what happened to the highlights?

the first being in material coordinates, the second in spatial coordinates. If $n = 2$

$$D\ell = \begin{pmatrix} \frac{\partial \ell_x}{\partial x} & \frac{\partial \ell_x}{\partial y} \\ \frac{\partial \ell_y}{\partial x} & \frac{\partial \ell_y}{\partial y} \end{pmatrix} = \begin{pmatrix} 1 + \frac{\partial u_x}{\partial x} & \frac{\partial u_x}{\partial y} \\ \frac{\partial u_y}{\partial x} & 1 + \frac{\partial u_y}{\partial y} \end{pmatrix} \qquad (4.26)$$

The consitutive equation gives the stress as a function $S(D\ell(\mathbf{x}), \mathbf{x})$ of the strain. S is a matrix whose $(i, j)^{th}$ component measures the force in direction i exerted by a small part of the body on the adjacent part displaced in direction j. As with strain, the stress can be given in material or spatial coordinates: we take it to be in spatial coordinates as this is where the force is acting. The case which we want to use in image processing is the hyperelastic case, defined by the fact that the body loses no energy to heat. In this case, the stress can be measured as a gradient of the stored energy as follows: Instead of the matrix-valued constitutive function S, we have a scalar function $e(D\ell(\mathbf{x}), \mathbf{x})$, called the strain energy density, whose integral (in material coordinates)

$$E(\ell) = \int_{\mathcal{D}} e(D\ell(\mathbf{x}), \mathbf{x}), d\mathbf{x}$$

is the total strain energy or energy stored in body by virtue of the deformation ℓ. Then the stress itself is the first variation of E as ℓ varies in the following sense:

$$\lim_{\epsilon \to 0} \frac{E(\ell + \epsilon \mathbf{w} \circ \ell) - E(\ell)}{\epsilon} = \iint \text{tr}(S(D\ell, \ell^{-1}\mathbf{y}) \cdot D\mathbf{w}(\mathbf{y})')dy$$

Here it is more natural to take the second integral in spatial coordinates $\mathbf{y}$.

The following conditions may be imposed on the constitutive equation:

- $e(J, \mathbf{x}) \geq e(I_n, \mathbf{x}) = 0$ so the reference position has minimum energy and e goes to infinity when either $||J||$ goes to infinity or $\det(J)$ goes to zero,

- $e(UJ, \mathbf{x}) = e(J, \mathbf{x})$, where U is orthogonal, called frame indifference. This means that if the body is translated or rotated, its stored energy doesn't change.

- $e(JU, \mathbf{x}) = e(J, \mathbf{x})$, where U is orthogonal, called isotropy, i.e., the body has the same response to deformation in each direction.

- $e(J, \mathbf{x})$ independent of $\mathbf{x}$, called homogeniety, i.e., the body has the same response to deformation at each point.

The first two are always assumed and imply that e may be written as a function of the strain $J'J$. If all four are assumed, it follows that e is a fixed symmetric function of the singular values of J. A simple example of a family of constitutive functions is given by the Hadamard formula:

$$e(J) = \alpha \text{tr}(J'J) + h(\det(J))$$

where h is convex, goes to infinity when its argument goes to zero or infinity, and $h(1) = -h'(1) = -2\alpha$.

We shall present the results of two sets of experiments with two constitutive equations, the first being the simplest possible choice, but one not satisfying any of the above conditions, and the other a simple choice which satisfies all the conditions. The first is the standard Gaussian prior, used by Horn and Schunck (81):

$$e_{prior1}[\ell] = \alpha_1 \text{tr} \left((D\ell(\mathbf{x}) - I)'(D\ell(\mathbf{x}) - I) \right) \tag{4.27}$$

$$= \alpha_1 \left(\frac{\partial u_x}{\partial x} \right)^2 + \left(\frac{\partial u_x}{\partial y} \right)^2 + \left(\frac{\partial u_y}{\partial x} \right)^2 + \left(\frac{\partial u_y}{\partial y} \right)^2 \tag{4.28}$$

The energy here is zero only for translations. This prior will be used as a baseline for comparison. Its most serious flaws are a lack of frame indifference (i.e., it is non-zero for rotations ℓ) and that the energy does not go infinity if $D\ell$ goes to zero. The fact that this prior penalizes rotations is not so serious in our experiment because we have already made a global coordinate change which included a rotation.

Another sort of constitutive equation is one for which the strain energy of a contraction is the same as that for an expansion, or equivalently, that the energy of the forward warp evaluated in material coordinates (in our case, over the model domain) is equal to the cost of the corresponding inverse warp evaluated in spatial coordinates (or over the input domain). If $\mathbf{y} = \ell(\mathbf{x})$ and ℓ maps $\mathcal{D}$ to $\mathcal{D}^*$ by a diffeomorphism, then this property of a penalty e can be written as

$$\int_{\mathcal{D}} e(D\ell) d\mathbf{x} = \int_{\mathcal{D}^*} e(D(\ell^{-1})) d\mathbf{y} \tag{4.29}$$

This constraint defines an entire family of priors for the Jacobian. In one dimension, we might use a penalty function

$$e_1(a) = a^p + \frac{1}{a^{p-1}} \tag{4.30}$$

for p, a positive integer. To see this, note that the integral of e_1 can be written symmetrically as $\int dx^{1-p} dy^p + dx^p dy^{1-p}$. A formula in two dimensions is obtained from considering the singular values λ and μ of $D\ell$ and is

$$e_{1'}(\lambda, \mu) = (\lambda^2 + \mu^2)(1 + (\lambda\mu)^{-1}) \tag{4.31}$$

which does in fact satisfy equation 4.29. Empirically it proves useful to break the property slightly by penalizing near-zero Jacobians even more heavily, using the penalty

$$e_2(\lambda, \mu) = (\lambda^2 + \mu^2)(1 + (\lambda\mu)^{-2}) \tag{4.32}$$

Since $(\lambda^2 + \mu^2) = \text{tr}(D\ell'D\ell)$ and $\lambda\mu = \det D\ell$, the energy functional can be written

$$E_{prior2}[\ell] = \alpha_2 \int_\mathcal{D} \left(\text{tr}D\ell(\mathbf{x})'D\ell(\mathbf{x})\left(1 + \frac{1}{\det D\ell(\mathbf{x})^2}\right) - 4\right) d\mathbf{x} \quad (4.33)$$

$$= \alpha_2 \int_\mathcal{D} \left(\left(\frac{\partial\ell_x}{\partial x}\right)^2 + \left(\frac{\partial\ell_x}{\partial y}\right)^2 + \left(\frac{\partial\ell_y}{\partial x}\right)^2 + \left(\frac{\partial\ell_y}{\partial y}\right)^2\right)$$

$$\left(1 + \left(\frac{\partial\ell_x}{\partial x}\frac{\partial\ell_y}{\partial y} - \frac{\partial\ell_x}{\partial y}\frac{\partial\ell_y}{\partial x}\right)^{-2}\right) - 4 \cdot d\mathbf{x} \quad (4.34)$$

where subtracting 4 sets the value of the prior to zero when ℓ is the identity map.

Though both E_{prior1} and E_{prior2} penalize local translations, shears, and rotations, they do so quite differently. E_{prior2} explicitly penalizes local shears, but not translations or rotations. The latter two though usually induce shears or scale changes in neighboring patches, which are indeed penalized, and so show up when the local cost is integrated over the entire domain. E_{prior1} lacks rotation invariance and so penalizes local shears and rotations explicitly, and local translations implicitly. More importantly, the extent to which E_{prior1} and E_{prior2} penalize these transforms varies considerably. Figure 4.7 shows plots of $\log(E_{prior2}/E_{prior1})$ versus each of four different local transforms: rotation, shear, uniform scaling and x-translation. The transformations are applied to the center four points of a four by four lattice, and the remaining boundary points have $\ell(\mathbf{x}_{ij}) = \mathbf{x}_{ij}$. The most heavily penalized transformations (by both priors) are of course rotations and translations, since any rotation of a subdomain will involve relatively large deformations with unbalanced eigenvalues along the outer edge of the rotated region, and translations will severely compress patches along boundaries (particularly in the case where boundary flow is fixed at zero). However, the plots show that E_{prior2} penalizes extreme rotations and translations much more severely than E_{prior1}, so we can assume that for a fixed value of the smoothing parameter α that E_{prior2} will tend to prefer smaller scale changes more evenly distributed over the lattice than, for example, large series of translations and a few scale changes nearer the boundaries. The significance of such preferences are of course modulated by the difference in the intensity values of the model and input images, but the robustness of the data term allows such preferences to be more pronounced than would otherwise be the case.

4.4.1.1 BOUNDARY CONDITIONS Currently $u(\mathbf{x})$ and $v(\mathbf{x})$ are set to zero at the boundary. This is fine as long as the boundaries of the model face domain lie within the boundaries of the input face domain. If the shape of the face is to be accurately captured, though, the derivatives of u and v should be set to zero at boundary.

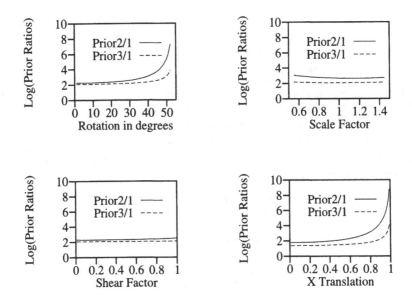

Figure 4.7. Plots of $\log(E_{prior2}/E_{prior1})$ for different deformations of a small patch within a grid. The translations and rotations applied cause some triangles to deform much more severely than with the shears and scales chosen, so the plots indicate by how much more than prior 1, prior 2 penalizes severe deformations.

4.4.2 The Algorithm

We use the probability distribution on the diffeomorphisms ℓ defined in the last section. The probability distribution of intensity differences is assumed to be exactly identical to the global warping case, i.e.,

$$E_{data}[\ell] = |\mathcal{D}|^{-1} \int_{\mathcal{D}} \psi\{I(\ell(\mathbf{x})) - S(\mathbf{x})\}d\mathbf{x} \qquad (4.35)$$

The gradient descent algorithm for local warping is simpler than in the case of global warping because all variables have the same units and priority, so there is no need for rescaling or epochs. The more important problem lies in ensuring that the discretization of $D\ell$ does not miss any of the triangular subdomains shown in Figure 4.2. Three numerical approximations are the centered difference D_c, the forward difference D_r, and the backward difference D_l.

$$D_c = \left(\begin{array}{cc} \left(\dfrac{(u_x(i+1,j)-u_x(i-1,j)-1)}{2} \right) & \left(\dfrac{(u_x(i,j+1)-u_x(i,j-1))}{2} \right) \\ \left(\dfrac{(u_y(i+1,j)-u_y(i-1,j))}{2} \right) & \left(\dfrac{(u_y(i,j+1)-u_y(i,j-1)-1)}{2} \right) \end{array} \right) \qquad (4.36)$$

$$D_r = \begin{pmatrix} (u_x(i+1,j) - u_x(i,j)) & (u_x(i,j+1) - u_x(i,j)) \\ (u_y(i+1,j) - u_y(i,j)) & (u_y(i,j+1) - u_y(i,j)) \end{pmatrix} \tag{4.37}$$

$$D_l = \begin{pmatrix} (u_x(i,j) - u_x(i-1,j)) & (u_x(i,j) - u_x(i,j-1)) \\ (u_y(i,j) - u_y(i-1,j)) & (u_y(i,j) - u_y(i,j-1)) \end{pmatrix} \tag{4.38}$$

Neither the forward nor backward approximations to the Jacobian will by themselves capture all the triangles since D_r skips the upper triangle and D_l skips the lower one, so these approximations must be combined or the algorithm will develop instabilities as we found. Alternately, D_c can be used, since it counts both the upper and lower triangles touching the center point $\mathbf{x}_{ij}$. Accordingly, we choose to discretize the cost functionals by

$$E_{data}[\{\mathbf{u}_{ij}\}] = N^{-1} \sum_{ij} \psi\{I(\mathbf{x}_{ij} + \mathbf{u}_{ij}) - M(\mathbf{x}_{ij}\} \tag{4.39}$$

$$E_{prior1}[\{\mathbf{u}_{ij}\}] = \alpha_1 \sum_{ij} \mathrm{tr}\left((D_c(\mathbf{x}_{ij}) - I)'(D_c(\mathbf{x}_{ij}) - I)\right) \tag{4.40}$$

$$E_{prior2}[\{\mathbf{u}_{ij}\}] = \alpha_2 \sum_{ij} \left(\mathrm{tr} D_r(\mathbf{x}_{ij})' D_r(\mathbf{x}_{ij}) \left(1 + \frac{1}{\det D_r(\mathbf{x}_{ij})^2}\right) - 4 \right)$$

$$+ \alpha_2 \sum_{ij} \left(\mathrm{tr} D_l(\mathbf{x}_{ij})' D_l(\mathbf{x}_{ij}) \left(1 + \frac{1}{\det D_l(\mathbf{x}_{ij})^2}\right) - 4 \right) \tag{4.41}$$

To minimize 4.41 we use steepest descent from the initial point 0. The inverse flow $\{\mathbf{v}_{kl}\}$ that is needed to compute the reconstruction $M(\ell^{-1}(\mathbf{x}))$ can be computed as shown in Figure 4.8. When changing resolutions, the flow fields are scaled up or down using bilinear interpolation.

4.4.3 Results

To test out different optimization strategies and implementation details, a set of experiments was run on several sets of images. The results can be summarized as follows:

- E_{prior1} must be weighted much more heavily than E_{prior2} to deliver the same quality of fit, suggesting that the approach of elasticity theory is reasonable in this application;

- The range of images for which results will be better for fixed alpha and robustness is larger for E_{prior2};

- Results for either prior can appear to be extremely good. The errors that plague both are a result of the functional being homogeneous, so the exact

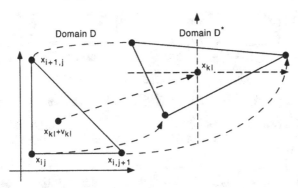

Figure 4.8. Calculating the inverse flow at a point $\mathbf{x}_{kl}$ in domain $\mathcal{D}$ involves finding the points $\mathbf{x}_{ij}$, $\mathbf{x}_{i+1,j}$, and $\mathbf{x}_{i,j+1}$ in the domain $\mathcal{D}$, such that the triangle defined by $\mathbf{x}_{ij} + \mathbf{u}_{ij}$, $\mathbf{x}_{i+1,j} + \mathbf{u}_{i+1,j}$, and $\mathbf{x}_{i,j+1} + \mathbf{u}_{i,j+1}$ contains the point $\mathbf{x}_{kl}$. Then the inverse flow displacement $\mathbf{v}_{kl}$ can be calculated by interpolation.

form seems less important than introducing a hierarchy of models or other forms of spatially-varying priors;

- Results are sensible even when the topographies of the model and input intensity landscapes differ.

The first set of experiments (Figures 4.9-4.11) demonstrates the effects of varying the priors, the smoothing parameters, and the robustness on a pair of binary images (see Figure 4.9), that is particularly difficult because of the closeness of the features in the model image and the extent of the deformations in the input image (e.g., the right eyebrow will blend into the background at a coarse resolution). For both sets of results, the strength of the smoothness term increases from left to right, and the degree of robustness decreases from top to bottom (i.e., the bottom row essentially results from a least squares norm). Also, for both

Figure 4.9. Left: model domain. Middle: model image. Right: input image.

Figure 4.10. Reconstructions $I(\ell(\mathbf{x}))$ for the model and input images given above using E_{prior1} with bilinear interpolation and boundary conditions $\mathbf{u} = 0$. The images should look as much like $M(\mathbf{x})$ as possible. The smoothing factor α_1 varies by column from left to right as: 50, 100, 200, 400, 800. The robustness factor h varies by row from top to bottom as 10, 50, 500. The Jacobians of the triangles go negative around the left eye.

priors, note that the mouth and nose are warped perfectly. However, the eyes are more difficult, both because of the magnitude of the deformation required and because of interactions between the eyes and the eyebrows, which merge at coarser resolutions. For E_{prior1} (4.10), the determinant of the Jacobian often goes negative (so the homeomorphism constraint is violated) for low smoothing and low robustness. The "split left eye" is in fact composed of two parts: a dilated closed eye from the input, and part of the inputs eyebrow, which jumped down at a low resolution. Similarly, at a low resolution, the right eyebrow can merge with the exterior boundary, making it quite difficult later for the entire eyebrow to move downwards. When the smoothness and robustness are at their highest (top right corner), the features maintain their integrity, but do not deform as much as needed. With E_{prior2} (Figure 4.11), the determinant of the Jacobian can still go negative for low values of the smoothing, constant, but not nearly as frequently.

Figure 4.11. Reconstructions $I(\ell(\mathbf{x}))$ for the model and input images given above using E_{prior2} with bilinear interpolation and boundary conditions $\mathbf{u} = 0$. The images should look as much like $M(\mathbf{x})$ as possible. The smoothing factor α_2 varies by column from left to right as: 50, 100, 200, 400, 800. The robustness factor h varies by row from top to bottom as 10, 50, 500.

The dark features are still heavily distorted at low values of smoothing, but they retain their connectedness. Also, a very reasonable solution finally emerges when high smoothing is combined with moderate robustness.

We conclude with examples demonstrating the range of performance of pure local warping. In each set of four images, the warped input image $I(\ell(\mathbf{x}))$ should look closest to the model image $M(\mathbf{x})$, while the warped model image $M(\ell^{-1}(\mathbf{x}))$ should look closest to the input $I(\mathbf{x})$. Unless otherwise indicated, all warps use E_{prior2} with the robustness factor h set to a moderate value of 50, and the smoothing factor α set to 100, which is lower than that needed for the best solution in the previous set of experiments, but which is adequate for the deformations required in this set.

$M(\mathbf{x})$ $I(l(\mathbf{x}))$ $\mathbf{I}(\mathbf{x})$ $M(l^{-1}(\mathbf{x}))$

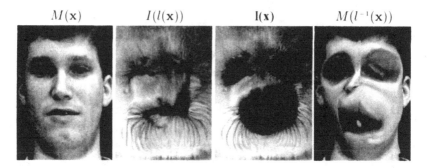

Figure 4.12. Example demonstrating what happens when a face is warped onto a non-face.

$M(\mathbf{x})$ $I(l(\mathbf{x}))$ $\mathbf{I}(\mathbf{x})$ $M(l^{-1}(\mathbf{x}))$

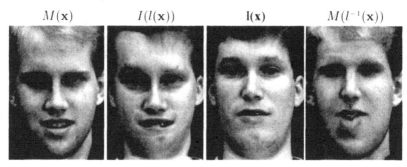

Figure 4.13. Example demonstrating what happens when faces are incorrectly aligned. Every facial feature is put in correct correspondence.

$M(\mathbf{x})$ $I(l(\mathbf{x}))$ $\mathbf{I}(\mathbf{x})$ $M(l^{-1}(\mathbf{x}))$

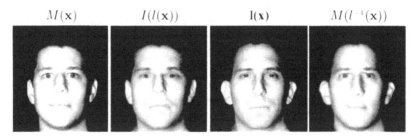

Figure 4.14. Example demonstrating what happens when the global warp is initially correct. The head outlines are correct, and the shape of the eyes and nose are nearly correct.

$M(\mathbf{x})$ $I(l(\mathbf{x}))$ $\mathbf{I}(\mathbf{x})$ $M(l^{-1}(\mathbf{x}))$

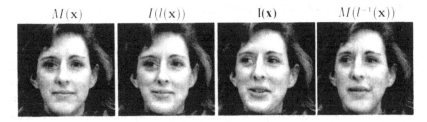

Figure 4.15. Example demonstrating that a local warp can successfully capture small changes in viewpoint. The eyes change their direction of gaze only slightly, because moving more would entail introducing portions of the whites that are not present in the input image (or conversely deleting whites from the model image).

$M(\mathbf{x})$ $I(l(\mathbf{x}))$ $\mathbf{I}(\mathbf{x})$ $M(l^{-1}(\mathbf{x}))$

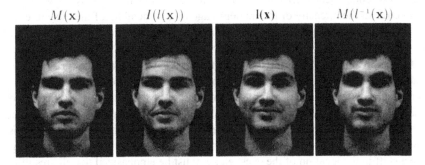

Figure 4.16. Example demonstrating what happens when there is a change of expression. The wrinkles induced by smiling have no match in the model and so can at best be shrunk into thinner lines or pushed into slightly more shaded areas. Dimples are similarly impossible to remove. The warping can easily distort wrinkles and dimples enough so that residue analyses may fail, unless they model the errors induced by the face model.

$M(\mathbf{x})$ $I(l(\mathbf{x}))$ $\mathbf{I}(\mathbf{x})$ $M(l^{-1}(\mathbf{x}))$

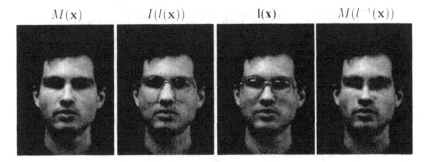

Figure 4.17. Example demonstrating what happens when there is a change of expression. The wrinkles induced by smiling have no match in the model and so can at best be shrunk into thinner lines or pushed into slightly more shaded areas. Dimples are similarly impossible to remove. The warping can easily distort wrinkles and dimples enough so that residue analyses may fail, unless they model the errors induced by the face model.

4.5   Inhomogeneous Local Warping

Ultimately no efficient coding of a face should require more parameters than there are pixels in the input data, even if we desire a representation rich enough to interpret expressions. However, the homogeneous local warping given above does exactly that. In fact, it is too general. ℓ simultaneously attempts to correct for variations in individual features and expressions, as well as viewpoint and shading errors. To actually analyze the face, the geometric warp must be written as the composition

$$\phi = \phi_{person} \circ \phi_{expressions} \circ \phi_{viewpoint}$$

where each component warp is highly restricted. To make things more difficult, the sets of component warps are not mutually exclusive in any way. A warp due to an error in the intensity of the model image (e.g., a bending of the nose to erase a poorly modeled cast shadow), can be indistinguishable from a bending of the nose by ϕ_{person}.

One approach to finding the component warps exploits the same type of statistical analysis as was used to construct the lighting basis vectors. This approach to modeling deformations decomposes the domain of the face into a collection of small patches (each corresponding to single pixel in the discretized model), and approximates any deformation of the face as a linear combination of eigenwarps, where an eigenwarp is essentially a discrete vector field corresponding to things like a shift in the location of the eyes, etc. It must be emphasized that the resulting eigenwarps are not required to be smooth in any way, and in particular, no underlying continuous model is assumed here that might allow the homeomorphism ϕ to be written as a linear combination of basis functions, each of which was continuous. (There are other approaches. ϕ can, for example, be expanded in terms of

Rank	VAF	Total VAF	Rank	VAF	Total VAF
1	0.1259	0.1259	11	0.0236	0.6836
2	0.1168	0.2427	12	0.0227	0.7063
3	0.1037	0.3464	13	0.0152	0.7215
4	0.0782	0.4246	14	0.0138	0.7353
5	0.0620	0.4866	15	0.0138	0.7491
6	0.0467	0.5333	16	0.0132	0.7624
7	0.0400	0.5732	17	0.0129	0.7752
8	0.0326	0.6058	18	0.0109	0.7862
9	0.0290	0.6348	19	0.0109	0.7971
10	0.0252	0.6600	20	0.0093	0.8064

Table 4.1. The variance-accounted-for (VAF) and running total of variance-accounted-for for the first 20 eigenwarps. Approximately 50 eigenwarps are required to approach a total VAF of 90 percent.

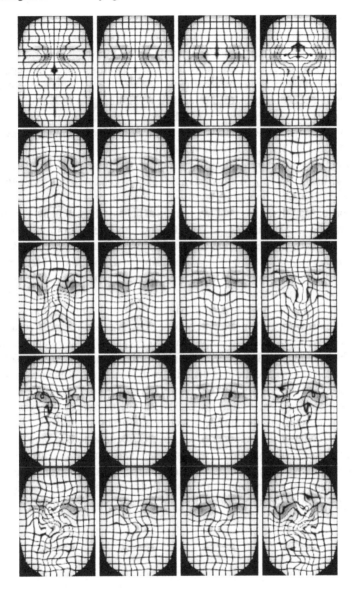

Figure 4.18. The first 5 eigenwarps ordered top to bottom. Each column contains the same orthonormal vector scaled by a different factor: From left to right: -100, -50, 50, 100. Factors -100 and 100 frequently generate violations of the ordering constraint.

an orthogonal basis on a suitable space of continuous functions (see Amit 94). In fact, even if a given eigenwarp from an orthonormal basis has a positive Jacobian everywhere, there will almost always be some factor by which it can be scaled to drive $\det J$ negative. Any smoothness of the eigenwarps will be induced solely by the prior used to insure that the original warps were smooth. Nonetheless, a principal components analysis of the local flows resulting from warping a model face onto a large set of input faces can be useful in determining what types of corrections are actually being made, and while the sets of corrections are easily anticipated for $\phi_{expressions}$, they are not so obvious for ϕ_{person}.

Accordingly, we performed a principal components analysis of all the local flows found using E_{prior2} to fit an individual face model to all 15 centrally-lit (latitude $\in [-30, +30]$, longitude $\in [0, +30]$) images of ten different people at a resolution of 2^6. The input set was doubled as in Chapter 3 by flipping the warps about the vertical axis to account for lighting effects from the other side. The input data was selected so that the resulting eigenwarps could be assigned to ϕ_{person}, though it was found $\phi_{viewpoint}$ contributed significantly. More carefully constructed databases than those taken in Chapter 3 would be needed to better isolate the component warps.

Table 4.1 shows the variance accounted for (VAF) and running total of VAF for the first 20 eigenwarps. Approximately 50 eigenwarps are required to approach a total VAF of 90 percent. This represents an excellent lossy compression ratio of order 50:1. Figure 4.18 displays the first 5 orthonormal eigenwarps scaled by different factors to exaggerate the distortions they capture. Eigenwarp 1 shifts eyes together or apart, and as a likely side effect of the smoothing prior, expands the nose. Eigenwarp 2 raises and lowers the nose with respect the eyes, while 3 lengthens the nose. Note though the effect on the eyebrows in both. This is the major disadvantage of the homogeneous prior; corrections to one part of the grid propagate to others (though this effect is exacerbated in the eigenwarps by the condition that the basis be orthogonal). Eigenwarps 4 and 5 appear to be shifting the nose, but are really compensating for small changes in viewpoint which create a nose shadow (that is not represented in the lighting basis vectors).

Chapter 5

Recognition from Image Data

In this chapter, we combine the intensity model of Chapter 3 and the warping model of Chapter 4 to build a model for faces that allows recognition under a wide range of lighting conditions. Our purpose here is to show that each component of the face model–shading, global warping and local warping–is necessary for recognition, and that the face model as a whole is sufficient for successfully recognizing faces under a wide range of lighting conditions. We do not claim that the algorithm used to minimize the fit of the deformable template is optimal by any criteria, but only that it is sufficient given suitably good initial conditions.

5.1 The Energy Functional

To find the best fit of the face model to an input image, we solve a minimization problem to find the best values of the vector of shading coefficients s introduced in Chapter 3 and the warping function $\phi(\mathbf{x})$ introduced in Chapter 4.

The actual form of $\phi(\mathbf{x})$ will vary depending on the face model chosen. We consider two models. The first, a generic male model, is built from the average of five men (see Figure 5.1). We have a mean face $S_0(\mathbf{x})$ and $L = 5$ eigenfaces $S_i(\mathbf{x})$, and we fit using a five-parameter global warp since most faces will have

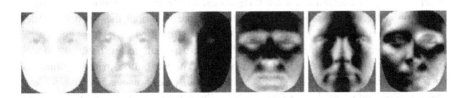

Figure 5.1. Mean image and eigenimages used to define the generic model. Image at far left is the mean. Then from left to right are S_1 through S_5.

105

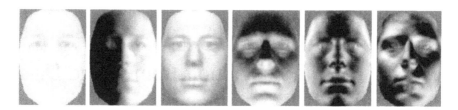

Figure 5.2. Mean image and eigenimages used to define the individual model. Image at far left is the mean. Then from left to right are S_1 through S_5.

different aspect ratios than average. The second is an individual model built from just one person (for an example, see Figure 5.2). In this case matching is done using a four-parameter global warp, since with this model we are seeking to reject all inputs not containing an image of the individual, and under weak perspective projection, there is just one scale factor applicable.

Given either model, the fundamental idea is that any image of a face, roughly frontally viewed and unoccluded by glasses, cigarettes or other objects and cropped to exclude the hair and background, can be approximated by the model we have built up:

$$I(\mathbf{x}) \approx \left(S_0 + \sum_{l=1}^{L} s_l S_l \right) (\phi^{-1}(\mathbf{x})) \tag{5.1}$$

This can be made into a probabilistic model by putting priors on the vector of shading coefficients s, and on the warping ϕ, and by putting a distribution on the residual difference between the left and right hand sides of this equation (the imaging model). We have not investigated the appropriate probability model for s, although this would be easy to do with a suitable database of natural images containing faces, so we leave out this prior term. Because the model is being fit to an input I, the coefficients s are constrained by the imaging model. The distribution on ϕ has been discussed in Chapter 4. Here we adopt the "prior2" model for the local component ℓ. Note that this model was defined by a stress energy E: when ℓ is given by a discrete approximation, then E leads to a probability model $\Pr(\ell) = \frac{1}{Z} e^{-E(\ell)}$ as usual. Defining a probability distribution in the continuous case is not so simple and has not been carried out (see, however, Trouve 99 and Dupuis, Grenander and Miller 98). Finally, the imaging model was discussed in Sections 4.1 and 4.2.

To fit this model, we seek to minimize -log(Pr). Subsituting the models we have discussed, this makes the problem one of minimizing:

$$
\begin{aligned}
E[\phi, \mathbf{s}] \;=\; & \underbrace{|\mathcal{D}|^{-1} \int_{\mathcal{D}} \psi\{I(\phi(\mathbf{x})) - (S_0(\mathbf{x}) + \sum_{l=1}^{L} s_l S_l(\mathbf{x}))\} dx}_{\text{intensity matching term}} \\[2ex]
+ \; & \underbrace{\beta |\mathcal{D}|^{-1} \int_{\mathcal{D}} \psi\{\Phi_e(I(\phi(\mathbf{x})); \sigma) - \Phi_e((S_0 + \sum_{l=1}^{L} s_l S_l)(\mathbf{x}); \sigma)\} dx}_{\text{edge matching term}} \\[2ex]
+ \; & \underbrace{k_1(\sigma_x - 1)^2 + k_2(\sigma_y - 1)^2 + k_3\left(\frac{\sigma_x}{\sigma_y} - 1\right)^2}_{\text{global priors}} \\[2ex]
+ \; & \underbrace{\alpha_3 \int_{\mathcal{D}} \left(\operatorname{tr} D\ell(\mathbf{x})' D\ell(\mathbf{x}) \left(1 + \frac{1}{\det D\ell(\mathbf{x})^2}\right) - 4\right) dx}_{\text{local prior}} \qquad (5.2)
\end{aligned}
$$

Here the term $S_0 + \sum s_l S_l$ will be called the model $M(\mathbf{x})$ for the input face, i.e., the reconstruction with correct shading, after being warped to standard position.

5.2 The Algorithm

There are two components to using the face model for recognition: (1) finding values for the parameters that minimize the total energy; and (2) applying a decision function to the total energy (or component energies) to determine whether the input is a particular person, or if it is a human face at all.

5.2.1 Matching

Solving Equation 5.2 for optimal values of g, ℓ, and $\mathbf{s}$ poses considerable problems in general because of the local minima involved. However, under the assumption that we have a good initial estimate of location, scale, and rotation, it turns out that a relatively simple algorithm works well. Since the local flow cannot be estimated until the global flow is found, and the latter depends critically on choice of the shading coefficients, we use the two stage algorithm given in the box below. First, we co-estimate g and $\mathbf{s}$ via a gradient descent method. Second, we estimate ℓ using gradient descent with the second prior of Section 4.4. In this case, we can directly warp $I(\mathbf{x})$ onto $M(\mathbf{x})$.

There are two ways to co-estimate g and $\mathbf{s}$. First, if the robust norm is actually close (or identical) to the L^2 norm, then optimization in $\mathbf{s}$ is just projecton of the image onto the linear span of the eigenfaces, and we can alternate between a gradient descent step for the parameters of g and a projection step for the shading coefficients. The second method involves gradient descent on both global and shading parameters simultaneously, where the derivative of E_{data} with respect to a shading coefficient s_l is given by

$$\frac{\partial E}{\partial s_l} \;\;=\;\; |\mathcal{D}|^{-1} \int_{\mathcal{D}} \psi' \left\{ I(g(\mathbf{x})) - M(\mathbf{x}) \right\} S_l(\mathbf{x}) d\mathbf{x} \qquad (5.3)$$

The detailed algorithm also uses a pyramid multi-resolution scheme and is shown in the box.

Optimizing g, ℓ and s
For r = lores to hires
    Apply gradient descent to minimize
    $E_{data}[g, \mathbf{s}] + E_{prior}[g]$
    using images at scale r
Set $\ell_{lores}(\mathbf{x}) = \mathbf{x}$ on the coarsest scale
For r = lores to hires
    Apply gradient descent to minimize
    $E_{data}[\ell_r] + E_{prior}[\ell_r]$
    where ℓ_r is defined on a grid of resolution r.
    Initialize ℓ_r from ℓ_{r-1} by interpolating the interior in
    and extrapolating near the boundaries.

5.2.2 Decision criteria

Two criteria are used, one measuring the degree of match of the raw intensities and one for the match of edge features. The goodness-of-fit function for intensities is:

$$\epsilon_i \;\;=\;\; 1 - \frac{\int_{\mathcal{D}} \psi\{I(\phi(\mathbf{x}) - M(\mathbf{x})\} d\mathbf{x}}{\int_{\mathcal{D}} \psi\{I(\phi(\mathbf{x}))\} d\mathbf{x}} \qquad (5.4)$$

The goodness-of-fit function for edges is:

$$\epsilon_e \;\;=\;\; 1 - \frac{\int_{\mathcal{D}} \psi\{\Phi_e(I(\phi(\mathbf{x})); \sigma) - \Phi_e(M(\mathbf{x}); \sigma)\} d\mathbf{x}}{\int_{\mathcal{D}} \psi\{\Phi_e(I(\phi(\mathbf{x})); \sigma)\} d\mathbf{x}} \qquad (5.5)$$

The reason for introducing the edge-based criteria is that ϵ_i for a half-black and half-white non-face image (one with maximum variance) may well be lower than ϵ_i for a centrally lit face since a considerable portion of the variance in the former image can be explained by a half-shadowed face model, while the latter face image has little variance and is distinguished as a face by higher frequency details. By considering ϵ_e, shading information is discounted and the amount of detail captured by the face model is more adequately measured.

5.3 Results

Two tasks are used to test the deformable face model: recognizing individuals and discriminating faces from non-faces. Both tests employ the same image database.

The database consists of one set of nonfaces (labeled *NF*), and twelve sets of faces of eleven different individuals labeled *wo, ww, ao, co, do, eo, go, lo, mo, no, ro, to* where the first letter marks the individual and the second letter determines whether the expression was neutral (o) or allowed to vary (w). Each face set consists of 63 images of one person lit from different directions. These are the same images collected in Chapter 3, except the top row with latitude +75 degrees is omitted because the five lighting basis vectors are not adequate to model such extreme conditions.

The 25 images in the non-faces set are of random outdoor and indoor scenes. They are each searched for the 20 best initial conditions (where best is a function of the face model in use), so that a total of 500 non-face inputs are tested on each model.

5.3.1 Separating Different People

The first recognition task involves using a model of one individual person to discriminate between that person and all other images, whether they are of faces or non-faces. The shading and global warping parameters, but *no local warping* are fitted, both because expressions are held neutral and because doing so accentuates the differences between E_{data} for different individuals.

Each model tested is built from sparse samples (see Chapter 3) of the lighting directions, leaving 43 images from that person's set remaining as test images. Here we present the results of applying each of five different models to all 13 datasets.

Using as a decision criterion a threshold on ϵ_e, the measured results match expectations:

- Each model is able to distinguish the face from which it was built from all other images.

- Non-faces and wrong faces do *not* have distinguishably different errors using this criterion.

- The generic model selects no one in particular.

- The worst false alarms and misses are often due to minimization errors.

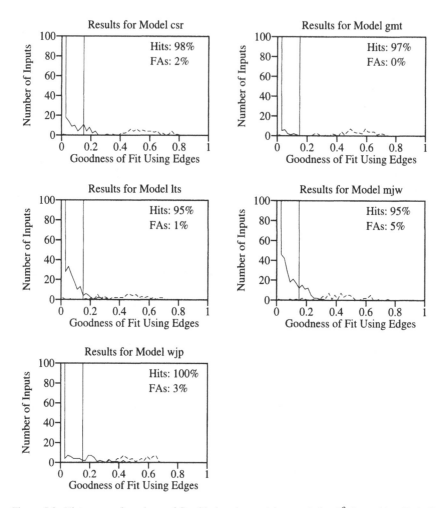

Figure 5.3. Histograms of goodness-of-fit with the edge model at resolution 2^6 for positive (dashed) and negative (solid) examples using 5 different models. The vertical bar indicates the threshold used to compute the recognition rates.

Figure 5.3 shows results for using individual models (left, a female subject and right, a male subject) to discriminate between approximately 63 positive and 1170 negative instances of each individual. Negative instances include non-faces as well as faces. Histograms of the goodness-of-fits of hipass-filtered intensity images are shown with dashed lines for positive instances and solid lines for negative instances. (N.B. For display purposes the histograms are clipped above

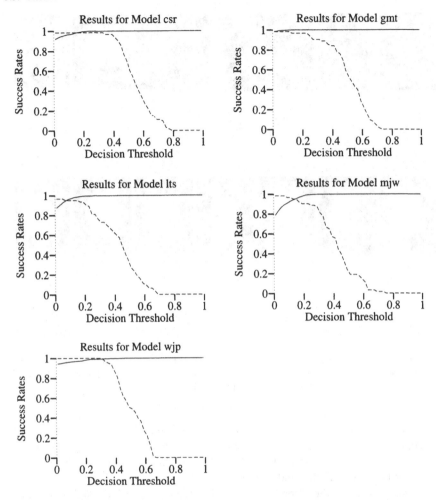

Figure 5.4. Variation in recognition rates by threshold in the edge model for 5 different models. When the decision threshold is one, there is 100% correct rejections and no correct acceptances. The crossover point defines a decision threshold at which the false alarm and miss rates are identical.

counts of 100.) The vertical lines indicate the goodness-of-fit at which the decision threshold was set to yield the hit and false alarm rates shown in each graph. In both cases the threshold was arbitrarily set to 0.15 (goodness-of-fit values lie in $(-\infty, 1]$). Other values may make more sense, depending on the relative cost of false alarms and misses, but in general, recognition rates will be good because the distributions of positive and negative instances are sufficiently well-separated by each of the face models.

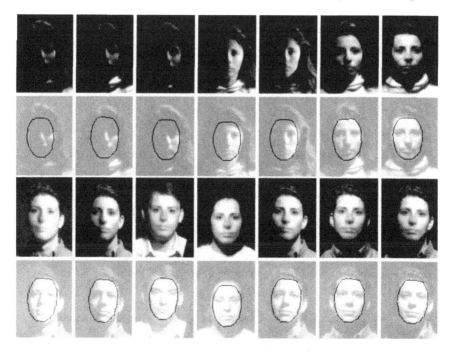

Figure 5.5. Reconstructions $M(\phi^{-1}(\mathbf{x}))$ of $I(\mathbf{x})$ top row: showing the 7 worst fits (worst is at far left) of model lts to positive examples and their boundaries (2nd row). The best fits of model lts (3rd row) to negative examples and their boundaries (4th row)

Figure 5.4 shows the success rates for positive and negative exemplar identification. The crossover point gives the threshold value for which the false alarm rate will equal the miss rate. Typically, a threshold can be found yielding small rates for both false alarms and misses.

Figure 5.5 shows the reconstructions $M(\phi^{-1}(\mathbf{x}))$ for the 7 worst fits of model lts to positive examples. The worst fits occur for the most unusual lighting conditions. The figure also shows the best fits of model lts to negative examples. Comparisons in both cases are between input and warped model images. Figure 5.6 provides the same information, but shows model and warped input images.

5.3.2   Separating Faces and Nonfaces

5.3.2.1   HOMOGENEOUS PRIORS.   The setup here is same as in the previous section, except that the models now are allowed to use local warping with prior2. For each model, faces and nonfaces were distinguished by thresholding ϵ_i. Results are given for individual models (Figures 5.11-5.14) or the task of discriminating (Figures 5.9, 5.10) between approximately 755 positive and 435 negative instances

Figure 5.6. Reconstructions $I(\phi(\mathbf{x}))$ (1st row) and model images $M(\mathbf{x})$ (2nd row) showing the worst fits of model lts to positive examples. 3rd and 4th rows: The same kinds of images for negative examples

of human faces. The interpretation of the graphs (Figures 5.7, 5.8) is the same as above, except that (a) histograms are of goodness-of-fits of unfiltered intensity images; and (b) the threshold is set to 0.70 for both models. Again, the face models are very successful at separating the distributions of fits for positive and negative instances, so recognition rates are very good.

5.3.2.2 FINDING FACES IN CLUTTERED SCENES   To corroborate the results given above, we ran the face/non-face detection scheme on very cluttered scenes having both natural and artificial objects. One such image is given in Figure 5.15. The set of initial conditions was obtained by uniformly sampling from the space of possible rigid deformations (global warps). The best fit of the generic male model is also shown in Figure 5.15.

5.3.2.3 EIGENWARPS   Finally, we demonstrate that recognition is only slightly impaired by using a basis of 50 eigenwarps in place of the generic local warping (see Figures 5.16, 5.17)

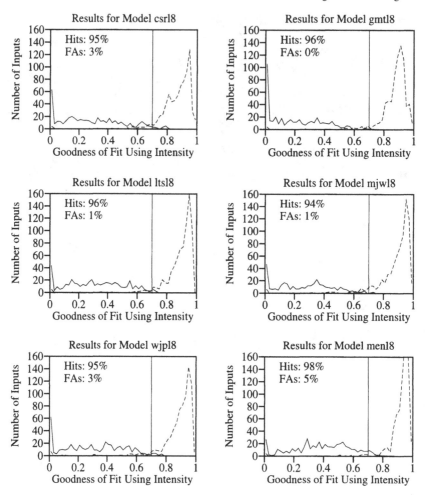

Figure 5.7. Histograms of goodness-of-fit with the intensity model at resolution 2^6 for positive (dashed) and negative (solid) examples using 6 different models. The vertical bar indicates the threshold used to compute the recognition rates.

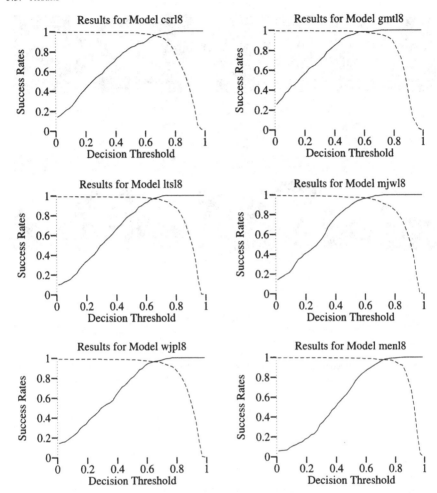

Figure 5.8. Variation in recognition rates by threshold in the intensity model for 6 different models. When the decision threshold is one, there is 100% correct rejections and no correct acceptances. The crossover point defines a decision threshold at which the false alarm and miss rates are identical.

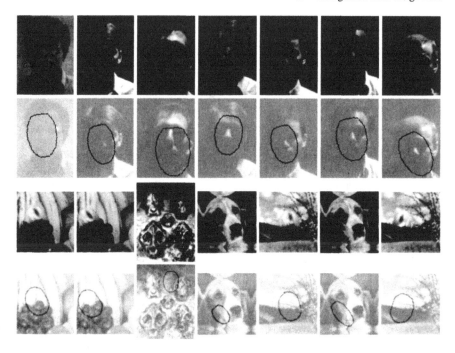

Figure 5.9. Top: Reconstructions $M(\phi^{-1}(\mathbf{x}))$ of $I(\mathbf{x})$ showing the worst fits of model lts to positive examples and their boundaries. Bottom: the best fits of model lts to negative examples and their boundaries

Figure 5.10. Top: Reconstructions $I(\phi(\mathbf{x}))$ (above) and model images $M(\mathbf{x})$ (below) showing the worst fits of model lts to positive examples. Bottom: The same kinds of images for negative examples

Figure 5.11. A set of input images lit from different directions, reconstructed in next figure

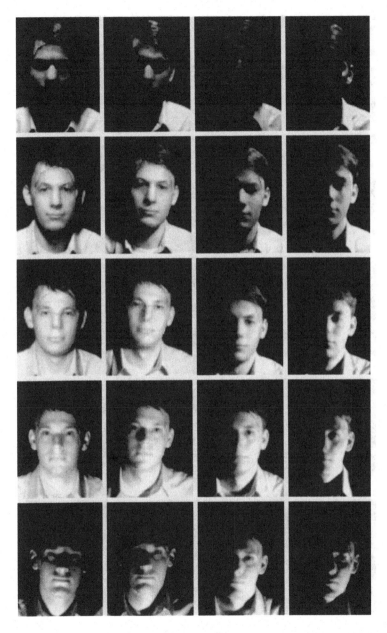

Figure 5.12. The input faces from Figure 5.11 replaced with warped model images, demonstrating the effectiveness of the deformable model over a wide range of lighting conditions.

Figure 5.13. Another set of input images lit from different directions

Figure 5.14. The input faces from Figure 5.13 replaced with warped model images, demonstrating the effectiveness of the deformable model over a wide range of lighting conditions.

Figure 5.15. The best fit of the face model within a cluttered scene.

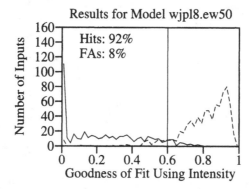

Figure 5.16. Histograms of goodness-of-fit of the intensity model at resolution 2^6 for positive (dashed) and negative (solid) examples using 50 eigenwarps for one model. The vertical bar indicates the threshold used to compute the recognition rates.

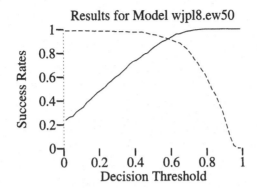

Figure 5.17. Variation in recognition rates by threshold using 50 eigenwarps for one model. When the decision threshold is one, there is 100% correct rejections and no correct acceptances. The crossover point defines a decision threshold at which the false alarm and miss rates are identical. Recognition rates using 50 eigenwarps

Chapter 6

Parabolic Curves and Ridges on Surfaces

6.1 Overview

We now turn to the study of the face as a three-dimensional object. We are interested in features of the face *which are invariant under rotations, translations and scaling*. This is not just an idle wish for mathematical elegance, but is the only possible way to find meaningful features since there is no distinguished coordinate system in the space around us and faces are always moving to new positions and orientations. The eigenhead approach of Atick et al. (96), for instance, depends on choosing a particular vertical axis through the head and expanding the function giving the distance of points on the face from this axis. In contrast, the principal curvatures of a surface (whose definition will be recalled below) are invariant under all Euclidean coordinate changes and lead to invariant features on every smooth surface. To motivate this excursion into differential geometry, it is helpful to see that they do express something significant about the face: Figure 6.1 shows an example of the two principal curvatures calculated for a face. It is an interesting exercise to 'explain' what these figures show by touching your own face and mentally estimating its principal curvatures at various points. These curvatures and the parabolic and ridge curves to be introduced shortly create a remarkable pattern on the human face and reveal how complex a surface the face really is.

The study of curvatures of surfaces goes back to Gauss but many of the basic results on these features have only been proven recently. The beautiful treatise by Koenderink (90) describes most of these results, but unfortunately it is so lacking in mathematical details that one is often hard-put to translate his terms into formulae or to know what has been proven. Since there is no complete treatment in the literature of these basic facts, we want to fill this gap here. In this chapter, we will give a systematic exposition of the local structure of points on smooth surfaces $M \subset \mathbf{R}^3$. After this dry discussion, we will return to the face

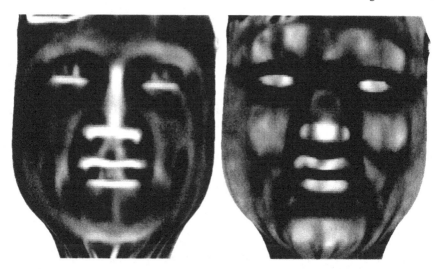

Figure 6.1. Principal curvatures for a single face. Left: maximum curvature κ_1, and right: minimum curvature κ_2, with value indicated by brightness. Thus in the right-hand figure, the dark bands indicate a large negative value for κ_2 while the highlight on the tip of the nose indicates a large positive value for κ_2.

and show how a face may be constructed, as by a sculptor, by adding layers of complexity each modifying the pattern of these curvature features.

To motivate the discussion which follows, it is useful to return to the ideas about simple closed-plane curves discussed in Section 1.5. We can define the curvature of such a curve at each point, positive at convex points, negative at concave points. There are two sets of special points on the curve: the points of inflection where the curvature is zero and the 'vertices' where the curvature has a local maximum or minimum. These are the local curvature features of a plane curve. Moreover, for 'generic' curves, the points of inflection always have a local equation of the form $y = bx^3 + \cdots$ in a suitable Euclidean coordinate system, for some $b \neq 0$; and the vertices always have a local equation of the form $y = ax^2 + cx^4 + \cdots$ for some $a \neq 0, c \neq a^3$. Here the word generic means that this is what happens for all but special curves, for which some combination of their derivatives has a special value at some point. Thus if, at the point of inflection $b = 0$, the point of inflection is degenerate and has fourth order contact[1] with its tangent line instead of third. And if $c = a^3$ at the vertex, the curvature doesn't have a simple local min or max: it has vanishing second as well as first derivative along the curve. Equivalently, this special sort of vertex is one where the osculating circle has more

---

[1] The order of contact is defined by taking a function whose locus of zeros is the tangent line and restricting this function to the curve. Then the order of contact is the order of zero of this function.

than fourth order contact with the curve. Put another way, at most points on most curves, there is a unique circle which has third order contact with the curve there. If the point is a vertex, this contact is actually fourth order. If $c = a^3$, this contact is at least fifth order!

For plane curves, inflection points and vertices are the most important local features and these have been often used to describe qualitatively the shape of curves. *Our goal is to generalize these simple features to surfaces.* As we might guess from the example of curves, the best way to understand these features is through the contact between these surfaces and planes and spheres. Contact of a surface M with planes determines the parabolic set and its special points such as cusps of Gauss (ruffles). Contact with spheres determines the ridge curves and the special points on them such as umbilics and turning points.[2] In particular, ridge curves can be defined by means of extrema of curvatures on the surface, and so are analogous to vertices of plane curves.

All this will be discussed in detail below. For now, we refer the reader to the 'road-map' at the end of this chapter which summarizes the situation that we will uncover. This road map shows how (i) a generic surface is broken up into three open sets — the elliptic convex points, hyperbolic points and elliptic concave points; (ii) there are two types of parabolic curves (the red and blue) separating them and four types of ridges on them, red and blue, elliptic and hyperbolic; and that (iii) there are special points, cusps of Gauss, umbilic points and turning points, each with several flavors, on these. This whole picture forms a sort of fingerprint for the surface, a way of making 'shape' explicit.

Similarly, it is possible to analyze the contact between a surface and *lines* in 3-space. This is related to projections of M to planes, and hence to the *apparent contours* of M. We will concentrate, however, on contact with planes and spheres in this book.

The mathematics which we will need is chiefly manipulation of Taylor series with simple algebra and calculus. We avoid tensors and differential forms as well as the machinery of singularity theory, although this means that some results can only be stated. The one key concept we need from differential geometry is that of principal curvatures, which can be defined in completely elementary terms as follows: If M is any smooth surface and $P \in M$ is any point, introduce coordinates so that P is the origin, and $z = 0$ is the tangent plane to M at P. Then M has a local equation of the form $z = \frac{a}{2}x^2 + bxy + \frac{c}{2}y^2 + \cdots$. If we make a rotation in the x, y-plane, we can eliminate the coefficient b so that M is now $z = \frac{a}{2}x^2 + \frac{c}{2}y^2 + \cdots$. Then a and c are called the *principal curvatures* of M at P and $x = z = 0$ and $y = z = 0$ are the *principal directions*. Much of our discussion in this chapter will consist of an analysis of the cubic (and

---

[2] In this book we are concerned with 'intrinsic ridges', which do not depend on being given a specific reference direction in space. There is another concept of ridge which is explored in the book by Eberly (96).

sometimes quartic) terms in the Taylor series for z as a function of x, y and in the geometric interpretation of these coefficients. (For general references to the underlying differential geometry which we assume here, we recommend O'Neill (66 or 97), Koenderink (90), or Cipolla and Giblin (to appear). Some of our discussion appears in a different form in Porteous (94), and many of the original ideas on ridge curves are due to Porteous, following pioneering work of R. Thom in the 1960s.)

We end this overview by describing the groups of transformations with respect to which our features will be invariant. It will turn out that each of them is invariant with respect to a larger group than the Euclidean group. Note that the families of lines and planes are invariant under arbitrary affine transformations of $\mathbf{R}^3$ and, more generally, under *projective transformations*, which act on $\mathbf{R}^3$ plus a plane 'at infinity' and are given by the formula:

$$T(\mathbf{x}) = \frac{\mathbf{a} + A(\mathbf{x})}{a_0 + \ell(\mathbf{x})}$$

Here A is a nonsingular 3×3 matrix, $\mathbf{a}$ is a vector, a_0 a constant and ℓ a linear function. Features on surfaces which are defined by contact with lines and planes will be invariant under all projective transformations. On the other hand, the families of spheres and circles are invariant under the group of *conformal transformations* whose general transformation can be defined by the formula:

$$T(\mathbf{x}) = \mathbf{a} + \lambda \cdot R \left(\frac{\mathbf{x} - \mathbf{b}}{\|\mathbf{x} - \mathbf{b}\|^2} \right)$$

where R is a rotation or reflection, $\mathbf{a}$ and $\mathbf{b}$ are vectors and λ is a constant. Features defined by the type of contact with spheres are preserved by all these transformations. In other words, if a surface and a sphere have a certain type of contact, then any conformal transformation of this surface will have the same contact with a sphere at the corresponding point.

6.2 Monge Patches

We will study surfaces locally by their equations:

$$
\begin{aligned}
z \;=\; & \frac{1}{2}\kappa_1 x^2 + \frac{1}{2}\kappa_2 y^2 + \frac{1}{6}(b_0 x^3 + 3b_1 x^2 y + 3b_2 xy^2 + b_3 y^3) + \\
& \frac{1}{24}(c_0 x^4 + 4c_1 x^3 y + 6c_2 x^2 y^2 + 4c_3 xy^3 + c_4 y^4) + \cdots \qquad (6.1)
\end{aligned}
$$

also called *Monge patches*. As above, the surface has been rotated about the z-axis so that the x- and y-axes are in principal directions at the origin and the numbers κ_i are the principal curvatures at the origin. So long as $\kappa_1 \neq \kappa_2$, these two directions are well defined.

We shall always assume that $\kappa_1 \geq \kappa_2$. Note that if we reverse the direction of the normal to M then both κ_1 and κ_2 change sign. So we assume that a specific normal has been chosen, and in particular we assume that our surface is orientable. In practice the surface will either be closed or will be a Monge patch. If M is closed, we assume $z > \frac{1}{2}\kappa_1 x^2 + \frac{1}{2}\kappa_2 y^2 + \cdots$ is the inside of M. Thus $\kappa_1, \kappa_2 > 0$ means M is convex near P and $\kappa_1, \kappa_2 < 0$ means M is concave near P. The *Gaussian curvature* K is defined to be $\kappa_1 \kappa_2$ and P is called *elliptic* if $K > 0$ (or $\mathrm{sign}(\kappa_1) = \mathrm{sign}(\kappa_2)$) and *hyperbolic* if $K < 0$.

Many of the conditions which we shall obtain below can, in the local case, be expressed simply in terms of the coefficients of the Monge form. For example, the third order coefficients b_i determine whether each of the principal curvatures at the origin has an extrema in a principal direction (see Section 6.4.2).

The origin is a called an *umbilic* point when the principal curvatures κ_1, κ_2 are equal. Despite appearances, this is two conditions and not one: if z has no linear terms and the general form of the quadratic terms is

$$a_0 x^2 + 2a_1 xy + a_2 y^2$$

then we require the roots of

$$\begin{vmatrix} a_0 - \lambda & a_1 \\ a_1 & a_2 - \lambda \end{vmatrix} = 0$$

to be equal. This is equivalent to $(a_0 + a_2)^2 = 4(a_0 a_2 - a_1^2)$, which rearranges to $(a_0 - a_2)^2 + 4a_1^2 = 0$, that is, *two* conditions $a_0 = a_2$ and $a_1 = 0$. So there cannot be an xy term in the quadratic terms when we require the principal curvatures to be equal. The condition in (6.1) is just $\kappa_1 = \kappa_2$. Note that unless $\kappa_1 = \kappa_2 = 0$ ('flat umbilic') the Gauss curvature K is necessarily > 0 at an umbilic: non-flat umbilics occur in elliptic regions of a surface.

It will be useful at several places to have local expansions of the principal curvatures κ_1 and κ_2 near the origin, as well as expansions of the lines of curvature through the origin. This involves a somewhat messy calculation of the initial terms in the power series expansions of (a) the first and second fundamental forms I, II; and (b) their eigenvalues and eigenvectors. It is, however, straightforward. Here are the results.

Recall that the first fundamental form of $z = f(x, y)$ is the expression for infinitesimal distances on the surface M as a function of the displacement in x, y. It is given by

$$\begin{aligned} ds^2 &= dx^2 + dy^2 + dz^2 \\ &= dx^2 + dy^2 + (f_x dx + f_y dy)^2 \end{aligned}$$

$$= (1 + f_x^2)dx^2 + 2f_x f_y dx dy + (1 + f_y^2)dy^2$$

$$= (\, dx \quad dy \,) \begin{pmatrix} 1 + f_x^2 & f_x f_y \\ f_x f_y & 1 + f_y^2 \end{pmatrix} \begin{pmatrix} dx \\ dy \end{pmatrix}$$

hence, substituting the Monge form and working *modulo terms of degree 3 or more*, we get

$$I = \begin{pmatrix} 1 + \kappa_1^2 x^2 & \kappa_1 \kappa_2 xy \\ \kappa_1 \kappa_2 xy & 1 + \kappa_2^2 y^2 \end{pmatrix} \tag{6.2}$$

The second fundamental form II is the expression for how the surface M diverges from its tangent planes. For a surface in Monge form this is given by the Hessian of f divided by $\sqrt{1 + f_x^2 + f_y^2}$, which works out, again *modulo terms of degree 3 or more*, to be:

$$\begin{pmatrix} \kappa_1 + b_0 x + b_1 y & b_1 x + b_2 y \\ +(\frac{c_0 - \kappa_1^3}{2}x^2 + c_1 xy + \frac{c_2 - \kappa_1 \kappa_2^2}{2}y^2) & +(\frac{c_1}{2}x^2 + c_2 xy + \frac{c_3}{2}y^2) \\ & \\ b_1 x + b_2 y & \kappa_2 + b_2 x + b_3 y \\ +(\frac{c_1}{2}x^2 + c_2 xy + \frac{c_3}{2}y^2) & +(\frac{c_2 - \kappa_1^2 \kappa_2}{2}x^2 + c_3 xy + \frac{c_4 - \kappa_2^3}{2}y^2) \end{pmatrix}$$
$$\tag{6.3}$$

The principal curvatures and principal directions are simply the eigenvalues and eigenvectors of the 'shape' matrix which is defined to be $I^{-1}II$. (The last few statements are all to be found in any textbook of differential geometry, for example, in O'Neill (66 or 97). These eigenvectors are only well-defined if $\kappa_1 \neq \kappa_2$, i.e., the origin is not umbilic. At umbilics a different analysis is called for (see Section 6.5). The patient reader will want to verify (by elementary but lengthy algebra) that the formulae given below for the four functions $K_1(x,y), K_2(x,y), S_1(x,y)$ and $S_2(x,y)$ satisfy:

$$II \cdot \begin{pmatrix} \kappa_1 - \kappa_2 \\ S_1 \end{pmatrix} = K_1 I \cdot \begin{pmatrix} \kappa_1 - \kappa_2 \\ S_1 \end{pmatrix} + O((x,y)^3)$$

$$II \cdot \begin{pmatrix} -S_2 \\ \kappa_1 - \kappa_2 \end{pmatrix} = K_2 I \cdot \begin{pmatrix} -S_2 \\ \kappa_1 - \kappa_2 \end{pmatrix} + O((x,y)^3)$$

(The $\cdot$ is used here only as a separator; it means ordinary matrix multiplication.) Thus the functions K_1 and K_2 give the leading terms in the Taylor series for the eigenvalues and the displayed vectors are the leading terms for the eigenvectors of the shape matrix. Thus K_1 and K_2 are the leading terms in the Taylor series for the principal curvatures. The formulae are:

$$K_1(x,y) = \kappa_1 + b_0 x + b_1 y + \left(\frac{c_0 - 3\kappa_1^3}{2} + \frac{b_1^2}{\kappa_1 - \kappa_2} \right) x^2$$

$$+ \left(c_1 + \frac{2b_1 b_2}{\kappa_1 - \kappa_2} \right) xy + \left(\frac{c_2 - \kappa_1 \kappa_2^2}{2} + \frac{b_2^2}{\kappa_1 - \kappa_2} \right) y^2$$

$$K_2(x,y) = \kappa_2 + b_2 x + b_3 y + \left(\frac{c_2 - \kappa_1^2 \kappa_2}{2} - \frac{b_1^2}{\kappa_1 - \kappa_2} \right) x^2$$

$$+ \left(c_3 - \frac{2b_1 b_2}{\kappa_1 - \kappa_2} \right) xy + \left(\frac{c_4 - 3\kappa_2^3}{2} - \frac{b_2^2}{\kappa_1 - \kappa_2} \right) y^2$$

$$S_1(x,y) = b_1 x + b_2 y + \left(\frac{c_1}{2} - \frac{b_1(b_0 - b_2)}{\kappa_1 - \kappa_2} \right) x^2$$

$$+ \left(c_2 - \kappa_1^2 \kappa_2 - \frac{b_1(b_1 - b_3) + b_2(b_0 - b_2)}{\kappa_1 - \kappa_2} \right) xy$$

$$+ \left(\frac{c_3}{2} - \frac{b_2(b_1 - b_3)}{\kappa_1 - \kappa_2} \right) y^2$$

$$S_2(x,y) = b_1 x + b_2 y + \left(\frac{c_1}{2} - \frac{b_1(b_0 - b_2)}{\kappa_1 - \kappa_2} \right) x^2$$

$$+ \left(c_2 - \kappa_1 \kappa_2^2 - \frac{b_1(b_1 - b_3) + b_2(b_0 - b_2)}{\kappa_1 - \kappa_2} \right) xy$$

$$+ \left(\frac{c_3}{2} - \frac{b_2(b_1 - b_3)}{\kappa_1 - \kappa_2} \right) y^2$$

6.3 Contact with Planes

We wish to classify the points P of a surface M by considering the contact of the surface M with planes through P, specifically its *contact with the tangent plane* T_P to M at P. What do we mean by 'contact'? We could describe the contact via the set which is the intersection $T_P \cap M$ near P. But this is not always very informative. Look at $T_P \cap M$ at $P = (0,0,0)$ in the two cases:

$$M : z = x^2 + y^2, \qquad M : z = x^4 + y^4$$

In both cases, the intersection is an isolated point; but surely one wants to say that in the quartic case T_P has higher order contact with M than in the quadratic case. Another approach to measuring the order of contact is to use the linear equation $F(x,y,z) = ax + by + cz = 0$ of T_P and describe the contact by the Taylor expansion at P of F restricted to M. In the above examples $F = z$, so in terms of local coordinates x, y on M, $f = F|_M$ is $x^2 + y^2$ in the first case, $x^4 + y^4$ in the second case, and these are certainly different. In general, the low order terms of the Taylor expansion of f are said to determine the 'type of singularity' of f, hence the type of contact of M and T_P. This concept will become clearer as we work out some examples.

Now assume M is in Monge form and $P = (0, 0, 0)$. Again F may be taken to be z and $f(x, y)$ is just the left hand side of equation (1). We can divide points P on M into 3 cases:

(a) the quadratic terms of f are a non-degenerate quadratic form, i.e., $\kappa_1, \kappa_2 \neq 0$;

(b) the quadratic terms of f are a degenerate quadratic form, i.e., $\kappa_1 \neq 0, \kappa_2 = 0$ or vice versa; and

(c) the leading terms of f are cubic or higher, i.e., $\kappa_1 = \kappa_2 = 0$.

In any case, recall that we assume $\kappa_1 \geq \kappa_2$ always. Then we can subdivide cases (a) and (b) further:

(a1) $\kappa_1 \geq \kappa_2 > 0$, which we describe by saying P is an *elliptic convex* point of M;

(a2) $\kappa_1 > 0 > \kappa_2$, P a *hyperbolic* point of M;

(a3) $0 > \kappa_1 \geq \kappa_2$, P an *elliptic concave* point of M;

(b1) $\kappa_1 > \kappa_2 = 0$, P a *red parabolic* point of M;

(b2) $0 = \kappa_1 > \kappa_2$, P a *blue parabolic* point of M.

See Figure 6.2. The term 'red' (resp. 'blue') will always be used to indicate something special happening with κ_2 and y (resp. κ_1 and x). Points of type (c) are called *planar* points of M. For a point to be planar, all 3 quadratic coefficients in the Taylor expansion of $z = f(x, y)$ must vanish. On a generic surface, this will never happen because this is three conditions and the points on a surface give us only a two-dimensional family of Monge forms. We defined 'generic' informally in the overview as meaning that there were no special points where some particular expression in the derivatives vanished which did not need to. A formal definition can be made by making the set of all smooth surfaces $M \subset \mathbf{R}^3$ into an infinite-dimensional space. Then if something happens on an open dense subset in the space of M's, it is said to happen generically. If M is a surface with a planar point, then any small random perturbation of M near this planar point will convert the planar point to a non-planar umbilic point. A complete discussion of this concept can be found in books on singularity theory.[3] All we need to use here is the fact that if some situation arises which requires three special conditions on the coefficients of the Monge form, then this will not happen on ageneric surface. (In the next chapter we will look at families of surfaces. If these

---

[3] An elementary case is dealt with in Chapter 9 of Bruce and Giblin (92); a more technical discussion can be found in Golubitsky and Guillemin (73, pages 42ff).

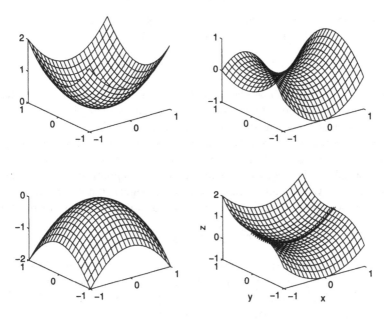

Figure 6.2. Four surface shapes close to $x = y = z = 0$. We orient them by taking the upward pointing normal. Top left: elliptic convex $z = x^2 + y^2$, where both curvatures are > 0; top right: hyperbolic $z = x^2 - y^2$, where curvatures have opposite signs; bottom left: elliptic concave $z = -x^2 - y^2$, where both curvatures are < 0; bottom right: $z = x^2 + y^3$ where there is a 'red' parabolic curve $y = 0$, marked with asterisks. This separates a convex '++' region from a hyperbolic '+−' region, the signs referring to the two curvatures κ_1, κ_2 respectively. At the origin, $\kappa_1 = 2 > 0 = \kappa_2$.

are *generic families*, nothing will happen which requires four special conditions to hold.)

Parabolic points are defined by the vanishing of the Gaussian curvature: $\kappa_1 \kappa_2 = 0$. For any surface $z = f(x, y)$ given as an arbitrary graph and not necessarily in the Monge form (i.e., f can have linear terms and an xy cross term), the set of parabolic points is given by the equation in x, y:

$$g(x, y) := f_{xx} f_{yy} - f_{xy}^2 = 0 \qquad (6.4)$$

So long as M is generic, $g(x, y) = 0$ is a smooth curve on M, called the parabolic curve, and it breaks up into disjoint red parabolic curves and blue parabolic curves. Red ones separate the elliptic convex and hyperbolic regions of M (they separate $\kappa_1 > \kappa_2 > 0$ from $\kappa_1 > 0 > \kappa_2$); blue ones separate hyperbolic and elliptic concave regions (they separate $\kappa_1 > 0 > \kappa_2$ from $0 > \kappa_1 > \kappa_2$).

To see why the parabolic curve is smooth on generic surfaces we use Monge form. The equation of the red parabolic curve is, from (6.4),

$$(\kappa_1 + b_0 x + b_1 y + \cdots)(b_2 x + b_3 y + \cdots) - (b_1 x + b_2 y + \cdots)^2 = 0$$

So long as $\kappa_1 \neq 0$ (P is non-planar) and either b_2 or b_3 is non-zero, this has a linear term so its solutions form a smooth curve. But $\kappa_1 = b_2 = b_3 = 0$ is a set of 3 conditions and never happens on a generic surface.

Parabolic curves can have special points on them even when they are smooth, however. We need to recall the classification of double points of curves, which is the first substantial result in singularity theory. Suppose we have a smooth function $f(x, y)$ vanishing to second order at the origin but not to third order. In a certain sense, almost all such functions f are equivalent to one of the functions:

$$x^2 \pm y^2; x^2 - y^3; x^2 \pm y^4; x^2 - y^5; \cdots$$

What does equivalent mean? It means that there is new set of coordinates $x' = u(x, y), y' = v(x, y)$ in some neighborhood of the origin such that $f(x, y) = a(x'^2 \pm y'^n)$, where a is a constant, and the sign can be eliminated if n is odd. When this holds, we say that f has a singularity of type A_{n-1}. Formally, this change of coordinates may be found by repeated application of completing the square to simplify the Taylor expansion of f:

$$ax^2 + xg(x, y) = a\left(x + \frac{1}{2a}g(x, y)\right)^2 - \frac{1}{4a}g(x, y)^2$$

where g has order ≥ 2 in x and y. Verifying the convergence of this process to local coordinates x', y' takes more work and can be found in references on singularity theory (see for example Bruce and Giblin (92), Chapter 10). Note that if n is odd then $f = 0$ is the curve of points $x' = t^n, y' = t^2$, which is said to have a cusp at the origin. If n is even and the sign is negative, then $f = 0$ consists of 2 smooth curves $x' = \pm y'^{n/2}$, which is said to be a node. Finally, if n is even and we use the upper sign, then the only solution of $f = 0$ near the origin is the origin itself. We call the singularity type A_{n-1}^+ in the isolated point case and A_{n-1}^- in the curve case.

In particular, at a red parabolic point P in Monge form, if $b_3 \neq 0$:

$$f(x, y) = \frac{\kappa_1}{2}\left(x + \frac{b_0}{6\kappa_1}x^2 + \frac{b_1}{2\kappa_1}xy + \frac{b_2}{2\kappa_1}y^2 + \cdots\right)^2 + \frac{b_3}{6}(y + \cdots)^3$$

has an A_2-singularity, called an ordinary cusp. However if $b_3 = 0$, then

$$f(x, y) = \frac{\kappa_1}{2}\left(x + \frac{b_0}{6\kappa_1}x^2 + \frac{b_1}{2\kappa_1}xy + \frac{b_2}{2\kappa_1}y^2 + \cdots\right)^2 + \frac{1}{24\kappa_1}(\kappa_1 c_4 - 3b_2^2)y^4 + \cdots$$

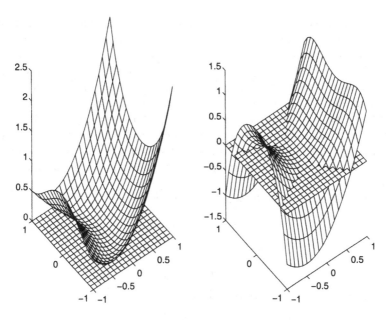

Figure 6.3. Left: an elliptic cusp of Gauss where the tangent plane meets the surface in a point. Right: a hyperbolic cusp of Gauss where the tangent plane meets the surface in a pair of tangential curves

So long as $b_2^2 \neq 3\kappa_1 c_4$, this has an A_3-singularity. Since $\kappa_2 = b_3 = 0$ is 2 conditions, while $\kappa_2 = b_3 = b_2^2 - 3\kappa_1 c_4 = 0$ is 3, these A_3-singularities occur on generic surfaces but A_4-singularities do not. These A_3-singularities are called *cusps of Gauss* and also *ruffles*. We divide them into 4 types:

(cog1) $\kappa_2 = b_3 = 0, \kappa_1 > 0, \kappa_1 c_4 - 3b_2^2 > 0$, red elliptic cusps of Gauss;

(cog2) $\kappa_2 = b_3 = 0, \kappa_1 > 0, \kappa_1 c_4 - 3b_2^2 < 0$, red hyperbolic cusps of Gauss;

(cog3) $\kappa_1 = b_0 = 0, 0 > \kappa_2, \kappa_2 c_0 - 3b_1^2 > 0$, blue elliptic cusps of Gauss;

(cog4) $\kappa_1 = b_0 = 0, 0 > \kappa_2, \kappa_2 c_0 - 3b_1^2 < 0$, blue hyperbolic cusps of Gauss.

The terminology comes from (a) red cusps of Gauss lie on red parabolic curves and blue cusps of Gauss on blue parabolic curves; and (b) elliptic cusps of Gauss P have the property P = an isolated point of $T_P \cap M$, i.e., locally M is all on one side of its tangent plane while for hyperbolic cusps of Gauss, $T_P \cap M$ is a pair of smooth curves through P (see Figure 6.3).

It is easy to locate the parabolic curves on a surface and not too hard to find the cusps of Gauss. When M is viewed from a point in the tangent plane T_P to

M at P, P is parabolic if and only if P is a point of inflection of any apparent contour[4] of M (i.e., contour like $y = x^3$) and P is a cusp of Gauss if and only if the apparent contour of M has fourth order contact with its tangent line (i.e., contour like $y = x^4$). For example, viewing either of the two surfaces in Figure 6.3 from a direction lying in the tangent plane at the origin, the apparent contour will have an 'undulation' — four-point contact with its tangent line. (There is an exceptional direction, namely the asymptotic direction, which in these figures is along the y-axis running bottom-right to top-left of the tangent plane.) It is not in practice very easy to tell four-point contact with a tangent line from ordinary two-point contact, since in both cases the curve lies locally on one side of the tangent line.

In fact, at an A_{n-1} point P, where M is given by

$$z \;=\; \frac{\kappa_1}{2}x'^2 + ay'^n$$
$$x' \;=\; x + O((x,y)^2)$$
$$y' \;=\; y + O(y^2)$$

then the contour of M when viewed along the x-axis is just:

$$z = ay'^n = ay^n + \cdots$$

Exercise: Find a cusp of Gauss on your face or hand.

6.4   Contact with Spheres; Ridge Points

We study the contact between a surface and one of its *spheres of curvature*. These are the spheres centered at one of the principal centers of curvature and having radius equal to the corresponding radius of curvature.

6.4.1   Ridge points via contact with spheres

We take our surface M in Monge form (6.1). Consider a sphere centered at $(0, 0, r)$ and passing through the origin, hence *tangent* to the surface M at the origin. This sphere has the equation

$$x^2 + y^2 + (z - r)^2 = r^2$$

The x, y values where this sphere meets the surface $z = f(x, y)$ are given by $g(x, y) = 0$ where

$$g(x, y) = x^2 + y^2 + (f(x, y) - r)^2 - r^2$$

---

[4] Given a view direction $\mathbf{v}$, this is the projection to a plane perpendicular to $\mathbf{v}$ of the 'contour generator' on M consisting of those points where $\mathbf{v}$ is a tangent direction to M. The only assumption about $\mathbf{v}$ above is that it is not tangent to the contour generator, which would produce a cusp on the apparent contour.

The function g is the *contact function* relevant to this situation. The equation $g = 0$ gives the curve of intersection of M with the sphere, in the sense that the intersection points are $(x, y, f(x, y))$ where $g(x, y) = 0$. But the function g itself measures the contact.

Expanding g as a power series in x and y gives

$$g(x, y) = x^2(1 - r\kappa_1) + y^2(1 - r\kappa_2) - \frac{r}{3}(b_0 x^3 + 3b_1 x^2 y + 3b_2 xy^2 + b_3 y^3)$$

$$-\frac{r}{12}(c_0 x^4 + \cdots) + \left(\frac{\kappa_1}{2}x^2 + \frac{\kappa_2}{2}y^2\right)^2 + \cdots \tag{6.5}$$

If $r \neq 1/\kappa_1$ and $r \neq 1/\kappa_2$ then g has an A_1 singularity, also called a *nondegenerate critical point* at $x = y = 0$. Additionally, the intersection of M and the sphere has an isolated point at the origin if (i) κ_1 and κ_2 have the same sign, and the center $(0, 0, r)$ of the sphere is *not* between the centers of curvature $(0, 0, 1/\kappa_1)$ and $(0, 0, 1/\kappa_2)$; or (ii) κ_1 and κ_2 have opposite signs, and the center of the sphere *is* between the two centers of curvature. When the intersection does not have an isolated point, it is, locally, two smooth intersecting curves. A typical sequence of intersections between a surface and spheres centered on the normal at a given point is shown in Figure 6.4. A specific sequence for the surface $z = x^2 + 2y^2 + 2x^3 + y^3$ is shown in Figure 6.5. These show how the branches link up as the radius increases.

When r takes one of the values $1/\kappa_i$, the contact function and, with it, the curve of contact, become more degenerate. Let us put $r = 1/\kappa_1$. Then, assuming $\kappa_1 \neq \kappa_2$, the contact function is of type A_2. The contact curve in that case is an *ordinary cusp*.

If $r = 1/\kappa_1$ again and $b_0 = 0$ then there is a further degeneration in the contact

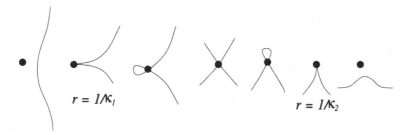

Figure 6.4. Local intersections between a surface and spheres (i) whose centers are on the line normal to the surface at a given point P; and (ii) which are tangent to the surface at P. From left to right the radius of the sphere increases. This shows the case where both principal curvatures have the same sign, and only indicates the intersection very close to P.

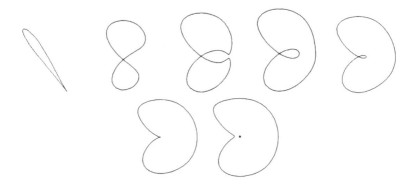

Figure 6.5. Local intersections between the surface $z = x^2 + 2y^2 + 2x^3 + y^3$ and spheres (i) centered on the normal line to the surface at the origin; and (ii) tangent to the surface there. From left to right the radius of the sphere is 0.25 (one radius of curvature; observe the cusp), 0.35, 0.38, 0.39, 0.43, 0.5 (the other radius of curvature, another cusp), 0.6 (isolated point at the origin). The pictures are not all to the same scale.

function and the curve of intersection:

$$
\begin{aligned}
\kappa_1 g(x,y) \;=\;& y^2(\kappa_1 - \kappa_2) - \frac{1}{3}(3b_1 x^2 y + 3b_2 xy^2 + b_3 y^3) \\
& - \frac{1}{12}(c_0 x^4 + \cdots) + \frac{\kappa_1^3}{4} x^4 + \cdots \\
\;=\;& (\kappa_1 - \kappa_2)\left(y - \frac{b_1}{2(\kappa_1 - \kappa_2)}x^2 - \frac{b_2}{2(\kappa_1 - \kappa_2)}xy - \frac{b_3}{6(\kappa_1 - \kappa_2)}y^2\right)^2 \\
& - \frac{1}{12(\kappa_1 - \kappa_2)}\left(3b_1^2 + (\kappa_1 - \kappa_2)(c_0 - 3\kappa_1^3)\right) x^4 + \cdots
\end{aligned}
$$

(Note that here, '$\cdots$' does not mean terms of higher *degree* but terms of higher 'weight', in the sense of giving the variable y weight 2 and the variable x weight 1. Then y^2 and x^4 are of lowest weight 4, and for example $x^2 y^2$ has higher weight 6.)

Generally, such a g can be reduced to the form A_3: $y^2 \pm x^4$ by smooth changes of coordinates. The condition for this to be possible is that the polynomial P_1 in the coefficients of the Monge form defined by the equation:

$$P_1 = 3b_1^2 + (\kappa_1 - \kappa_2)(c_0 - 3\kappa_1^3) \tag{6.6}$$

is *not equal to 0*. More precisely, if we have $P_1 < 0$, then the reduction is to $y^2 + x^4$ and the singularity is called elliptic or of type A_3^+. In that case the local intersection of the surface and the sphere is an isolated point. On the other hand if we have $P_1 > 0$, then the reduction is to $y^2 - x^4$, the singularity is said to be hyperbolic or of type A_3^-, and the local intersection is two smooth tangential curves (a 'tacnode').

Similarly, if we start with $r = 1/\kappa_2$ and $b_3 = 0$ then we find that reduction to type A_3^- : $-x^2 + y^4$, is possible provided $P_2 > 0$, and reduction to type A_3^+ : $-x^2 - y^4$ is possible provided $P_2 < 0$, where

$$P_2 = 3b_2^2 + (\kappa_2 - \kappa_1)(c_4 - 3\kappa_2^3)$$

We can sum this up as follows: A *ridge point of a smooth surface* is a point where one of the spheres of curvature has more degenerate contact than the usual (A_2) contact. A ridge point is *elliptic* if the local intersection of the surface with its sphere of curvature is an isolated point, and *hyperbolic* otherwise — generically the local intersection is then two tangential branches (see Figure 6.6). In Monge form, away from umbilics, i.e., assuming $\kappa_1 \neq \kappa_2$, these can be recognized as follows (where 'blue' always refers to the *larger* curvature κ_1 and 'red' to the *smaller*[5] curvature κ_2):

(r1) Blue elliptic ridge point: $b_0 = 0, P_1 < 0$,

(r2) Blue hyperbolic ridge point: $b_0 = 0, P_1 > 0$,

(r3) Red elliptic ridge point: $b_3 = 0, P_2 < 0$,

(r4) Red hyperbolic ridge point: $b_3 = 0, P_2 > 0$.

The elliptic ridge points are the *perceptually salient* ones, which are of most significance to surface shape.

As an example, suppose that the plane $x = 0$ is a *plane of symmetry* of the surface, that is, (x, y, z) belongs to the surface if and only if $(-x, y, z)$ does. Then the Monge form of the surface must contain only *even* powers of x, and in particular the coefficient of x^3 will be zero. This shows that the curve C in which a surface meets a plane of symmetry is always a ridge curve — corresponding to the principal directions running perpendicular to C. See Figure 6.7 for a simple example.

An important special case arises when the curvature κ_1 say is zero. Then it is a *plane* rather than a *sphere* which has degenerate contact with the surface at the origin. In that case the origin is a blue cusp of Gauss (see Section 6.3). Thus *parabolic curves cross ridges of the same color at cusps of Gauss*. Note that the cusp of Gauss is elliptic if and only if the ridge is elliptic.

How can we derive an equation for the curve of ridge points? Ridge curves are third derivative phenomena and the formulae for them are always more complex than those for parabolic curves. For a general point P on a surface (not at the origin) we can apply the same definitions as above: P is a ridge point corresponding

---

[5] 'larger' and 'smaller' only in the sense that $\kappa_1 \geq \kappa_2$; no absolute values are being used here.

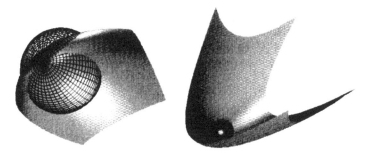

Figure 6.6. The surface $z = 4x^2 + y^2$. Left: a view from underneath of the surface and the sphere of curvature corresponding to the smaller curvature $\kappa_2 = 2$ at $x = y = 0$ (the sphere is drawn as a wire frame for greater clarity). This sphere intersects the surface in two tangential curves through the origin, which is a hyperbolic ridge point. Right: a view from higher up of the surface and the sphere of curvature corresponding to the larger curvature $\kappa_1 = 8$ at $x = y = 0$. This sphere intersects the surface only at the origin, which is an elliptic ridge point.

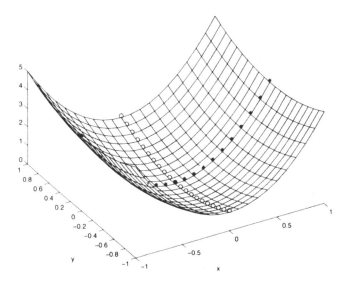

Figure 6.7. The surface $z = 4x^2 + y^2$, which has an elliptic blue ridge, marked by small circles, where the larger (blue) principal curvature has a maximum along the blue line of curvature, and a hyperbolic red ridge, marked by asterisks, where the smaller (red) principal curvature has a maximum along the red line of curvature. In this example, both ridges are curves of symmetry of the surface, and the relevant lines of curvature run perpendicular to the ridges.

to κ_1 provided the corresponding sphere of curvature has degenerate contact with the surface at P. This leads to a method for detecting ridge points, but we warn the reader in advance that it is hard to apply in practice. In the next section we give an alternative method.

Let the surface be parametrized, at least locally, by $X(u,v), Y(u,v), Z(u,v)$, with P corresponding to $u = u_0, v = v_0$. Let the center of the sphere of curvature at $u = u_0, v = v_0$ be (a, b, c). Then the contact function is

$$g(u,v) = (a - X(u,v))^2 + (b - Y(u,v))^2 + (c - Z(u,v))^2$$

This will automatically have the properties

$$g_u = g_v = 0, \quad g_{uu}g_{vv} = g_{uv}^2 \quad \text{at } (u_0, v_0)$$

since these just say that (a, b, c) is one of the principal centers of curvature. The last condition states that the quadratic terms of the Taylor expansion of g at (u_0, v_0) form (plus or minus) a perfect square, i.e.,

$$g_{uu}u^2 + 2g_{uv}uv + g_{vv}v^2 = \pm(Au + Bv)^2$$

Here A, B do not depend on u and v, only on u_0, v_0 (and the surface, of course), and the derivatives are all evaluated at (u_0, v_0). If $g_{uu} \neq 0$ then we can write, equivalently,

$$g_{uu}^2 u^2 + 2g_{uu}g_{uv}uv + g_{uu}g_{vv}v^2 = (g_{uu}u + g_{uv}v)^2$$

and similarly when $g_{vv} \neq 0$. If both g_{uu} and g_{vv} are zero, then also $g_{uv} = 0$, the case of a 'flat umbilic' or 'planar point'. In that case the contact is *worse* than A_3: the point P counts as a degenerate ridge point.

The additional condition which describes degenerate contact (A_3 or 'worse') can then be expressed by

$$Au + Bv \text{ is a factor of the cubic terms of } g \text{ at } (u_0, v_0)$$

This says that

$$g_{uuu}B^3 - 3g_{uuv}AB^2 + 3g_{uvv}A^2B - g_{vvv}A^3 = 0$$

where again all derivatives are evaluated at (u_0, v_0). Since this condition can be multiplied through by any nonzero constant, we can, by the above remarks, replace A by g_{uu} and B by g_{uv}, unless these are both zero, and we can also replace A by g_{uv}, B by g_{vv}, unless these are both zero. The result is an equation in u_0, v_0 which determines the blue ridge points with parameters $u = u_0, v = v_0$.

This criterion is in practice quite difficult to apply. In the next section we give an alternative method for determining ridge points.

6.4.2   Ridge points via extrema of principal curvatures

It is also possible to interpret b_0, b_3 and indeed the other two cubic coefficients, in a different way. We can use the equations for S_i in Section 6.2 to determine the local equations of the lines of curvature at the origin. Thus suppose that the line of curvature corresponding to κ_1 is $y = \alpha x^2 + \beta x^3 + \cdots$. (Note that it is tangent to the principal direction which is the x-axis at the origin so there is no x term.) In the notation of Section 6.2 we have, for the slope of the principal curve through (x, y, z),

$$\frac{S_1(x, \alpha x^2 + \beta x^3 + \cdots)}{\kappa_1 - \kappa_2} = 2\alpha x + 3\beta x^2 + \cdots$$

Using the formula for S_1 and comparing coefficients of x and x^2 we find for the blue line of curvature corresponding to κ_1

$$y = \frac{b_1}{2(\kappa_1 - \kappa_2)}x^2 + \frac{1}{6}\left(c_1 - \frac{b_1(2b_0 - 3b_2)}{\kappa_1 - \kappa_2}\right)x^3 + \cdots \qquad (6.7)$$

Similarly for the red line of curvature corresponding to κ_2 we get

$$x = -\frac{b_2}{2(\kappa_1 - \kappa_2)}y^2 + \frac{1}{6}\left(c_3 + \frac{b_2(2b_3 - 3b_1)}{\kappa_1 - \kappa_2}\right)y^3 + \cdots$$

We can expand both the first and second principal curvatures as functions of x on the blue line of curvature. The results, which follow immediately from (6.7) and the formulae for K_1 and K_2 in Section 6.2, are

$$\begin{aligned}
\kappa_1(x) &= \kappa_1 + b_0 x + \frac{1}{2}\left(c_0 - 3\kappa_1^3 + \frac{3b_1^2}{\kappa_1 - \kappa_2}\right)x^2 + \cdots \\
&= \kappa_1 + b_0 x + \frac{P_1}{2(\kappa_1 - \kappa_2)}x^2 + \cdots, \\
\kappa_2(x) &= \kappa_2 + b_2 x + \frac{1}{2}\left(c_2 - \kappa_1^2\kappa_2 + \frac{b_1 b_3 - 2b_1^2}{\kappa_1 - \kappa_2}\right)x^2 + \cdots
\end{aligned}$$

Figure 6.8 shows level sets of κ_2 together with the corresponding red lines of curvature and a ridge line. Note that the lines of curvature are tangent to the level sets at points of the ridge. This makes them easy and stable to find, given good second derivatives for the surface.[6]

Similar results hold when expanding the first and second principal curvatures on the *red line of curvature*, that is the one tangent to the y-axis and so corresponding with the smaller principal curvature κ_2.

---

[6] The equation of the surface is $z = 0.1x^2 + 0.02y^2 + 0.021x^3 + 0.0052y^3 - 0.001exp(-8x^2 - 8y^2)$, which can be considered as generic surface patch (the first 4 terms) perturbed by a tiny bump, invisible to the naked eye but putting a clear ripple in the second derivatives.

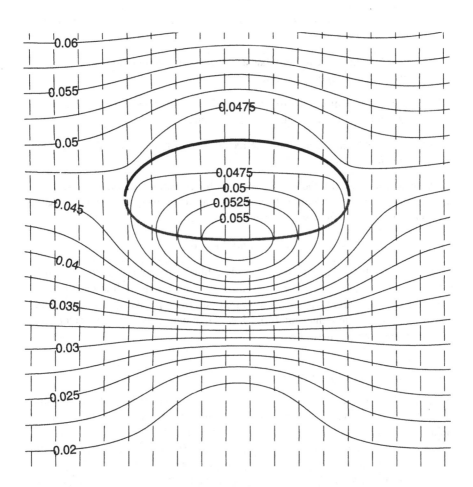

Figure 6.8. In the x, y parameter plane, the field of red principal directions is shown as nearly vertical dashes: the red lines of curvature are almost vertical. The level sets of κ_2 are shown as solid lines. The thick black line is a 'red minimum' (salient) ridge and the gray line is a 'red maximum' (non-salient) ridge. It is clear that the level sets are tangent to the lines of curvature along the lower ridge segment and that κ_2, taken along a line of curvature, has a maximum at each of these ridge points. The lines of curvature are also tangent to the level sets along the upper ridge segment; this is not so obvious from the level sets drawn, but it is clear from the labels on the level sets that, along a line of curvature, κ_2 reaches a minimum and then rises again. This minimum occurs at a point of the upper ridge segment. Where the ridge itself is tangent to the line of curvature it changes from red minimum to maximum; these are turning points.

This gives us the following interpretations when the origin is not an umbilic:

$b_0 = 0$: κ_1 has an extremum on the blue (κ_1) line of curvature. The origin is a blue ridge point;

$b_1 = 0$: The blue line of curvature has a (geodesic) inflection, and also κ_1 has an extremum along the red line of curvature;

$b_2 = 0$: The red line of curvature has a (geodesic) inflection, and also κ_2 has an extremum along the blue line of curvature;

$b_3 = 0$: κ_2 has an extremum along the red (κ_2) line of curvature. The origin is a red ridge point.

We can also read off the conditions for the curvatures to have a *maximum* or *minimum* from the quadratic terms of the above expansion. Thus κ_1 has a maximum along the blue line of curvature provided

$$b_0 = 0 \text{ and } P_1 < 0$$

This is a blue elliptic ridge point. Similarly a blue hyperbolic ridge point will be a 'blue minimum', that is, κ_1 will have a minimum along its line of curvature. Applying the same argument to κ_2, at red elliptic ridge points κ_2 has a minimum and at red hyperbolic ridge points κ_2 has a maximum, in each case along the corresponding line of curvature.

6.4.3   Local equation of a ridge

We can use the above criteria for ridges and the formulae of Section 6.2 to determine the local equation of a ridge at the origin, when the origin is itself a ridge point. This is done as follows: Suppose that $x = \alpha y + \beta y^2 + \cdots$ is the blue ridge curve through the origin, when $\kappa_1 \neq \kappa_2$ and $b_0 = 0$. We take the expression for $K_1(x, y)$ in Section 6.2 and substitute the above expression for x as a power series in y. Now the principal direction at (x, y, z) is given by $((\kappa_1 - \kappa_2), S_1(x, y))$, where again we refer to Section 6.2 for the formula for S_1. We know that at ridge points the derivative of K_1 in the principal direction is zero, that is, substituting for x as a power series in y in S_1,

$$\frac{\partial K_1}{\partial x}(\kappa_1 - \kappa_2) + \frac{\partial K_1}{\partial y}S_1 = 0$$

for all values of y. Then comparing coefficients of y we get an expression for α, and, with more effort, we could get an expression for β and higher terms too. The result of this is that the blue ridge (when $b_0 = 0$) has local equation

$$P_1 x + Q_1 y + \cdots = 0 \tag{6.8}$$

where P_1 was defined above (6.6) and Q_1 is given by:

$$Q_1 = 3b_1b_2 + (\kappa_1 - \kappa_2)c_1$$

Similarly, the local equation of the red ridge is

$$Q_2x + P_2y + \cdots = 0$$

where

$$Q_2 = 3b_1b_2 - (\kappa_1 - \kappa_2)c_3$$

Finally a ridge point is called a *turning point* if the corresponding curvature has first and second derivatives zero along the principal direction – that is a degenerate extremum. In general the third derivative will be non-zero, and the contact with the sphere of curvature centered at $(0, 0, 1/\kappa_1)$ will be exactly of type A_4 (compare (6.6) above). A very important property of generic turning points (where the contact is exactly of type A_4) is that the ridge *changes* there from elliptic to hyperbolic: blue maximum changes to blue minimum, or red minimum to red maximum. Of course the change can also go the other way, from hyperbolic to elliptic ridge (see Figure 6.8 for an example).

For blue ridge points, the turning point condition is $b_0 = P_1 = 0$. At such points, the intersection curve with the surface depends on further terms of the Taylor expansion of the surface. For an A_4 point, when the contact function can be reduced to the form $y^2 + x^5$, the intersection is a 'rhamphoid cusp'. This rhamphoid cusp has parametrization $(-t^2, t^5)$; often the version $(t^2, t^4 - t^5)$ is used when drawing a rhamphoid cusp, since this looks more 'rhamphoid' (beak-like). The two are locally diffeomorphic (see Figure 6.9). The condition that it is not an A_5 point, i.e., an x^5 term remains after completing the square, is easily seen to be:

$$R_1 = (\kappa_1 - \kappa_2)^2 d_0 + 10(\kappa_1 - \kappa_2)b_1c_1 + 15b_1^2b_2 \neq 0$$

6.4.4 Two remarks on umbilic points

In all the above, we have assumed that the surface point (taken as the origin) is not an umbilic. We study umbilics in greater detail in Section 6.5, but it is worth making an observation here. Suppose the origin in (6.1) is an umbilic, that is to say $\kappa_1 = \kappa_2$. Suppose also that not all the cubic terms of the Monge expansion (6.1) are zero. The contact function in (6.5), for $r = \kappa_1 = \kappa_2$ is then dominated by the cubic terms, and the intersection between the surface and its sphere of curvature at the umbilic is given, locally, by the vanishing of a homogeneous cubic form in x and y. This intersection can never be an isolated point, since cubics always have real roots. We deduce the following:

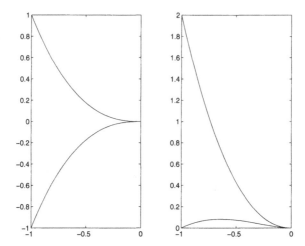

Figure 6.9. Left: a rhamphoid cusp $(-t^2, t^5)$: Right: a more beak-like rhamphoid cusp $(-t^2, t^4 + t^5)$.

Proposition 6.1 *If a ridge curve passes through an umbilic of a surface (at which the cubic terms of the surface do not vanish identically) then at the umbilic, and hence nearby, the ridge curve must be hyperbolic.*

We shall see in Section 6.5 that either one or three ridges pass through a generic umbilic.

Secondly, we make explicit the connection between contact with spheres and umbilics. In Section 6.4.1 we supposed the point under consideration was at the origin. Let us now take any surface given as a graph, $z = f(x, y)$, any point $P = (x_0, y_0, f(x_0, y_0))$ on it, and any point $A = P + \lambda(-f_x, -f_y, 1)$ on the normal at P. Here and below, all partial derivatives of f are evaluated at (x_0, y_0). Any sphere S centered at A and passing through P will be tangent to the surface there. We can parametrize the surface close to P by

$$(x_0 + u, y_0 + v, f(x_0 + u, y_0 + v))$$

and $f(x_0+u, y_0+v) = f(x_0, y_0) + uf_x + vf_y + \frac{1}{2}(u^2 f_{xx} + 2uv f_{xy} + v^2 f_{yy}) + \cdots$

Substituting this parametrization of the surface into the equation of the sphere S, we find the contact function for these two surfaces. This is a function of u and v and works out to be

$$u^2(1 + f_x^2 - \lambda f_{xx}) + 2uv(f_x f_y - \lambda f_{xy}) + v^2(1 + f_y^2 - \lambda f_{yy}) + \cdots$$

The condition for P to be an umbilic is that *all the quadratic terms of the contact function should vanish.* This gives us three conditions, or, eliminating λ, two conditions on x_0 and y_0, confirming the fact that umbilics are isolated points in general. The conditions for an umbilic point then can be expressed by the matrix

$$\begin{pmatrix} 1 + f_x^2 & f_x f_y & 1 + f_y^2 \\ f_{xx} & f_{xy} & f_{yy} \end{pmatrix}$$

has rank 2, i.e., that all 2×2 minors are zero. This is the same as saying that the first and second fundamental form matrices, I and II, are proportional, which is another criterion for umbilics. When the surface is in Monge form, with $f_x = f_y = 0$ then this reduces, of course, to $f_{xy} = 0, f_{xx} = f_{yy}$.

6.4.5 Symmetry sets and ridges

Finally, we mention one other way of defining (and visualizing) ridges. First recall some concepts for plane curves (which we will generalize to surfaces). The *symmetry set* of the curve is the locus of centers of circles tangent to the curve in two places, called 'bitangent' circles. The *evolute* of the curve is the locus of centers of circles of curvature, i.e., circles having 3-point contact[7] with the curve. When the two tangency points of a bitangent circle coincide, the circle becomes the circle of curvature at a *vertex* of the curve: these are the points where the circle has 4-point contact with the curve and the evolute of the plane curve has a cusp. The *medial axis* of the curve is the subset of the symmetry set given by the centers of bitangent circles which are contained inside the curve, i.e., the minimum distance from the center of such a circle to the curve equals the radius of the circle.

For surfaces, we may consider the set of all spheres tangent to a surface M at two different places: 'bitangent' spheres. This is a 2-dimensional set called the *symmetry set* of M. If these points of contact tend to coincidence at P, then P is a ridge point. Thus ridge points are the 'vertices of surfaces'. Note that this analogy also fits in with the definition of a ridge point in terms of extrema of principal curvatures, for a vertex is an extremum point of the curvature of a plane curve. (See Bruce et al. (85), Giblin and Brassett (85) for general work on symmetry sets; and, for the vision perspective, Leyton (87) and Yuille and Leyton (90).)

Moreover, in the surface case the locus of centers of the spheres of curvature, called the *focal set*, has a cuspidal edge over the ridges on the surface. The symmetry set of the surface M has a boundary along these cuspidal edges. The

---

[7] This refers to three points of intersection which have come into coincidence, whereas at an ordinary '2-point contact' only two points of intersection have coincided. Note that a bitangent circle has, generally, ordinary 2-point contact at two different planes on the curve.

symmetry set has more complex structure (swallowtails, and more) at certain special points, but most ridge points are simply points where a bitangent sphere has accumulated all its intersections with the surface at a single point. The elliptic ridge points are then those ridge points corresponding to limiting bitangent spheres which intersect the surface locally at only one point.

By analogy with the curve case, we consider the *medial axis* of the surface to consist of the subset of the symmetry set given by the centers of bitangent spheres contained inside the surface, i.e., the minimal distance from the center of such a sphere to the surface equals the radius of the sphere. The center of the appropriate sphere of curvature at a ridge point can only contribute to the medial axis when the ridge point is elliptic — for the sphere must not intersect M away from the ridge point. However, not all spheres of curvature at elliptic ridge points contribute to the medial axis, for we have to make sure that there are no other points of intersection between the M and the sphere, possibly remote from the ridge point itself.

Here is a simple example, where the surface has planes of symmetry which make ridges easy to detect. Consider the surface M defined by

$$z = 2x^2 + y^2$$

which has two planes of symmetry, $x = 0$ and $y = 0$, and these intersect the surface, necessarily, in ridges. (Figure 6.6 shows a similar surface.) Consider first the plane $x = 0$, which meets the surface in the curve R_1 given by $z = y^2$; this is both a line of curvature and a ridge. At any point of this curve, the principal directions are parallel to the x-axis and tangent to R_1, and the corresponding principal curvatures are

$$\frac{4}{(4y^2 + 1)^{1/2}} \text{ and } \frac{2}{(4y^2 + 1)^{3/2}}$$

Clearly the first of these is the larger. Thus R_1 is a red line of curvature and a blue ridge, in fact a blue elliptic ridge.

By symmetry, we shall be able to find a sphere tangent to M at two points of the form

$$(x_1, y_1, 2x_1^2 + y_1^2) \text{ and } (-x_1, y_1, 2x_1^2 + y_1^2)$$

For a sphere of radius r, we write down the condition that the points a distance r along the normals to M at these two points coincide, which gives $r = \frac{1}{4}(16x_1^2 + 4y_1^2 + 1)^{1/2}$ and the center of the sphere (the point on the symmetry set) as

$$\left(0, \frac{y_1}{2}, \ 2x_1^2 + y_1^2 + \frac{1}{4}\right) \tag{6.9}$$

When $x_1 = 0$, the points of contact coincide, and the point on the symmetry set becomes $(0, \frac{1}{2}y_1, y_1^2 + \frac{1}{4})$. This is the 'rib line' lying over the ridge whose

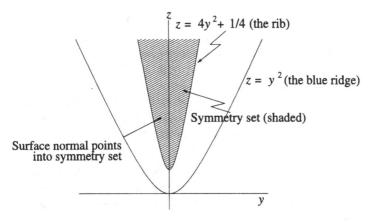

Figure 6.10. One sheet of the symmetry set of the surface $z = 2x^2 + y^2$, lying in the plane $x = 0$, and terminating on the rib line lying over the (elliptic blue) ridge in this plane. This sheet is also part of the medial axis of the surface.

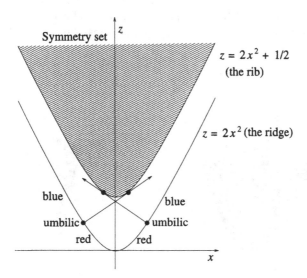

Figure 6.11. One sheet of the symmetry set of the surface $z = 2x^2 + y^2$, lying in the plane $y = 0$, and terminating on the rib line lying over the ridge in this plane. The ridge is partly red and partly blue, and all hyperbolic. This part of the symmetry set is not part of the medial axis of the surface. Note that the surface normal at an umbilic point is tangent to the rib.

points are $(0, y_1, y_1^2)$. The rib line consists of the 'blue' centers of curvature of the ridge points, that is, the centers of the spheres which have exceptionally high contact with the surface there. The symmetry set itself, given by (6.9), consists of points 'on or above' the rib, since $x_1^2 \geq 0$. Furthermore, it is easy to check that the normal to M, drawn from the point of M to the corresponding rib point, is oriented *into* the symmetry set. This gives force to the idea that the spheres centered on the symmetry set and tangent to M in two places are those *inside* M, that is, spheres whose centers contribute to the medial axis. This is illustrated in Figures 6.10, 6.12 and 6.13.

If we consider the ridge R_2 given by intersecting M with the plane $y = 0$, we are looking at spheres tangent to M at points of the form $(x_1, y_1, 2x_1^2 + y_1^2)$ and $(x_1, -y_1, 2x_1^2 + y_1^2)$. These are not maximal spheres; they are tangent to M externally. Calculating the radius r, we find $r = \frac{1}{2}(16x_1^2 + 4y_1^2 + 1)^{1/2}$, and the center of the sphere is at

$$\left(-x_1, 0, , 2x_1^2 + y_1^2 + \frac{1}{2} \right)$$

When $y_1 = 0$, the two contact points coincide and the center is $(-x_1, 0, 2x_1^2 + \frac{1}{2})$ on the rib lying over the ridge. This point is the center of curvature corresponding to the principal curvature at $(x_1, 0, 2x_1^2)$ with principal direction $(0, 1, 0)$, parallel

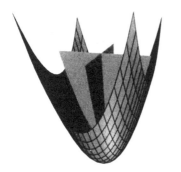

Figure 6.12. Both sheets of the symmetry set of the surface $z = 2x^2 + y^2$, shown with the surface and without it. The darker sheet lies in the plane $x = 0$ and is the one corresponding to the bitangent spheres whose intersection with the surface is locally just two points. Its boundary is the rib line lying over the blue elliptic ridge on the surface.

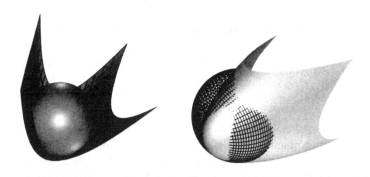

Figure 6.13. Left: A bitangent sphere for the surface $z = 2x^2 + y^2$ which meets the surface locally in two points — its center is on the sheet of the symmetry set illustrated in Figure 6.10. The surface has a grid drawn on it for greater clarity. Right: A bitangent sphere (drawn as wireframe) where each intersection with the surface is locally a pair of crossing curves. Its center is on the sheet of the symmetry set illustrated in Figure 6.11.

to the y-axis. In fact, the principal curvatures work out to be

$$\frac{4}{(16x^2 + 1)^{3/2}} \text{ and } \frac{2}{\sqrt{16x^2 + 1}}$$

corresponding to principal directions tangent to the curve R_2, and parallel to the y-axis, respectively. The second of these is larger for $|x| > \frac{1}{4}$, and the first is larger for $|x| < \frac{1}{4}$. When $x = \pm\frac{1}{4}$ we have an *umbilic* at $(x, 0, 2x^2)$. The situation is sketched in Figure 6.11.

6.5 Umbilics

In Section 6.2 we gave formulae for the first and second fundamental forms of a surface close to a non-umbilic point. Now, we want to extend our analysis to umbilic points, and some more calculations are necessary. The principal curvatures are equal at an umbilic point, but all directions are principal there. Nevertheless, there are, in the generic case, well-defined *limiting* principal directions at umbilics. The configuration of these is one way of distinguishing umbilics from one another; we shall also need some other features, such as whether the principal curvatures have local maximum or minimum values there. Recall that we always assume $\kappa_1 \geq \kappa_2$; hence we can ask whether κ_1 has a local minimum and κ_2 has a local maximum. It turns out that this hinges on whether the cubic terms in the Monge form represent one or three real lines through the origin.

6.5.1   Principal directions close to an umbilic

As before, we will use a Monge patch; at an umbilic this takes the form

$$z = \frac{1}{2}\kappa(x^2 + y^2) + \frac{1}{6}(b_0 x^3 + 3b_1 x^2 y + 3b_2 xy^2 + b_3 y^3)$$

$$+ \frac{1}{24}(c_0 x^4 + 4c_1 x^3 y + 6c_2 x^2 y^2 + 4c_3 xy^3 + c_4 y^4) + \cdots \quad (6.10)$$

We shall assume that the umbilic is *isolated*. This happens on all but very special surfaces, since umbilics are defined by two conditions (see Section 6.2), which can be expected to produce only isolated solutions. It follows that at every nearby point the principal directions are well-defined; we want to see how these principal directions change as we make a circuit of the umbilic. The formulae (6.2) and (6.3) are still valid and they show that, for small x, y,

$$I = I_2 + O((x, y)^2); \quad II = \kappa I_2 + \begin{pmatrix} b_0 x + b_1 y & b_1 x + b_2 y \\ b_1 x + b_2 y & b_2 x + b_3 y \end{pmatrix} + O((x, y)^2)$$
$$(6.11)$$

where I_2 is the 2×2 identity matrix. The displayed matrix in the formula for II is the hessian (matrix of second partial derivatives) of the cubic terms of z. The principal directions are then the eigenvectors of $I^{-1}II$ which to first order in x, y means that the principal directions are the eigenvectors of the hessian matrix. Think of the eigenvector as $(1, m)$, where $m = \tan\theta$ and θ is the slope of the principal direction. For any 2×2 symmetric matrix

$$\begin{pmatrix} A & B \\ B & C \end{pmatrix}$$

we have $A + Bm = \lambda$, $B + Cm = \lambda m$ for some λ (the eigenvalue), giving $(A - C)m = B(1 - m^2)$. Hence

$$\tan 2\theta = \frac{2m}{1 - m^2} = \frac{2B}{A - C} = \frac{2(b_1 x + b_2 y)}{(b_0 - b_2)x + (b_1 - b_3)y}$$

in our case. Now, as (x, y) traverses a small counter-clockwise circle centered at the origin, the point $((b_0 - b_2)x + (b_1 - b_3)y, 2(b_1 x + b_2 y))$ will travel counter-clockwise or clockwise accordingly, as the determinant

$$S = \begin{vmatrix} b_0 - b_2 & b_1 - b_3 \\ b_1 & b_2 \end{vmatrix} \quad (6.12)$$

is positive or negative. On a generic surface, $S \neq 0$, hence one of these holds. (Also, $S \neq 0$ implies the umbilic is isolated because the shape matrix does remain equal to a multiple of the identity.) Because the above formula involves 2θ rather

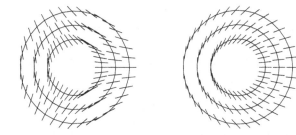

Figure 6.14. Left: a direction field with index $-\frac{1}{2}$ giving rise to a 'star', $S < 0$: Right: a direction field with index $+\frac{1}{2}$ giving rise to a 'lemon' (or a 'lemonstar'), $S > 0$.

than θ, the principal direction turns through only π when (x, y) makes a complete circuit of the origin: *the index of the principal vector fields is* $\pm\frac{1}{2}$, the sign being given by that of (6.12). Of course at each point away from the origin, there are two principal directions at right-angles: the two angles θ with a given value of $\tan 2\theta$ will be perpendicular. Figure 6.14 shows a direction field for one set of principal directions, round three circles centred at the origin. The index is $-\frac{1}{2}$ on the left and $+\frac{1}{2}$ on the right. These lead to one family of lines of curvature, and the pattern is called a 'star' for the left picture ($S < 0$) and a 'lemon' for the right ($S > 0$). In Figures 6.15 and 6.16 we show an example of each of the different kinds of umbilic, including those distinguished by the finer classification of Section 6.5.4 below. For the present, the sign of S divides all umbilics with $S \neq 0$ into 2 topologically distinct families, and is the first step in the classification of umbilic points. Being topological, this distinction is very robust and easy to make from numerical data, as we shall see with faces.

6.5.2 Principal curvatures close to an umbilic

Next we consider the principal curvatures, which by (6.11) are, to first order in x and y, the curvature $\kappa = \kappa_1(0, 0) = \kappa_2(0, 0)$ plus the eigenvalues of the hessian matrix of the cubic terms of z. Explicitly, this gives

$$\kappa + \frac{(b_0 + b_2)x + (b_1 + b_3)y}{2} \pm \sqrt{\left(\frac{(b_0 - b_2)x + (b_1 - b_3)y}{2}\right)^2 + (b_1 x + b_2 y)^2}$$

(6.13)

The upper sign gives $\kappa_1(x, y)$ and the lower sign $\kappa_2(x, y)$. It follows from this formula for the first order behavior of κ_i that the full graph of κ_i is a smooth function plus or minus the square root of a positive smooth function with non-degenerate quadratic term. Thus these two graphs look like the top and bottom parts of a tilted cone.

Consider the set of (x, y) for which the expression after κ is *zero*. If this is a single point, namely $(x, y) = (0, 0)$, then the graphs of κ_1 and κ_2 will be separated by a horizontal plane, and κ_1 will have a local minimum at $(0, 0)$ while κ_2 will have a local maximum. A little manipulation shows the expression after κ is zero if and only if

$$x^2(b_1^2 - b_0 b_2) - xy(b_0 b_3 - b_1 b_2) + y^2(b_2^2 - b_1 b_3) = 0$$

and this quadratic form is definite – thereby taking a constant sign for all x and y — if and only if

$$D = 4(b_1^2 - b_0 b_2)(b_2^2 - b_1 b_3) - (b_0 b_3 - b_1 b_2)^2 > 0 \qquad (6.14)$$

On the other hand it can be checked that this is the condition for the cubic form

$$b_0 x^3 + 3b_1 x^2 y + 3b_2 xy^2 + b_3 y^3$$

to have three real roots, that is, to factorize into three real linear factors. On generic surfaces $D \neq 0$ at an umbilic and the sign of D is a second way to divide umbilics into 2 distinct types. We say the umbilic is *elliptic* if the cubic term of its Monge form has three distinct real roots or, equivalently, κ_1 has a local minimum and κ_2 has a local maximum at the umbilic. On the other hand, we say it is *hyperbolic* if the cubic has only one real root or, equivalently, there are

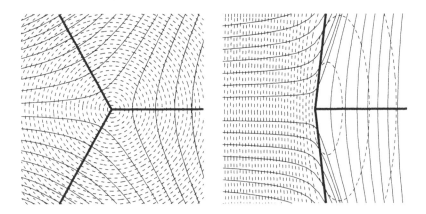

Figure 6.15. Arrangements of blue lines of curvature (solid) and level sets of the blue principal curvature κ_1 (dashed) corresponding with the two types of elliptic umbilic. The thick gray line is the blue ridge. Note that a red ridge will continue each branch of the blue ridge: the color changes at an umbilic. First: symmetric elliptic umbilic $D > 0, S < 0, T < 0$; second: unsymmetric elliptic umbilic $D > 0, S < 0, T > 0$. Note that these are automatically star umbilics and that κ_1 has a minimum at the umbilic in each of these cases. Also κ_2 will have a maximum. See Section 6.5.2.

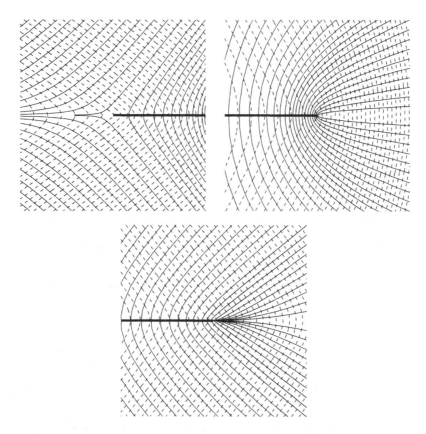

Figure 6.16. Arrangements of blue lines of curvature (solid) and level sets of the blue principal curvature κ_1 (dashed) corresponding with the three types of hyperbolic umbilic. The thick gray line is the blue ridge. Note that a red ridge will continue the blue ridge: the color changes at an umbilic. First: hyperbolic star umbilic $D < 0, S < 0$; second: lemon hyperbolic umbilic $D < 0, S > 0, U > 0$; third: lemonstar ('monstar') hyperbolic umbilic $D < 0, S > 0, U < 0$. In all these cases, κ_1 does not have an extremum at the umbilic (Section 6.5.2).

curves through the umbilic where $\kappa_1 = \kappa$ and $\kappa_2 = \kappa$. If we consider the vector field $\nabla \kappa_1$ defined by the gradient of κ_1 at all non-umbilic points (κ_2 would do just as well), then we see a topological distinction between these two types of umbilics. At elliptic umbilics where κ_1 has a minimum, the level curves of κ_1 are simple closed curves encircling P and the index of $\nabla \kappa_1$ is +1. On the other hand, at hyperbolic umbilics, $\nabla \kappa_1$ has a removable singularity at P (by letting the coefficient of the square root term in (6.13) go to zero) and its index is 0.

The lemon/star and elliptic/hyperbolic distinctions are not completely independent: an elliptic umbilic must be a star. If the point is elliptic, the cubic

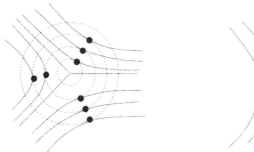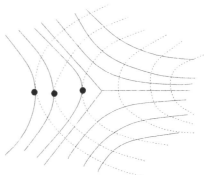

Figure 6.17. The dashed lines represent level sets of one principal curvature. Left: there is a maximum at the origin, which is an elliptic star. Right: there is no maximum for the hyperbolic star. The solid curves are the lines of curvature. We expect three ridge lines to form out of the umbilic on the left, joining the dots where the principal curvature has an extremum along the line of curvature, and one ridge line on the right.

polynomial $b_0 t^3 + 3b_1 t^2 + 3b_2 t + b_3$ must have three real roots, and so its derivative $3(b_0 t^2 + 2b_1 t + b_2)$ has two real roots, so $b_1^2 > b_0 b_2$. But $D > 0$, which by the expression (6.14) implies $(b_1^2 - b_0 b_2)(b_2^2 - b_1 b_3) > 0$, hence $b_2^2 > b_1 b_3$. Adding these two shows that the determinant in (6.12) is negative.

In the case of an elliptic umbilic, which is necessarily a 'star' of the lines of curvature, we know that the principal directions have index $-\frac{1}{2}$ while $\nabla \kappa_1$ has index $+1$. On topological grounds, there are at least 3 directions in which the level curves of κ_1 are tangent to the blue principal directions, hence lie on blue ridges. We need to verify that asymptotically, these vector fields have the simplest possible form and it then follows that there are 3 blue ridges which end at such an umbilic. Likewise, there will be 3 red ridges. Note also the important fact that the 'color' of the ridge will change as we pass through the umbilic: if on one side κ_1 has a minimum, along the corresponding lines of curvature at each ridge point, then on the other side κ_2 will have a maximum along its corresponding lines of curvature.

At a hyperbolic umbilic, a similar argument is based on the facts that the principal directions have index $\pm \frac{1}{2}$ while $\nabla \kappa_1$ has index 0. It follows that there is now one red and one blue ridge passing through the umbilic, one of them changing into the other as it passes through. The situation is shown in Figure 6.17.

For further details, see Chapter 11 of Porteous (94).

6.5.3   The main classification of umbilics

We can sum up the calculations of the last few sections as follows:

At an *elliptic umbilic*, there are three ridge curves passing through the umbilic, all of which are necessarily hyperbolic ridges (see Section 6.4.4). The larger curvature κ_1 has a local minimum, and the smaller curvature κ_2 has a local maximum. The index of each principal vector field is $-\frac{1}{2}$ (elliptic star). In addition, taking any particular ridge curve through the umbilic, its 'color' changes at the umbilic, from a 'blue minimum' (κ_1 having a local minimum along the corresponding lines of curvature) to a 'red maximum' (κ_2 having a local maximum along the corresponding lines of curvature) (see Figure 6.15).

At a *hyperbolic star*, there is one ridge curve passing through the umbilic, which is necessarily a hyperbolic ridge (see Section 6.4.4) and which changes color at the umbilic. The principal curvatures do not have local extrema at the umbilic. The index of each principal vector field is $-\frac{1}{2}$ (see the first part of Figure 6.16).

At a *hyperbolic lemon*, there is one ridge curve passing through the umbilic, which is necessarily a hyperbolic ridge (see Section 6.4.4) and which changes color at the umbilic. The principal curvatures do not have local extrema at the umbilic. The index of each principal vector field is $+\frac{1}{2}$ (see the second and third parts of Figure 6.16).

There is a further distinction in the hyperbolic case which is not computationally very robust: some lemons are called lemonstars (or monstars) (see Section 6.5.4 and Figure 6.16 below).

Note: The terminology 'elliptic' and 'hyperbolic' is not so geometrically consistent for umbilics as it is for surface points and ridge lines, and from our point of view is rather unfortunately confusing. We could perhaps use the terms '3-ridge umbilic' and '1-ridge umbilic' instead. The ridges which pass through umbilics are always hyperbolic ridges, as pointed out in Section 6.4.4. However in this chapter we stick to the traditional terminology. Ian Porteous (Porteous 94) uses the terms 'fertile ridge' for hyperbolic ridge and 'sterile ridge' for elliptic ridge, referring to the kind of ridge on which umbilics can be born as fertile. As we have seen, umbilics can only exist at all on hyperbolic (fertile) ridges.

The same book (Section 7.4) contains a discussion of the classification of cubic forms, and hence umbilics, by a complex parameter. This is based on the observation that the usual cubic part of the Monge form can be rewritten as

$$\frac{1}{6}\mathrm{Re}(\alpha z^3 + 3\beta z^2\bar{z})$$

where $z = x + iy$ and $\alpha = \alpha_1 + i\alpha_2, \beta = \beta_1 + i\beta_2$ are complex numbers. In fact $b_0 = \alpha_1 + 3\beta_1$, $b_1 = \alpha_2 - \beta_2$, $b_2 = \alpha_1 + \beta_1$ and $b_3 = \alpha_2 - 3\beta_2$. At an umbilic we can rotate coordinates about the z-axis without affecting the quadratic terms; a rotation through θ has the effect of rotating the complex number α through 3θ and β through θ. Thus a rotation can be chosen which makes α real and positive, and then by scaling we can choose $\alpha = 1$. This classifies cubic forms by a single complex number β, and the positions of β in the complex plane determine the type of umbilic. (For the details, see Porteous (94) or Bruce et al. (96a).) Note that as well as using rotation to make α real we could also use it to eliminate the coefficient of x^2y. For since α and β rotate at different speeds, we can make $\alpha_2 = \beta_2$ for a suitable θ. The same applies to eliminating the coefficient of xy^2.

6.5.4   Finer classification of umbilics

In this section, we give two distinctions between umbilics which are not so significant computationally as those listed in Section 6.5.3.

The first relatively insignificant distinction between umbilics is between so-called 'lemon' and 'lemonstar' or 'monstar' umbilics. In Section 6.5.1, equation (6.11), we saw that the principal directions close to an umbilic are approximately the eigenvectors of the hessian matrix

$$\begin{pmatrix} b_0x + b_1y & b_1x + b_2y \\ b_1x + b_2y & b_2x + b_3y \end{pmatrix}$$

Put another way, this says that the principal directions at the point with $x = x_0, y = y_0$ are approximately the factor lines of the quadratic form

$$(b_1x_0 + b_2y_0)x^2 + ((b_2 - b_0)x_0 - (b_1 - b_3)y_0)xy - (b_1x_0 + b_2y_0)y^2 \quad (6.15)$$

If we approach the umbilic along a line of curvature — say, close to the umbilic, along the line obtained by multiplying x_0 and y_0 by λ and letting $\lambda \to 0$ — then one principal direction will always be in the same direction as (x_0, y_0), so that this direction (x, y) will be a factor line of the cubic form in x and y obtained by replacing x_0, y_0 by x, y in (6.15):

$$b_1x^3 + (2b_2 - b_0)x^2y - (2b_1 - b_3)xy^2 - b_2y^3 \quad (6.16)$$

This cubic form is called the 'Jacobian' cubic form and its factor lines are the tangents to lines of curvature which end at the umbilic. A special case arises when two of these factor lines coincide: this marks the transition from three limiting principal directions to one, and separates two types of 'lemon', the true lemon and the 'lemonstar' or 'monstar'. (A more crucial case is $S = 0$, which marks the birth of umbilics. Then (6.16) has two perpendicular root lines. See (6.12) and Section 7.2.5.)

The condition in terms of the coefficients of the Monge cubic form is that (6.16) should have a repeated factor line. Writing the Jacobian cubic as

$$B_0x^3 + 3B_1x^2y + 3B_2xy^2 + B_3y^3 = b_1x^3 + (2b_2 - b_0)x^2y - (2b_1 - b_3)xy^2 - b_2y^3$$

we let

$$U = 4(B_1^2 - B_0B_2)(B_2^2 - B_1B_3) - (B_0B_3 - B_1B_2)^2 \quad (6.17)$$

be its discriminant. Then we have the distinction:

- If $U > 0$ then there are three limiting principal directions at the umbilic; this is a *star* if $R < 0$ and a *lemonstar* = *monstar* if $R > 0$;

- If $U < 0$ then there is one limiting principal direction at the umbilic; this is a true *lemon* and necessarily $R > 0$.

It is the transition between lemons and lemonstars which occurs as U passes through 0, and this is not computationally robust.

Note: The factor lines of the Jacobian cubic form above are the tangents to the lines of curvature which end at the umbilic. We might call such tangent lines 'limiting principal directions' at the umbilic, but there is a danger here. It is not, in general, true that, taking an arbitrary path into the umbilic, the limits of the principal directions at points along that path are among the factor lines of the Jacobian cubic. Indeed, this would require that these factor lines were in perpendicular pairs, which is hardly possible for one or three real factor lines! There is an example in the discussion immediately following which brings out this point.

The second distinction divides elliptic stars into 2 subgroups depending on whether the red and blue ridges ending at the umbilic alternate R,B,R,B,R,B or have the order R,R,R,B,B,B. The transition between the two can be found by considering the case where the cubic part of the Monge form of our surface has three real factors and that two of these factor lines are *orthogonal*. That is, assuming $b_0 \neq 0$,

$$b_0 x^3 + 3b_1 x^2 y + 3b_2 x y^2 + b_3 y^3 = b_0(x - py)\left(x + \frac{y}{p}\right)(x - qy)$$

for some numbers p, q. Eliminating p and q we find that the condition is $T = 0$ where

$$T = b_0^2 + b_3^2 + 3(b_0 b_2 + b_1 b_3) \tag{6.18}$$

If $T = 0$ holds, let us align the x and y axes along the two orthogonal factor lines through the umbilic. The cubic form then has the shape $xy(rx + sy)$ for some r and s, so that the cubic terms in the Monge form satisfy $b_0 = b_3 = 0$. Then consider points (x_0, y_0) near the umbilic on the line $rx + sy = 0$. Using (6.15) above we find that the principal directions as we approach the umbilic along this particular line are approximately along $xy = 0$, that is, along the x- and y- axes. Their limiting direction is along these two axes. (Note, however, that it is not true that the x- and y- axes are among the tangents to the lines of curvature through the umbilic: they are not factor lines of the Jacobian cubic (see above).) Likewise we can use the formulae at the end of Section 6.2 to calculate the limits of $\nabla \kappa_1$ and $\nabla \kappa_2$: they are also the x- and y-axes, using $b_0 = b_3 = 0$. It follows that both a red and a blue ridge pass through the umbilic tangent to the line $rx + sy = 0$: two ridges have become tangential. Thus $T = 0$ separates the elliptic umbilics in a relatively minor way into two classes:

- *symmetrical*, where $T < 0$: ridge lines alternate colors round the umbilic;

- *unsymmetrical*, where $T > 0$: the three blue ridges are followed by the three red ones round the umbilic.

6.5.5 Direction of ridges at an umbilic

It is not so easy to predict the directions of the ridges at an umbilic, but it does follow from the cubic part of the Monge form. Here is an indication of how this works.

From (6.8) we know the angle which a blue ridge makes with the x-axis (the corresponding principal direction) at a non-umbilic point in Monge form, namely θ, where

$$\tan \theta = -\frac{P_1}{Q_1} = \frac{-3b_1^2 - (\kappa_1 - \kappa_2)(c_0 - 3\kappa_1^3)}{3b_1 b_2 + c_1(\kappa_1 - \kappa_2)}$$

As we approach the umbilic, $\kappa_1 - \kappa_2 \to 0$, and the above value of $\tan \theta$ approaches $-b_1/b_2$. Further, the principal direction tends to a real factor line of the cubic form at the umbilic.

So the angle between a ridge and a factor line of the cubic form of the surface at the umbilic has tangent $-b_1/b_2$, provided the x-axis is aligned along the factor line, to make the coefficient of x^3 equal to zero.

As an example of this, consider the surface

$$z = \frac{\kappa}{2}(x^2 + y^2) + x^2 y - \lambda^2 y^3$$

which has three real factor lines of the cubic form, namely $y = 0, x = \pm \lambda y$. Turning the axes about the z-axis through an angle θ amounts to replacing x and y by

$$x \cos \theta - y \sin \theta, \quad x \sin \theta + y \cos \theta$$

respectively. When we do this, the quadratic terms are unaffected and the coefficients of $x^2 y$ and xy^2 become b_1, b_2 where

$$\tan \phi = -\frac{b_1}{b_2} = -\frac{1 - (3\lambda^2 + 2)\tan^2 \theta}{\tan \theta (\tan^2 \theta - (3\lambda^2 + 1))}$$

The relevant values of θ are 0 and $\arctan(\pm 1/\lambda)$ and, for each of these, $\theta + \phi$ gives us the angle which the corresponding ridge makes with the x-axis.

For instance, let $\lambda = 2$. Then the factor lines of the cubic are $y = 0$ and $y = \pm \frac{1}{2}x$. For the factor line $y = 0$ the ridge makes an angle $\frac{\pi}{2}$ with the x-axis,

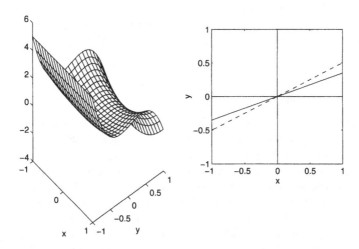

Figure 6.18. Left: the surface $z = x^2 + y^2 + x^2y - 4y^3$: Right: dashed line is the factor $y = x/2$ and the solid line is the ridge tangent at an angle $\arctan(4/11)$ to the factor line.

and for the factor line $y = \frac{1}{2}x$ the angle ϕ works out at $\arctan \frac{-4}{11}$ so the ridge makes an angle $\arctan \frac{1}{2} - \arctan \frac{4}{11}$ with the x-axis (see Figure 6.18).

Note: It is plausible from this that, given a real factor line of the cubic form, we shall determine a direction for a ridge to pass through the umbilic. This confirms the result that at elliptic umbilics (three real factor lines) there are three ridges, and at hyperbolic umbilics (one real factor line) there is one ridge.

Remark: There is an interesting general result which applies to any curve, not necessarily a ridge, passing through an umbilic. (The result is proved in Porteous (94), page 200.) Using the usual cubic part of the Monge form of a surface at the origin, as in (6.1), the corresponding trilinear form is defined to be

$$\frac{1}{6}\big(b_0 x_1 x_2 x_3 + b_1(x_1 x_2 y_3 + x_1 y_2 x_3 + y_1 x_2 x_3)$$

$$+ b_2(x_1 y_2 y_3 + y_1 x_2 y_3 + y_1 y_2 x_3) + b_3(y_1 y_2 y_3)\big)$$

This is linear in each of the three points (x_i, y_i) and, when $x_i = x, y_i = y$ for each i it reduces to the cubic part of the Monge form. The result is as follows: Given a smooth curve γ through the origin, which is assumed to be an umbilic, let (x_1, y_1) and (x_2, y_2) be the limiting principal directions at points of γ approaching the origin. These are necessarily perpendicular, of course. Let (x_3, y_3) be tangent to γ at the origin. Then the result states that the above trilinear form vanishes.

In particular, if the limiting principal directions are along the x and y axes, then $(x_1, y_1) = (1, 0)$ and $(x_2, y_2) = (0, 1)$, and the result says that the tangent to γ satisfies $b_1 x_3 + b_2 y_3 = 0$. We have seen above that this is true when γ is a ridge curve.

6.6 The Road Map

We can pull together everything we have done so far in a big diagram, in which we assume Monge form as in (6.1) and take the surface oriented by the normal which at the origin is $(0, 0, 1)$.

Note that everything which is labelled 'blue' is related to the larger of the two principal curvatures κ_1 and is governed by the constants b_0, P_1, Q_1 and R_1, while everything 'red' is related to the smaller of the two curvatures and is governed by b_3, P_2, Q_2 and R_2. Almost everything descibed as elliptic concerns points where the surface lies on one side of a key plane or sphere, and almost everything described as hyperbolic concerns points where their intersection is locally non-isolated. (The exceptions are elliptic ('3-ridge') umbilics and hyperbolic ('1-ridge') umbilics.) The arrows indicate which curves are on the boundary of which patches, and which special points are in the closure of which curves. *However*, note that red ridges may meet blue ridges, red ridges may meet blue parabolics and blue ridges may meet red parabolics: we do not give such intersection points special status (though Porteous calls the first of these 'purple flyovers'). We do not specifically prohibit a red turning point from being on a blue parabolic or vice versa. Nor do we prohibit a red cusp of Gauss from being on a blue ridge or vice versa. Such situations are non-generic but have no special significance: the red and blue worlds go on more or less independently, except that red switches to blue on a ridge at an umbilic point.

Finally the constants referred to in the boxes are defined by:

$$
\begin{aligned}
P_1 &= (\kappa_1 - \kappa_2)(c_0 - 3\kappa_1^3) + 3b_1^2 \\
Q_1 &= (\kappa_1 - \kappa_2)c_1 + 3b_1 b_2 \\
R_1 &= (\kappa_1 - \kappa_2)^2 d_0 + 10(\kappa_1 - \kappa_2)b_1 c_1 + 15b_1^2 b_2 \\
P_2 &= (\kappa_2 - \kappa_1)(c_4 - 3\kappa_2^3) + 3b_2^2 \\
Q_2 &= (\kappa_2 - \kappa_1)c_3 + 3b_1 b_2 \\
R_2 &= (\kappa_2 - \kappa_1)^2 d_5 + 10(\kappa_2 - \kappa_1)b_2 c_3 + 15b_1 b_2^2 \\
D &= 4(b_1^2 - b_0 b_2)(b_2^2 - b_1 b_3) - (b_0 b_3 - b_1 b_2)^2 \\
S &= (b_0 - b_2)b_2 - (b_1 - b_3)b_1 \\
T &= b_0^2 + b_3^2 + 3(b_0 b_2 + b_1 b_3) \\
U &: \quad \text{see (6.17)}
\end{aligned}
$$

Elliptic Convex (resp. Concave) Patch	**Hyperbolic Patch**
$\kappa_1 > \kappa_2 > 0$, (resp. $0 > \kappa_1 > \kappa_2$)	$\kappa_1 > 0 > \kappa_2$
$b_0 \neq 0, b_3 \neq 0$	$b_0 \neq 0, b_3 \neq 0$
projective invariant	*projective invariant*

Ridge Curve
blue: $b_0 = 0, \kappa_1(\kappa_1 - \kappa_2)P_1 \neq 0$
red: $b_3 = 0, \kappa_2(\kappa_1 - \kappa_2)P_2 \neq 0$
elliptic: $P_1 > 0$ (resp. $P_2 > 0$)
hyperbolic: $P_1 < 0$,
(resp. $P_2 < 0$)
conformal invariant

Parabolic Curve
blue: $0 = \kappa_1 > \kappa_2, b_0 \neq 0$
red: $\kappa_1 > \kappa_2 = 0, b_3 \neq 0$
projective invariant

Umbilic Point
$\kappa_1 = \kappa_2 \neq 0$
elliptic: $D > 0, S < 0$
(symmetric elliptic:
$T < 0$,
unsymmetric: $T > 0$)
hyp.star: $D < 0, S < 0$
hyp.lemon:
$D < 0, S > 0$
(hyp.true lemon: $U > 0$,
hyp.lemonstar: $U < 0$)
conformal invariant

Turning Point
blue: $b_0 = P_1 = 0$,
$\kappa_1(\kappa_1 - \kappa_2)Q_1 R_1 \neq 0$
red: $b_3 = P_2 = 0$,
$\kappa_2(\kappa_1 - \kappa_2)Q_2 R_2 \neq 0$
conformal invariant

Cusp of Gauss
blue:
$b_0 = 0 = \kappa_1 > \kappa_2$,
$b_1 P_1 \neq 0$
red: $\kappa_1 > \kappa_2 = 0 = b_3$,
$b_2 P_2 \neq 0$
elliptic: $P_1 > 0$ or
$P_2 > 0$
hyperb: $P_1 < 0$ or
$P_2 < 0$
projective invariant

Chapter 7

Sculpting a Surface

7.1 Overview

A fundamental issue in all of computer vision is to separate the small details from the large structures in images. The same issue arises with the description of surfaces. If we have three-dimensional data on the shape of a face and work out the parabolic curves and ridge curves on it, we find a huge mess. The reason is that the mathematical treatment of surface features is purely infinitesimal and does not distinguish minor noisy irregularities from major features. To apply this kind of mathematical tool, it is essential to use it in conjunction with some kind of smoothing.[1] You can also view this smoothing in reverse: i.e., think of yourself as a sculptor starting with the simplest shape and gradually forming more and more detail in the shape and in the process, creating the parabolic and ridge curves. We want to describe how this works in this chapter. In the first section, we shall study arbitrary families of surfaces and classify all generic ways in which the pattern of parabolic and ridge curves can change. In the second section, we shall look at the creation of two very simple shapes: a bell-shaped protrusion on a surface and a dimple-shaped intrusion. We break the formation of these shapes into a sequence of the generic changes of Section 7.2. These cases were first worked out by Koenderink (90), but we add some detail to his exposition. In the third section, we will take range data of an actual face and, using a family of smoothings of the face, see how its parabolics and ridges form as the sculptor molds the face, brow, eyes and mouth.

7.2 Transitions

In the last chapter we proposed representing surfaces in terms of geometric descriptors such as parabolic curves and ridges (see the ROADMAP at the end of

---

[1] Some general work on the creation of structure by smoothing appears in Yuille (88).

Chapter 6). When we deform a surface these descriptors may change qualitatively. For example, a hyperbolic patch might acquire an elliptic 'island' so that a
parabolic curve appears from nowhere. Thus transitions may occur in which, for
example, one of the curvatures passes through zero and changes sign. In mathematical shorthand, these transitions occur when one or more of the inequalities in
the ROADMAP become equalities.

The material of this section is an adaptation of Bruce et al. (96a, 96b) which
are written for a computer vision readership, and Bruce et al. (95, 98), which are
written for a mathematical readership and contain more of the mathematical details.

A transition[2] is a generic family of surfaces M_t, defined say for a parameter
t = 'time' close to $t = 0$, where something special happens at $t = 0$. What does
generic mean? In the family M_t, a three-dimensional set of Monge patches is
present. Therefore generic imples that the Monge forms of the points of M_0 can
satisfy 3 special identities, but not 4. We concentrate below on the conditions
which must be satisfied by the transitional surface M_0. The reader will note that
we characterise each transition by means of inequalities and equalities among the
various expressions which occurred in the ROADMAP of Chapter 6. It then becomes clear that each one is a degenerate case ($<$ or $>$ becoming $=$) of something
which appears in the ROADMAP.

There is naturally also a condition on the family itself, which guarantees that
the way in which the surface is evolving at time $t = 0$ is sufficiently general for
the transition under discussion to occur, and not some more degenerate transition.
These 'generic family' conditions can also be worked out, using the methods of
Bruce et al. (95, 98), but they tend to be very complicated and unhelpful and we
do not go into them here.

7.2.1 Singular parabolic set: creation and collision of parabolic loops

Consider the case of a blue cusp of Gauss, so that the origin is both a blue parabolic
point and a blue ridge point. Thus $\kappa_1 = 0 > \kappa_2$, $b_0 = 0$, $P_1 = 3b_1^2 - \kappa_2 c_0 \neq 0$.
Here, we add the condition $b_1 = 0$, so that $P_1 \neq 0$ reduces to $c_0 \neq 0$. The result is
to make the parabolic curve *singular* at the origin: generically, it consists locally
of an isolated point or a crossing of two smooth curves. In the above-cited papers,
this is called a 'non-versal A_3 transition of the family of height functions'.

Using the formulae for principal curvatures close to the origin in Section 6.2,
we find that the Gauss curvature is $K(x, y)$ where

$$2K(x, y) = \kappa_2 c_0 x^2 + 2\kappa_2 c_1 xy + (c_2 \kappa_2 - 2b_2^2)y^2 + \cdots$$

From this we can deduce the condition for *every* point near the origin to be elliptic,
indicating an isolated point of the parabolic set at the origin surrounded by an

---

[2] In the mathematical literature a transition is also known as a bifurcation or a perestroika.

elliptic region: we require simply that the discriminant of the above quadratic equation is negative and that the coefficient of the x^2 term is positive. Likewise, an isolated point in the parabolic set surrounded by a hyperbolic region means that the discriminant is still negative but that the coefficient of the x^2 term is negative.

When the discriminant of the quadratic is positive there are locally two parabolic curves through the origin, dividing the plane locally into four sectors. We can distinguish two cases accordingly as the ridge which necessarily passes through the origin runs through the elliptic or the hyperbolic sectors. Using the formula of (6.8), the ridge tangent is in the direction $(c_1, -c_0)$, and it quickly follows that we require $c_0 < 0$ for the ridge to run through elliptic regions. In this transition, two parabolic curves collide, reform by linking up their branches in the opposite order and move apart in the other direction (see Figure 7.1). Putting this together, for the blue case ($\kappa_1 = 0 > \kappa_2, b_0 = b_1 = 0$) we have the following conditions:

(i) Parabolic curve isolated: $\kappa_2 c_1^2 > c_0(\kappa_2 c_2 - 2b_2^2)$

    (a) elliptic region: $c_0 < 0$. The transition here creates a parabolic loop encircling a hyperbolic island in an elliptic sea;

    (b) hyperbolic region: $c_0 > 0$. The transition here creates a parabolic loop encircling an elliptic island in a hyperbolic sea;

(ii) Parabolic curve locally a crossing: $\kappa_2 c_1^2 < c_0(\kappa_2 c_2 - 2b_2^2)$

    (a) ridge curve passes through the elliptic sectors: $c_0 < 0$. This transition sees the appearance or disappearance of two hyperbolic cusps of Gauss;

    (b) ridge curve passes through the hyperbolic sectors: $c_0 > 0$. This transition sees the appearance or disappearance of two elliptic cusps of Gauss.

The situation with a red ridge is similar. Here, we have $\kappa_1 > \kappa_2 = 0, b_2 = b_3 = 0$ and

(i) Parabolic curve isolated: $\kappa_1 c_3^2 < c_4(\kappa_1 c_2 - 2b_1^2)$

    (a) elliptic region: $c_4 > 0$;

    (b) hyperbolic region: $c_4 > 0$;

(ii) Parabolic curve locally a crossing: $\kappa_1 c_3^2 > c_4(\kappa_1 c_2 - 2b_1^2)$

    (a) ridge curve passes through the elliptic sectors: $c_4 < 0$;

    (b) ridge curve passes through the hyperbolic sectors: $c_4 > 0$.

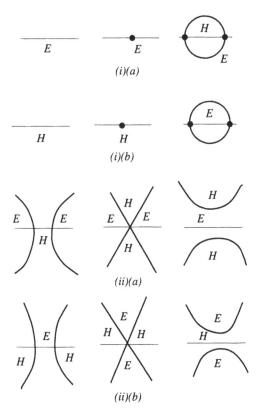

Figure 7.1. The four cases for evolution of parabolic sets through a singular parabolic set; see Section 7.2.1 Ridges are drawn lightly and parabolic sets heavily. Dots are cusps of Gauss, and 'H, E' stand for hyperbolic and elliptic respectively.

Example of families of surfaces which exhibits these latter transitions are

$$z = x^2 + \epsilon_1 x^2 y^2 + \epsilon_2 y^4 + t y^2$$

where (i)(a) $\epsilon_1 = \epsilon_2 = 1$; (i)(b) $\epsilon_1 = \epsilon_2 = -1$; (ii)(a) $\epsilon_1 = 1$, $\epsilon_2 = -1$; (ii)(b) $\epsilon_1 = -1$, $\epsilon_2 = 1$. The '$t y^2$' term is sufficient to guarantee a generic transition (see Bruce et al. 95).

7.2.2   Birth of cusps of Gauss: collision of parabolic curve and ridge

This is a specialization of both cusp of Gauss and turning point, called an 'A_4 transition of the family of height functions' in the papers cited above. In the 'blue'

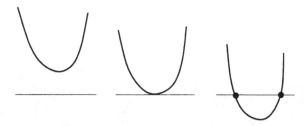

Figure 7.2. A parabolic curve (thick line) collides with a ridge of the same colour (thin line), creating two cusps of Gauss (dots).

case we have

$$b_0 = 0, \ 0 = \kappa_1 > \kappa_2, \ P_1 = 0, \ R_1 \neq 0$$

The last two give $3b_1^2 = c_0\kappa_2$ and $\kappa_2^2 d_0 - 10\kappa_2 b_1 c_1 + 15b_1^2 b_2 \neq 0$. Similarly in the 'red' case we have

$$b_3 = 0, \ \kappa_1 > \kappa_2 = 0, \ P_2 = 0, \ R_2 \neq 0$$

In both cases a ridge and a parabolic curve of the same colour, locally disjoint from each other, collide tangentially on the surface and continue past, now crossing at two cusps of Gauss, one of which is elliptic and the other hyperbolic (see Figure 7.2). An example of the 'red' case is

$$z = x^2 + y^5 + 2xy^2 + y^4 + ty^3$$

For the 'blue' case, interchange x and y.

7.2.3 Flat elliptic umbilic

We now take up flat umbilics, special umbilics in which both principal curvatures are zero. In the papers cited above these are called 'D_4 transitions of the family of height functions'. In all these cases, for $t \neq 0$, the surface M_t has a unique non-planar umbilic near the flat umbilic on M_0. But there is a distinction depending on whether the umbilic is elliptic or hyperbolic. We take up the elliptic case first where $\kappa_1 = \kappa_2 = 0$ and $D > 0$.

From Section 6.5.2 we know that κ_1 has a local minimum and κ_2 a local maximum. Hence, close to the umbilic, the Gauss curvature $K = \kappa_1\kappa_2$ is negative: the surface is locally hyperbolic. The transition involves the disappearance and reappearance of a ring of parabolic points, which must therefore enclose an elliptic island. For $t \neq 0$, the umbilic is non-planar and therefore lies in this elliptic island and is crossed by three ridges. Three cusps of Gauss, which are necessarily

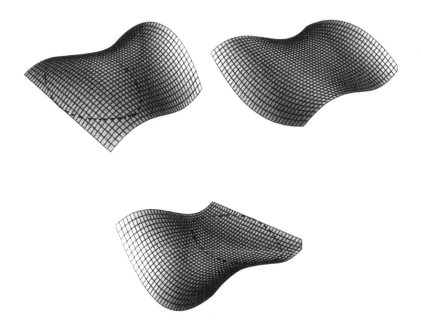

Figure 7.3. A sequence of surfaces passing through a flat elliptic umbilic. The dashed line is the parabolic curve. Note the change from convex elliptic region to concave.

hyperbolic since the ridges near any umbilic are hyperbolic (Section 6.4.4), merge and reappear opposite their original positions. Each ridge changes colour at the umbilic, so the cusps of Gauss are initially all red, e.g., but emerge as all blue. The parabolic curve has changed from red to blue. This is an important feature of this transition: *the elliptic island changes from concave to convex or vice versa.* There is an illustration of this in Figure 7.3.

There are two cases which differ only in the order in which ridges occur round the umbilic and are distinguished by $T < 0$ (the symmetric case) and $T > 0$ (the unsymmetric case) (see Figure 7.4).

7.2.4 Flat hyperbolic umbilic

Here $\kappa_1 = \kappa_2 = 0$ and $D < 0$ (automatically $S < 0$). Using the formula (6.13), we see easily that the Gauss curvature will now be zero locally along

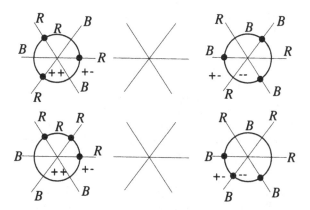

Figure 7.4. Evolution of a parabolic curve (thick line) through a flat elliptic umbilic, through which pass three hyperbolic ridges (thin lines). Three hyperbolic cusps of Gauss (dots) merge and reappear. The island inside the parabolic curve is always elliptic, but the parabolic line has *changed colour* from left to right. Thus the elliptic island changes from convex (++) to concave (−−), or vice versa, the signs indicating respectively those of κ_1 and κ_2. The letters R and B stand for red and blue; all of these could also be reversed. The lower diagram shows the alternative 'unsymmetric' case.

two curves through the umbilic, separating the surface locally into four sectors, one elliptic convex, two hyperbolic and one elliptic concave. For $t \neq 0$, the hyperbolic sectors merge but the umbilic moves into one elliptic region or the other. Thus the transition may be described as a red and blue parabolic curve coming together instantaneously and then pulling back apart *but exchanging an umbilic point when they meet*. There must also be a unique (necessarily hyperbolic) ridge line through the umbilic at the moment of transition and it will cut across the two elliptic sectors, or else the two hyperbolic sectors. A cusp of Gauss (necessarily hyperbolic since it lies on a hyperbolic ridge) is transferred from one branch of the parabolic curve to the other, changing colour (red to blue or vice versa) as it does so. This results in the schematic diagrams of Figure 7.5.

To calculate whether the ridge passes through elliptic or hyperbolic sectors at the transitional moment, we proceed as follows. Take the x-axis along the unique real factor line of the cubic part of the surface's Monge form, so that the equation of the surface is locally

$$z = \frac{1}{6}(3b_1x^2y + 3b_2xy^2 + b_3y^3) + \cdots$$

There is only one real factor line, so $3b_2^2 < 4b_1b_3$ (this just says $D < 0$). The local formula giving the sign of the Gauss curvature $K = \kappa_1\kappa_2$ is calculated from $z_{xx}z_{yy} - z_{xy}^2$, giving leading terms

$$-b_1^2x^2 - b_1b_2xy + (b_1b_3 - b_2^2)y^2$$

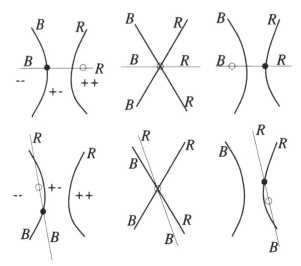

Figure 7.5. Evolution of a parabolic curve (thick line) through a flat hyperbolic umbilic, through which passes one hyperbolic ridge (thin line). The two components of the parabolic curve are of different colors, and the one which is the same color as the ridge intersects the ridge in a cusp of Gauss (solid dot). The unfilled dot is a hyperbolic umbilic, which is not flat except in the middle picture. It is possible for the ridge curve to intersect the hyperbolic (+ −) region at the transitional moment, despite the fact that before and after this moment the umbilic must lie in an elliptic (++ or − −) region. This is shown in the lower figure.

Note that this quadratic part always has real solutions so that the parabolic curve forms two branches through the origin. For small x, y, when the quadratic expression is positive, the Gauss curvature of the surface is also positive. Now consider the (unique) ridge curve through the origin, which has local equation $y = (-b_1/b_2)x$ (see Section 6.4.3 and Section 6.5.5). Substituting this into the above expression, we find that $K > 0$ close to the origin on the ridge if and only if $b_1 b_3 > b_2^2$. We know that $b_1 b_3 > \frac{3}{4}b_2^2$ from $D < 0$, but this allows $b_1 b_3 - b_2^2$ to have either sign. If the planar umbilic is a lemon, however, one easily checks that the ridge must lie in the elliptic sectors.

See Figure 7.5 for the way that the parabolic set is evolving here. There is in fact a further subtle distinction which is visible only on the image of the parabolic set under the Gauss map, and which depends on the degree 4 terms of the surface (see Bruce et al. 96a, p.299).

7.2.5   Creation of lemon/star pairs of umbilics

This is a highly significant transition since it is the only one in which umbilics are created (or destroyed). This has

$$\kappa_1 = \kappa_2 \neq 0, \; D < 0, \; S = 0, \text{ necessarily } U < 0$$

$$\underline{\hspace{2cm}R\hspace{2cm}} \qquad \underline{\hspace{1.5cm}R\hspace{0.3cm}}_{\circ} \qquad \underline{\hspace{0.8cm}R\hspace{0.3cm}}_{\circ}\underline{\hspace{0.3cm}B\hspace{0.3cm}}_{\circ}\underline{R}$$

Figure 7.6. Two hyperbolic umbilics (unfilled dots) created from one degenerate umbilic on a hyperbolic ridge. The R and B labels can be interchanged throughout; the point is that the new piece of ridge in the middle is the opposite color to the pre-existing ridge.

When $S = 0$, the linear terms in the second fundamental form (6.11) at points (x, y) near the umbilic have eigenvectors independent of (x, y), hence the principal directions return to their initial values without winding round when you go around the umbilic on a small circle, i.e., the index is 0. By rotation of coordinates about the z-axis, which will not affect the quadratic terms at an umbilic, we can always remove the $x^2 y$ term (or the xy^2 term) from the cubic part of the Monge form. (See the note at the end of Section 6.5.3.) By making $b_1 = 0$ and using $S = 0$ we see that either $b_1 = 0$ or $b_0 = b_2$. Thus the cubic terms can be put in the normal form $\frac{1}{6}(b_0 x^3 + b_3 y^3)$ or, alternatively, the normal form $\frac{1}{6}(b_0 x^3 + 3b_0 xy^2 + b_3 y^3)$. In the first normal form, the x- and y-axes are the tangents to lines of curvature which end at the umbilic (see (6.16)). In the second, (6.16) becomes $y(b_0 x^2 + b_3 xy - b_0 y^2)$, which again has two perpendicular root lines. This perpendicularity of root lines of the Jacobian cubic is a feature of the birth of umbilics.

There is a unique ridge through such an umbilic. In one direction in the family, the umbilic is destroyed and we have a simple ridge but no other features; in the other direction, there are two hyperbolic umbilics, one a star and one a lemon,[3] connected by a small piece of the ridge. Note that we need both a star and a lemon because the total index must be zero. And the ridge must change color at each umbilic, so it is one color away from both umbilics and the other between them (see Figure 7.6). We will see many examples of this transition on the face.

A simple example is given by the equation:

$$z = \frac{1}{2}(x^2 + (1 - t)y^2) + \frac{1}{6}(x^3 + 3xy^2)$$

This family is symmetric around the plane $y = 0$, thus $y = 0$ is the ridge for all t. For $t < 0$, there are no umbilics and for $t > 0$, it has two with coordinates $(\pm\sqrt{t} + \cdots, 0)$.

7.2.6 *Hyperbolic to elliptic umbilic*

In this transition, referred to as the 'D_5 transition of the family of distance-squared functions' in the papers cited above, an elliptic umbilic changes into a hyperbolicumbilic, at the moment of transition becoming 'parabolic', that is, two

---

[3] In fact it is a lemonstar, or 'monstar'.

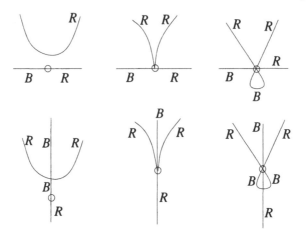

Figure 7.7. A hyperbolic umbilic (unfilled dot, left) on a hyperbolic ridge collides with another hyperbolic ridge and produces an elliptic umbilic. Top: the unsymmetric case $T > 0$. Bottom: the symmetric case $T < 0$, which is *non-generic* in a one-parameter family of surfaces: the nonsingular ridge and the cuspidal ridge are tangential in the middle picture. This splits up into the unsymmetric transition followed by an 'unsymmetric to symmetric' transition (Section 7.2.9): visualise the horizontal ridge in the upper diagram rotating until it is in the position of the lower diagram. Note that 'B' = blue and 'R' = red could be reversed throughout each sequence.

factor lines of the cubic Monge form coincide. The conditions are

$$\kappa_1 = \kappa_2 \neq 0, \ D = 0, \ S < 0, \ T \neq 0$$

The effect on the ridge curves is shown in Figure 7.7. An example is

$$x^2 + y^2 + 2xy^2 + x^2y + y^3 + t(x^3 + x^2y + xy^2 + y^3)$$

7.2.7 Singular ridge: creation or collision of ridge loops

In this transition, which is analogous to the transition described in Section 7.2.1 for parabolic curves, the ridge curve becomes singular, generically an isolated point or a crossing of two nonsingular branches. The 'blue' conditions are

$$\kappa_1 \neq 0, \ \kappa_1 \neq \kappa_2, \ b_0 = P_1 = Q_1 = 0, \ R_1 \neq 0$$

and similarly for the 'red' case.

The effect on the ridge curves is shown in Figure 7.8. Note that inevitably the process involves turning points, where the ridge is tangential to the corresponding lines of curvature. In both scenarios, two turning points merge and disappear.

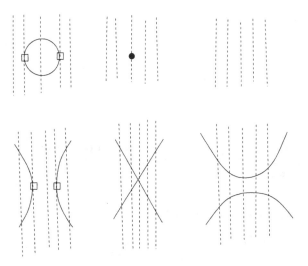

Figure 7.8. A ridge (thin line) becoming singular. The dashed lines are lines of curvature of the same color as the ridge, and the open squares are turning points where the ridge is tangent to one of these lines of curvature. Two turning points are gained or lost in the transition. Note that at turning points the ridge changes from hyperbolic to elliptic or vice versa, so the 'upper' half of each ridge will be hyperbolic and the lower half elliptic, or vice versa.

This is referred to as a 'non-versal A_4 transition of the family of distance-squared functions' in the papers cited above. The creation case of this transition is very important because this is the only case in which curvature features emerge from nothing, i.e., there are no ridges or parabolic curves at all before the creation. New structure must begin with such a transition.

7.2.8 Inflection between ridge and line of curvature: creation of elliptic or hyperbolic parts of a ridge

In this transition, referred to as the 'A_5 transition of the family of distance-squared functions' in the papers cited above, two turning points are created or destroyed by a process in which a ridge remains non-singular but momentarily makes an inflection with the corresponding line of curvature. The 'blue' conditions are

$$\kappa_1 \neq 0, \ \kappa_1 \neq \kappa_2, \ b_0 = P_1 = 0, \ Q_1 \neq 0, R_1 = 0$$

and in addition a condition which ensures that when we complete the square on the distance-squared function a term in x^6 remains. This will involve the degree 5 terms of the Monge form (see Figure 7.9).

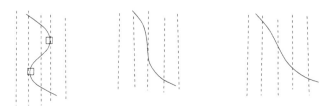

Figure 7.9. A ridge inflecting the lines of curvature of the same colour. Note that two turning points (marked by open squares), where the ridge is tangential to the lines of curvature, disappear in the transition from left to right.

7.2.9   Symmetric to unsymmetric umbilic

This minor transition has

$$\kappa_1 = \kappa_2 \neq 0, \ D > 0, \ S < 0, \ T = 0$$

At the moment of transition, two ridges are tangential (see Figure 7.10). An example is

$$x^2 + y^2 + 2x^3 - 2xy^2 + t(x^3 + xy^2)$$

7.3   The Evolution of the Bell and the Dimple

There are two major events which we describe in some detail in which a perceptually salient feature is created on some featureless piece of surface. One involves pushing the surface *out* to make what Koenderink called a 'bell', and the other pushing the surface *in* to make what he called a dimple. The astonishing aspect

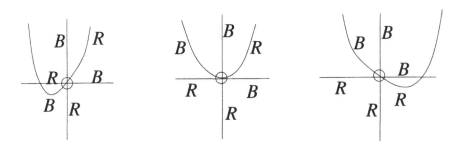

Figure 7.10. Conversion of a symmetric elliptic umbilic to an unsymmetric one. R stands for red and B for blue: on the left, red and blue alternate, and on the right they do not. All ridges involved are hyperbolic. The open circle is the elliptic umbilic.

of both of these is how many of the elementary transitions just listed are required for each such feature.

7.3.1 The bell

In this evolution, a convex elliptic region on a surface first acquires a hyperbolic island (see Section 7.2.1) bounded by a red parabolic curve (red because a '++' convex region abuts on a '+−' hyperbolic region so the smaller, red curvature passes through zero). The eventual shape has a convex (++) island within this hyperbolic region. A typical such surface is shown in the first image of Figure 7.11.

A schematic diagram of how the parabolic curve behaves is shown in Figure 7.12; compare Koenderink (90, p.536). Note that parabolic curves can only be created on ridges (Section 7.2.1). Note also that it is only possible to create a *convex* elliptic region in the middle of the surface this way.

Consider the principal directions along the inner parabolic curve surrounding the bell. On this curve, $\kappa_2 \equiv 0$ while $\kappa_1 > 0$. The red principal direction corresponding to κ_2 is everywhere transverse to this curve (e.g., because there are no cusps of Gauss on the parabolic; this is also clear from the geometry since the negative curvature lines of curvature in the hyperbolic region always point inwards). Thus the index of the principal directions around this parabolic curve must be +1. This requires that the bell itself must have 2 lemon umbilic points in it in the generic case. Thus we must have two transitions in which lemon/star umbilic pairs are created. The generic sequence with all the transitions is shown in Figures 7.13 and 7.14 which display the full red structure: the red principal directions, the red parabolics and ridges and the umbilics. It is given by the family of surfaces

$$z = ax^2 + by^2 + cx^3 + 3dx^2y + 3fxy^2 + gy^3 + t\exp(-s(x^2 + y^2)) \quad (7.1)$$

where t is the parameter in the family and the rest of the coefficients are constants. In point of fact, the values chosen were
$a = 0.1$, $b = 0.02$, $c = 0.02135$, $d = 0.0001$, $f = -0.0001$, $g = 0.005195$, $s = 8$, $t < 0$.
The range of values of x and y in the figures is $-1 \le x \le 1$ and $-1 \le y \le 1$.

Here is a commentary on the action between time frames in Figures 7.13 and 7.14.

1. One closed red ridge has formed (Section 7.2.7). Note that one half will be elliptic (red minimum) and one half hyperbolic (red maximum), separated by the points at which the ridge is tangent to the displayed red principal direction field. Time $t = -0.001$.

2. A second closed red ridge has formed; $t = -0.002$.

3. A red parabolic curve has formed (Section 7.2.1(i)(a)); $t = -0.004$.

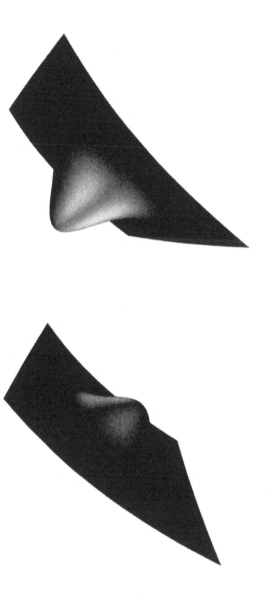

Figure 7.11. First: a bell surface which has a hyperbolic region between two elliptic convex regions, taking the 'inward' normal, which points generally upwards in this figure. Second: a dimple fully formed. Note that with a generally 'upward' normal, the outer part is convex and the inner part concave.

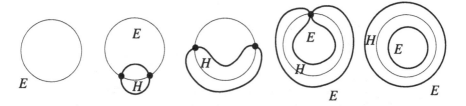

Figure 7.12. In principle a bell might be created this way (compare Koenderink (90, p.536). The thin lines are ridges and the thick lines are parabolic curves. A parabolic curve is created at a point of an elliptic ridge of the same color. The parabolic curve expands to close up at another ridge point, leaving two disjoint components. Dots are elliptic cusps of Gauss. In practice the sequence tends to be more complicated (see Section 7.3.1).

4. Another red parabolic curve has formed; $t = -0.008$.

5. A lemon/star pair of hyperbolic umbilics have formed, leaving a gap in the red ridge which is filled by the blue ridge (not shown) (Section 7.2.5). Note that the bottom half of the ridge must have been the hyperbolic half since it has given birth to umbilics (see 1 above); $t = -0.011$.

6. The hyperbolic star umbilic has turned to an elliptic umbilic (Section 7.2.6, which generically would be unsymmetric (the tangent lines to the ridges all lie in a half-plane); but almost immediately turns symmetric since the tangent lines are not in a half-plane in the figure. Strictly speaking, this is 2 transitions in succession; $t = -0.013$.

7. The red ridge collides with itself (Section 7.2.7); $t = -0.014$.

8. Another collision of red ridges has occurred (Section 7.2.7); $t = -0.017$.

9. Another lemon/star pair of hyperbolic umbilics have formed (Section 7.2.5), and the red parabolic curve has become singular (Section 7.2.1(ii)(b)); $t = -0.02$.

10. A hyperbolic star umbilic has turned into a symmetric elliptic umbilic (Section 7.2.6, case $T < 0$); $t = -0.025$

11. There have been two collisions of red ridges (Section 7.2.7), as in 7 and 8 above; $t = -0.03$.

12. The parabolic curve collides with itself to produce two red parabolic loops (Section 7.2.1(ii)(b)). Two lemon umbilics have been trapped inside the inner parabolic loop; $t = -0.04$. The elliptic star umbilic on the left seems to have reverted or being about to revert to being a hyperbolic star.

7.3.2 The dimple

The dimple has a *concave* $(--)$ elliptic region formed from an initially convex $(++)$ elliptic piece of surface, via the creation of two parabolic loops, which have to be of opposite color. Thus two ridges of opposite colours are involved in

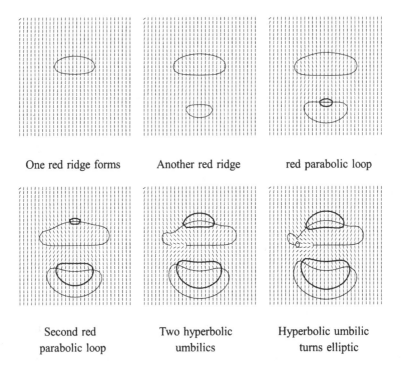

One red ridge forms   Another red ridge   red parabolic loop

Second red   Two hyperbolic   Hyperbolic umbilic
parabolic loop   umbilics   turns elliptic

Figure 7.13. First part of the sequence constructing the bell as in Section 7.3.1. The diagrams show
the parameter plane of an evolving surface. Thin lines are red ridges and thick lines are red parabolic
curves, assuming that the surface normal points 'inwards' so that we start with a convex (++) elliptic
region. The background is the field of red principal directions. See the text for details of the transitions
involved.

the process. The concave region includes two hyperbolic umbilics. Figure 7.15
illustrates one formation of a dimple, using the same family as in (7.1) but with
$t > 0$. A slightly exaggerated picture of the final surface is in the second image
of Figure 7.11.

Here is a summary of what is happening in Figure 7.15.

1. Two red ridges have formed (Section 7.2.7); $t = 0.002$.

2. A red parabolic curve forms on one of the ridges, separating a convex (++)
region from a hyperbolic (+−) region (Section 7.2.1(i)(a)); $t = 0.004$.

3. A blue parabolic curve is born on the *blue* ridge passing through the center of
the picture (not shown). This parabolic curve separates a hyperbolic (+−) region
from a concave (−−) one (Section 7.2.1(i)(b)); $t = 0.0128$.

4. A lemon/star pair of hyperbolic umbilics is born on the blue ridge (not shown),
causing a short piece of red ridge (shown: it is the short vertical piece above the
red parabolic) to appear (Section 7.2.5); $t = 0.014$.

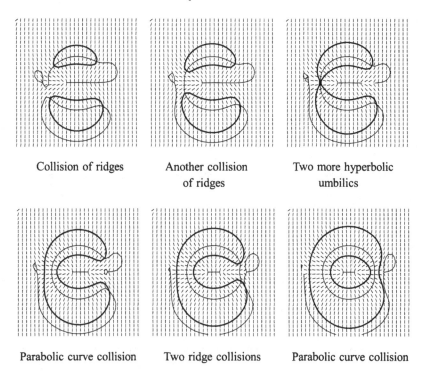

Collision of ridges   Another collision   Two more hyperbolic
                      of ridges   umbilics

Parabolic curve collision   Two ridge collisions   Parabolic curve collision

Figure 7.14. Second part of the sequence constructing the bell of Section 7.3.1. Thin lines are red ridges and thick lines are red parabolic curves. The background is the field of red principal directions. See the text for a running commentary on what is happening between the time frames.

5. The short piece of red ridge has attached itself to the red ridge loop via a hyperbolic-to-elliptic transition (Section 7.2.6). This does not materially affect the dimple. But the same thing as 4 above has happened on the other red loop of the ridge, so that we now have two lemon umbilics about to penetrate the outer parabolic (red) loop by the transition (Section 7.2.4) which did not occur in the bell case; $t = 0.019$.

6. Two umbilics have now moved inside the inner (blue) parabolic curve (Section 7.2.4); $t = 0.03$.

Note the difference in the red principal directions in the final figures of the bell and dimple evolutions. Both have two umbilics within the inner parabolic, but the red principal directions are rotated by 90° between the two cases. For the bell, the red principal directions cross the inner parabolic (which is red) transversally so there are no cusps of Gauss; for the dimple, the red principal directions are more or less tangent to the inner parabolic (which is blue), so the blue principal directions cross it transversally and again there are no cusps of Gauss.

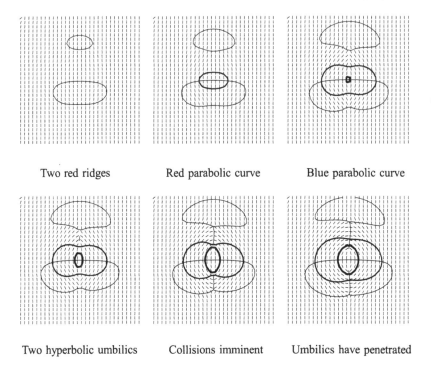

Two red ridges	Red parabolic curve	Blue parabolic curve

Two hyperbolic umbilics	Collisions imminent	Umbilics have penetrated

Figure 7.15. The creation of a dimple in stages, showing the parameter plane of an evolving surface. Thin lines are red ridges and thick lines are parabolic curves: red ones are medium thickness and blue ones are thickest. The background is the field of red principal directions. See the text for a running commentary on what is happening between the time frames.

7.4   How to Sculpt a Face

We have seen the elementary transitions in the parabolic/ridge fingerprint of a surface and we have seen how they can be assembled into scenarios as bells and dimples are formed on a surface. We now want to look at a 'real' example. From long and intimate familiarity, we tend to think of the face as a rather simple sort of shape: a protrusion forming the nose, paired intrusions forming the two eye sockets, etc. In fact, well over a 100 transitions must be employed to form a surface which resembles a face.

The experiment in this section is based on laser range data of a young woman, part of the same data used in the following two chapters. The data was acquired by a Cyberware scanner in cylindrical coodinates (r, θ, y) based on a vertical y-axis roughly through the center of the head. It consists in measurements $r_{i,j} = f(\theta_i, y_j)$ giving points $(r_{i,j}, \theta_i, y_j)$ on the surface of her head for 512 angles θ_i all around the head, and 256 samples y_j on a segment of the vertical axis of length 40 cm.

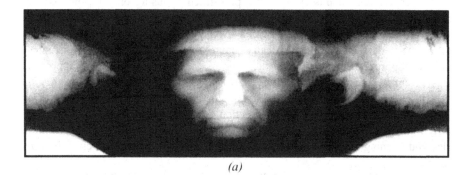

(a)

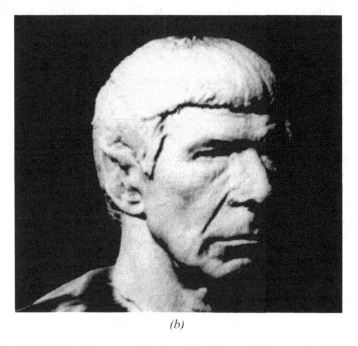

(b)

Figure 7.16. (a) Depth of face parameterized as $f(\theta, y)$ (Leonard Nimoy as Spock), (b) rendered polygonal model of face composed from coarse sampling of depth data.

The data from this scanner was estimated as being accurate up to a Gaussian distributed error of standard deviation $\pm.15$ millimeter. Figure 7.16(a) shows an example depth file in parameter space displayed with nearer points lighter, further points darker. Figure 7.16(b) shows a view of the same data set rendered from a polygon model made by connecting nearest neighbors in a subsampled depth map.

The experiment in this section was performed by using only the portion of this data extending from the top of the brow down to the middle of the chin and from one cheek to the other, which excluded all hair. This window in the data consisted of 75 samples vertically (approximately 12 cm.), and 88 samples radially (approximately $\pm 30°$ on each side of the frontal view). The approach was to create a family *interpolating between this data with all its fine detail and an ellipsoid which describes in simplest terms the overall global shape of a head.* Running this scenario in the direction from the featureless ellipsoid to the fully formed face gives a striking impression of a sculptor starting with a lump of clay and forming the features, starting with the largest and progressively filling in detail.

The ellipsoid was created carefully so as to approximate the true face around the edges of the 75×88 window of face data. We use the fact that an ellipsoid

$$\frac{x^2}{a^2} + \frac{y^2}{b^2} + \frac{z^2}{c^2} = 1$$

in cylindrical coordinates has the nice expression

$$r_{ell} = \frac{ac}{b} \cdot \frac{\sqrt{b^2 - y^2}}{\sqrt{c^2 \sin^2 \theta + a^2 \cos^2 \theta}}$$

We choose b so that the numerator fits the top and bottom 5 rows of the face data; a, c so that the denominator fits the left and right 5 columns of the face data. This fits the ellipsoid to the boundary of the skin area of the face. (If the whole face is used, the ellipsoid tries to fit the nose and eyes which are hardly ellipsoidal; but using only the border, we allow the eyes and nose to be features that grow.)

Then the face data r_{data} and the ellipsoid r_{ell} are interpolated by:

$$r_a = r_{ell} + e^{-\frac{5}{a}} (r_{data} - r_{ell}) * G_a, 0 \le a < \infty$$

where we convolve with the Gaussian kernel:

$$G_a(\theta, y) = \frac{a\pi}{4} e^{-(\theta^2 + y^2)) \frac{\pi^2 a}{4}}$$

and θ and y are scaled so that the window size is 1 (it is, in fact, roughly square in physical space).[4]   Note that as $a \to 0$, the interpolant $r_a \to r_{ell}$, i.e., we approach the ellipsoid; and that as $a \to \infty$, then $r_a \to r_{data}$, i.e., we approach the face itself. To calibrate the meaning of a on this scale, we can check that the standard deviation of the smoothing comes out as about $36/\sqrt{a}$ pixels. If the discrete cosine transform is used to implement the convolution, then we also get a

---

[4] The odd constants arise because the convolution is implemented by a discrete cosine transform and this happened to be the simplest way to measure a.

simple way to interpolate the smoothed data on a finer grid. This turns out to be important, esp. near the star umbilics where cubic terms have a major influence. To do this, one pads the DCT with a frame of zeros representing high frequencies and takes the inverse DCT. In some cases, we have refined the grid by a factor of 2 or 4 in order to get an accurate picture near umbilic points.

7.4.1 The scenario

7.4.1.1 THE STARTING POINT   We shall show how the curvature fingerprint of the surfaces r_a elaborates itself as a increases. Why do we choose an ellipsoid as the starting point rather than a sphere? The reason is not simply that a sphere is not as good an approximation to the face as an ellipsoid, but that a sphere is completely degenerate and special from a curvature point of view, whereas an ellipsoid fits our scheme by possessing only points with generic curvature behavior. In fact, an ellipsoid has *3 ridges along its 3 planes of symmetry*. If the ellipsoid is longest along the y-axis and shortest along the x-axis, the length along the z-axis being in the middle, these ridges are colored as follows: The ridge in the plane $x = 0$ containing the 2 largest directions is blue and elliptic, i.e., a perceptually salient protruding ridge; the ridge in the plane $y = 0$ containing the 2 shortest directions is red and elliptic, i.e., a perceptually salient intruding (or, if the curvatures are still positive as in this case, maximally flattened) ridge; and the third ridge in the plane $z = 0$ containing the longest and the shortest axis is hyperbolic, hence not salient, and switches from red to blue at 4 lemon umbilic points.

This corresponds very well to what we find on a face. Here the longest axis on the approximating ellipsoid is the vertical one through the head, which we are calling y, the shortest is the axis through the ears, which we are calling x, and the medium-length axis is the front to back axis, from the nose to rear of the head. Thus the symmetry plane $x = 0$ of the ellipsoid is also the plane of (approximate) bilateral symmetry of the head, and its intersection with the face is the curve from the middle of the forehead down across the bridge of the nose, along the nose, through the mouth to the middle of the chin. The elliptic blue ridge along this curve foreshadows the nose ridge, which is one of the most prominent curvature features of the face (see Figure 6.1). On the other hand, the elliptic red ridge passes approximately from one ear to the other across the top of the nose, and this foreshadows the left to right furrow across the eye sockets and nose bridge which is another prominent feature in Figure 6.1.

This is the starting point of our mathematical 'sculpture' and is shown in Figure 7.17, part (a). This figure, like the ones which follow, has a 3-D mesh of the surface with parabolic curves marked on it as starred lines (there are none yet), the elliptic blue ridges marked with solid black lines, the elliptic red ridges with dotted black lines and the hyperbolic ridges with solid and dotted gray lines (color, of course, makes these figures even better). The turning points are where elliptic ridges change to hyperbolic, or the black lines become gray. The star umbilics are marked by large triangles; the lemon umbilics by large circles.

7.4.1.2   THE RED ELLIPTIC RIDGES ACROSS THE NECK AND MOUTH   The first step in the creation of more structure on the face is the formation of hyperbolic red ridges across the nose and chin and an elliptic red ridge across the mouth. To see this, think of the sculptor as molding the profile of the clay along the vertical line of symmetry where the nose will form: he must make the nose and chin protrude and the mouth recede. Now this vertical line is the elliptic blue ridge in Figure 7.17 and a line of curvature for κ_2, the smaller of the 2 principal curvatures. κ_2 must be given a local maximum on this line at the nose and chin and a local minimum on the mouth, which means hyperbolic red ridges running across the nose and chin from left to right and an elliptic red ridge running from left to right across the mouth. In fact, all the vertical cross-sections near the plane of symmetry change from being ellipses to having protrusions at the nose tip and chin and being flatter across the mouth. This change takes place in the range $4.5 \leq a \leq 6$. The first transition happens off our diagram: a ridge loop appears as a result of the chin protruding and the neck being indented, creating an elliptic red ridge on the neck (not on our figure) and a hyperbolic red ridge across the chin, seen in Figure 7.17(b). Then a second red ridge loop is created at $a = 4.9$, Figure 7.17(c), with its elliptic part across the mouth, hyperbolic part across the future nose tip. At $a = 5.1$, Figure 7.17(d), an elliptic segment is created in the middle of the hyperbolic lower red ridge and at $a = 5.2$, Figure 7.17(e), these two ridges collide. Finally at $a = 6$, Figure 7.17(f), the elliptic red mouth furrow appears.

7.4.1.3   A HYPERBOLIC ISLAND FORMS ACROSS THE EYES   The next set of events takes place at $8 \leq a \leq 9$: first, a blue event takes place at $a = 8.0$, the creation of a blue ridge loop on the right cheek. This is due to the protruding of the cheek bone and the flattening of the cheek itself effecting the blue structure, which is given by the left-to-right lines of curvature. It is interesting that the corresponding ridge loop on the left cheek isn't created until $a = 9.5$: the deviations from bilateral symmetry in faces are actually quite substantial! In the meantime, without it causing any transitions, the furrow across the eyes and nose bridge that was represented by an elliptic red ridge already on the ellipsoid has not been standing still. In fact, it has been deepening and moving slightly up. At $a = 8.3$, this furrow gets deep enough so that a parabolic loop enclosing a hyperbolic island is created on the nose bridge. It enlarges rapidly and by $a = 10$, it has become a band of hyperbolic points crossing the face from ear to ear, reflecting the bone structure of the eye sockets. These events are depicted in Figure 7.18.

7.4.1.4   UMBILIC PAIRS FORM ON EACH CHEEK   As we have seen in the previous section, in order to form a 'bell', two lemon umbilics must be created in order to reorient the lines of curvature and give the bell index 1. Geometrically, the

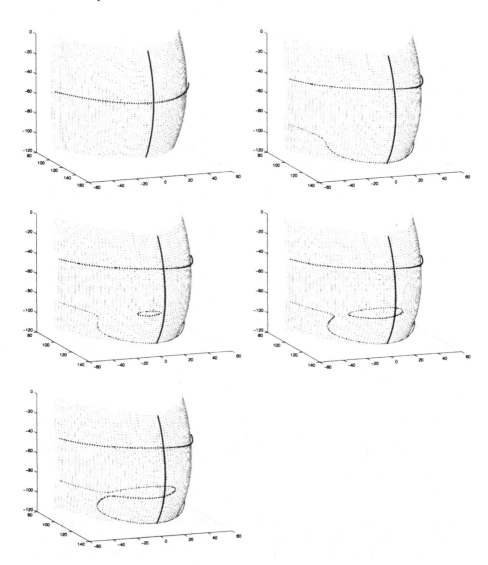

Figure 7.17. The earliest steps in sculpting the face: In part (a) we see the ellipsoid which is the starting point. Blue ridges are shown with solid lines, red ridges with dotted lines. κ_1 is the larger curvature which is found in roughly horizontal sections and it has maximima on the vertical ridge in the center of the face; κ_2 is the smaller curvature which is found in roughly vertical sections and it has a minimum in the horizontal ridge in the center. (b-f) The vertical contour is molded (very slightly!), becoming flattened across the mouth and protruding on the nose and chin. This creates in stages a pattern of 3 red ridges, hyperbolic (dotted gray lines) across the nose and chin, elliptic (dotted black lines) across the mouth.

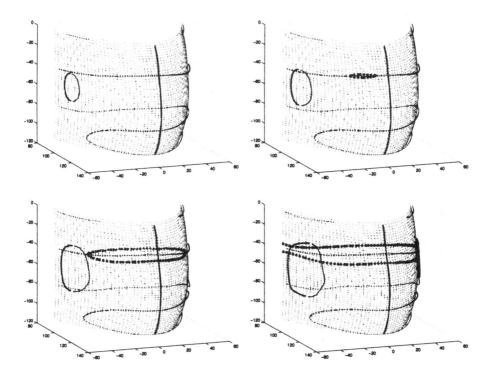

Figure 7.18. The deepening of the eye furrow and the formation of a hyperbolic band across the eyes. At the same time, the protrusion of the cheek bones and the flattening of the cheeks themselves causes blue ridge loops to form. As before, red ridges are solid, blue ridges are dotted, elliptic ridges are black and hyperbolic ridges are gray. The parabolic curve is the starred curve. In the four parts, a is respectively 8.0, 8.3, 9.0 and 10.0.

nose is a very prominent 'bell' on the face and as it protrudes, two pairs of umbilics must be created, with the lemons in each pair migrating to its tip, and the stars staying on the cheeks. The first lemon/star umbilic pair is created at about $a = 11.88$. In order to best follow the evolution of this geometry, we now use three different types of figures: the mesh plot of the evolving face in 3-D with ridges and parabolics shown in Figure 7.20, and flattened 2-D plots of the red and blue stories respectively shown in Figure 7.20. In these red and blue plots, we show (i) level curves of κ_1 and κ_2 respectively (shown with dotted lines); (ii) blue and red ridges respectively (shown by thick solid black and gray lines); and (iii) a sample of the blue and red lines of curvature respectively (shown by thin black lines). It is easy to 'see' why the ridges are where they are from these plots,

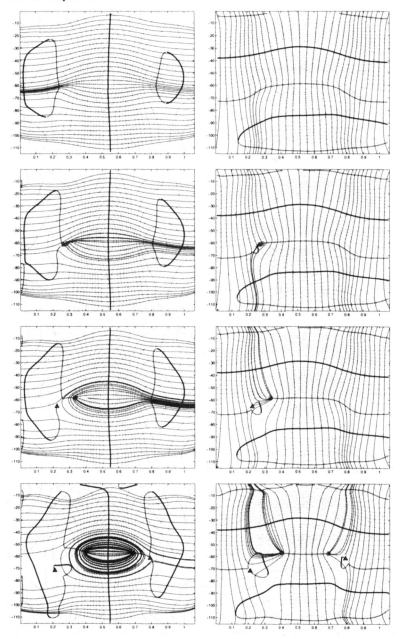

Figure 7.19. Two lemon/star umbilic pairs form, one on each cheek, creating an island around the nose with index +1. On the left, the blue lines of curvature, blue ridges and the level sets of κ_1 are shown. On the right, the red lines of curvature, ridges and level sets of κ_2. $a = 11$, 11.77, 12.5 and 15 in the four rows.

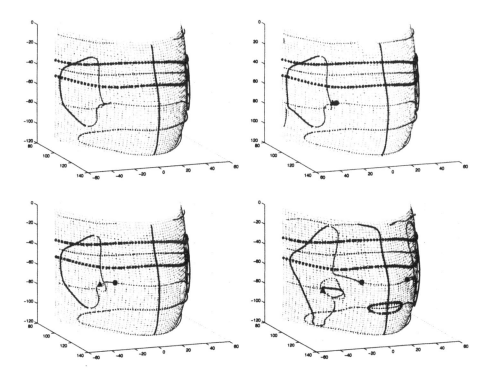

Figure 7.20. The creation of the two lemon/star umbilic pairs in 3-D new. $a = 11$, 11.88, 12.2 and 15. See text for full discussion.

because in each of these figures, the lines of curvature become tangent to the level curves of curvature exactly on the ridges.

As with the cheek ridges, the right side of this person's face is more developed than the left, so its structures form first. Looking at Figures 7.19(a) and 7.19(b), we see the appearance of the level sets and lines of curvature when $a = 11$ just before the first umbilic appears. Note that κ_1 has a max on the nose tip and minima on each cheek, and that the blue lines of curvature still run left to right but have begun to clump together on each cheek. κ_2 also has a maximum on the nose tip, minima on the nose bridge and center of the mouth, and a maximum on the chin. The red lines of curvature all run more or less vertically but are beginning to bend on the right cheek. Complicating the situation, at $a = 11.8$, just before the umbilic pair is formed, a small piece of the red ridge on the right cheek becomes elliptic (see Figure 7.20(a)). In fact, κ_1 and κ_2 are both nearly constant at this part of the cheek and the bifurcation is not so easy to follow. In Figures 7.19(c) and 7.19(d), we see the same picture at the point at which the umbilic pair is created on the right cheek. Note that it is created on the red ridge, thus there will be a tiny piece of blue ridge between the pair (too small to see). But also a blue ridge is lurking in the vicinity, shown in Figure 7.19(c), though not touching the umbilic. Both the red and blue picture are superimposed in Figure 7.20(b). What apparently happens is that immediately after the umbilic pair is formed, a second bifurcation happens in which the big blue ridge collides with the tiny newly formed blue ridge, resulting in what is seen in Figure 7.20(c) where $a = 12.2$. Here the ridges reform. At $a = 12.5$, Figure 7.19(e) and 7.19(f), we see the red and blue lines of curvature: the umbilic pair captures a whole mass of blue lines of curvature which loop between them. The second umbilic pair is about to form. In Figure 7.19(g-h), we skip ahead to $a = 15$ when both umbilic pairs are well-formed. Now the blue lines of curvature spiral strongly about the pair of lemon umbilics forming an area around which the index of the lines of curvature is +1. In the 3-D view, we see that a hyperbolic island has also formed around the mouth and we get a curious caricature of a face. It is not clear, without heavy double-precision computation, whether the star umbilic on the left cheek is now elliptic: the blue picture makes it look elliptic, while the red makes it look hyperbolic: the problem is that both curvatures are so nearly constant on this part of the cheek that the difference is not very robust.

7.4.1.5 STRINGS OF UMBILICS FORM ON THE BROW AND CHIN
What happens next at first looks quite confusing: 9 more umbilics are formed by $a = 20.0$ and the lines of curvature become quite complicated. In fact, this has a very simple explanation. Consider a surface of revolution, rotationally symmetric about the vertical y-axis. It is easy to see that its principal directions are always given by $y = \text{cnst.}$ and $x/z = \text{cnst.}$, and its lines of curvature are the circles on the surface around the y-axis and the intersections of the surface with the pencil of vertical planes through the y-axis. Sounds simple! *But*, in concave portions of the surface, the vertical curvature is negative, hence equal to κ_2, while the horizontal curvature is positive, hence equal to κ_1; and in strongly convex parts of the surface, e.g., where the contour has a sharp protruding corner, the vertical curvature is very large, hence equal to κ_1, and the horizontal curvature is relatively small and positive, hence equal to κ_2. What is happening is that there are whole rings of degenerate umbilic points where all the lines of curvature take 90° turns, even though they look like they continue smoothly, i.e., the red and blue lines swap. If you make a small perturbation of this degenerate situation, such a ring of umbilics breaks up into a string of alternating lemons and stars, and the lines of curvature do a very elegant dance, turning alternately 90° clockwise and counter-clockwise between umbilics.

This is very close to what happens on the face at both the chin and the brow. Both of these structures are roughly surfaces of revolution. Look at the chin. On the chin itself, the larger curvature is in the vertical direction and the smaller runs horizontally around the head. But in the neck, the vertical direction is concave, hence has negative curvature, and the horizontal direction remains positive, and is even a bit larger as the neck has smaller diameter. Thus the red and blue lines of curvature must all take roughly 90° turns on crossing the chin. The same happens on the brow. To make this work, a string of umbilics is formed on both the chin and brow, 5 on the brow and 4 on the chin in our window (a fifth umbilic must lie in the middle of the chin just outside the window). This is seen in Figure 7.21(a), where the 3-D view is shown. At this stage, the picture with all ridges and parabolics is getting a bit confused. In Figure 7.21(b), we see the situation better by looking only at the blue ridges and blue lines of curvature. Across the eyes and mouth, the maximum curvature lies on left-to-right lines, but at the brow and on the chin, the maximum curvature lies on more or less vertical lines. The umbilics allow these lines to make this turn.

Note that an elliptic blue ridge has formed on the brow. Note too how well-defined the nose has become: the lines of curvature now are almost circular on a still barely visible nose protrusion. We can also see how some of the umbilic stars have become elliptic: The two umbilic stars (shown by triangles) on the chin are clearly elliptic as is the umbilic on the bridge of the nose. The umbilic star on the left cheek (on the right of the figure) is also apparently elliptic, though just past the bifurcation, there is a tiny blue ridge loop hidden under the triangle (compare Figure 7.7). The other three stars seem to be hyperbolic. As a general matter, we will observe that something like half of the umbilic stars we will find on the face for various values of a seem to hover near the hyperbolic to elliptic transition and, if elliptic, have one pair of ridges through it forming a small tight loop.

7.4.1.6 COMPLETION OF AN ELLIPTIC RED RIDGE AROUND THE NOSE   As the nose forms, a shift takes place from having hyperbolic depressions across the mouth and the eyes to having a whole hyperbolic ring around the nose with an elliptic red ridge in the middle. Several bifurcations in which red ridges collide and reform, and in which parabolics collide and reform, take place. The first takes place at about $a = 18$, when the elliptic red ridges on the mouth and cheeks collide, and make a more extended red ridge around the bottom of the nose and smaller red ridges turning down from the mouth corners: see Figure 7.22(a), where we show the red parabolics and red ridges and level sets of red curvature. Then at $a = 22$, the red parabolics around the mouth and eyes collide on the left cheek (note that the red ridge runs through the point of collision). At about $a = 22.7$, they collide similarly on the right cheek so that the nose is now an isolated convex elliptic island. At about $a = 28.8$, the red ridges below the nose and along the left eye collide. Note that yet more umbilics have been created on the brow and chin and that small hyperbolic islands have formed at the ends of the mouth. Finally at $a = 32$, the red ridges around the nose and right eye collide. The final part of Figure 7.22 shows the completed red ridge around the nose at $a = 33$.

Note that at $a = 18$, there are 2 elliptic cusps of Gauss on the face which occur where the red mouth ridge crosses the red parabolic around the mouth. After reforming, at $a = 23$ and thereafter, there are two hyperbolic cusps of Gauss below the eyes. A characteristic of the bell, however, is that there are no cusps of Gauss on the parabolic around the nose: the ridges which cross this parabolic are all blue, not red.

7.4.1.7 FORMATION OF CONCAVITIES NEXT TO THE EYES   The most prominent concavities on the face are the deep concavities immediately on each side of the bridge of the nose, between the eyes and the bridge. These are like dimples, as discussed above, but not exactly. To study these, note that concavities are surrounded by *blue* parabolic lines. The first of these forms at about $a = 29$ and is shown in Figure 7.23(a). In this figure we are showing the *blue ridges*, the blue parabolics with curves made up of triangles, and the level sets of the κ_1, the larger of the two curvatures. We see its evolution as a increases: when $a = 32$, Figure 7.23(b), we see both concave elliptic islands have formed, and that both have two cusps of Gauss on them, where the hyperbolic blue ridge crosses them. At $a = 40$, we get a very interesting bifurcation at both islands. This is the "flat hyperbolic umbilic" discussed above. The red and blue parabolics meet at a planar point around which we have an elliptic convex segment, two hyperbolic segments and an elliptic concave segment. The umbilic moves from the elliptic convex region, through the planar umbilic, to the elliptic concave region, as in Figure 7.5. To show this, we have drawn in Figure 7.23(c) both sets of parabolic

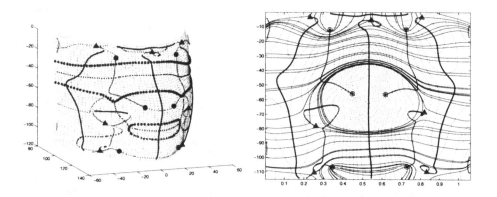

Figure 7.21. At $a = 20$, two strings of umbilics have formed, one just below the brow and one just above the chin, allowing the lines of curvature to make 90 degree turns as they go from the eyes to the forehead and from the mouth to the chin. In part (a), we see the 3-D picture with all the ridges; in part (b), we see the blue ridges and blue lines of curvature.

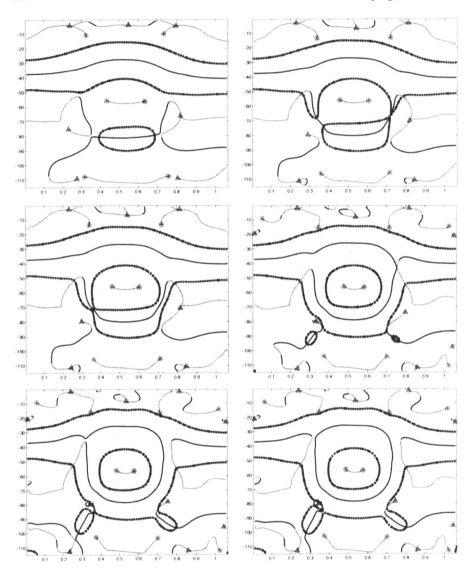

Figure 7.22. The formation of a hyperbolic moat around the nose with an elliptic red ridge inside. The 6 parts show $a = 18.0, 22.0, 22.7, 28.8, 32.0$ and 33.0. Note how the red parabolic and the red ridge progressively assemble themselves by a sequence of collisions and reformations.

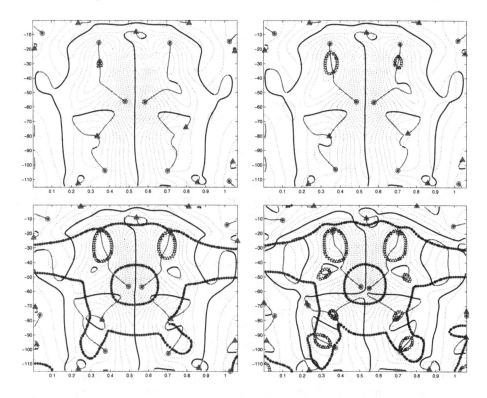

Figure 7.23. Two concavities form in the eye furrows on each side of the nose bridge. In parts a and b, we see the blue ridges, blue parabolics and the level sets of the maximum curvature for $a = 29$ and 32. Two concave elliptic islands are created. In parts c and d, we also show the red parabolic curves. In part c, at $a = 40$, the red and blue parabolics collide at planar points and an umbilic is exchanged from the convex to the concave region. The final form of this concave island is shown in part d at $a = 60$.

curves (but not the red ridges). The story at $a = 60$ is shown in Figure 7.23(d). In fact, this concave island never gets a second umbilic inside it, hence never becomes a fully formed dimple. It always has index $+1/2$. Although these parts of your face seem superficially like symmetric intrusions, they retain a cusp of Gauss on their edges.

7.4.1.8 A LOOK AT THE FINAL PICTURE The final face has a great deal more subtle structure that forms as a increases further. Let's first try to get a sense of how many parabolic regions the face acquires as more detail is added. This is shown in the sequence of Figures 7.24 where 3-D views of the face are given for $a = 25, 40, 60, 100, 200$ and 500. For clarity, only the parabolic curves are drawn, the blue ones in gray and the red ones in black. Thus the concave pockets on the face are surrounded in black. It is striking how complex the final picture is: this perhaps explains why Hilbert was disappointed when he had the parabolic curves drawn by one of his students on the bust of Apollo. The thing to bear in mind is that when one of the curvatures is near zero, mathematically, a tiny positive to negative deviation causes a parabolic curve just like those of the major features. Note, for instance, that going up the middle part of the nose, κ_2 hovers around zero, going from positive to negative to positive to negative and creating a small elliptic convex patch on the middle of the nose. Likewise, in the cheeks, κ_2 hovers around zero and this creates irregular hyperbolic and convex elliptic regions.

Some features are clear and significant, e.g., for face recognition (see the next 2 chapters). Around each eye are *three* concave patches, the one discussed in the last subsection and two more, one below and one at the outside corner of the eyes. Note that the eyeballs themselves and the lips are clearly visible at $a = 200$ as elliptic convex regions surrounded by hyperbolic regions. Another striking feature of this picture is the number of near planar points where a red and blue parabolic are on the verge of colliding. These are *not* collisions of parabolics of the same color, but rather the bifurcation called a 'flat hyperbolic umbilic' in Section 7.2.4. If we had drawn in the umbilics as well, this would be clear.

In a second sequence of figures (7.25), we have drawn the elliptic ridges on the same 3-D views for the same sequence of values of a. We have drawn the blue ridges in black and the red ridges in gray. Note that these ridges end in turning points, because we have not drawn the hyperbolic ridges to avoid too much confusion. The important strong features of the face, such as the blue nose ridge and blue brow ridge, remain at the largest value of a, but as with the parabolic curves, it is striking how much junk is found, e.g., on the cheeks: in these nearly smooth featureless patches, many tiny undulations cause short pieces of elliptic ridge. This underlines the importance of using mathematical tools like ridge curves in conjunction with smoothing techniques to separate the major features from the minor ones. However, some small features are perceptually important to us: only at $a = 500$ do we find blue ridges all the way across the upper and lower lips, although the red ridge between the lips is formed by $a = 200$. Also note how the strength of the blue brow ridge contrasts to the rather random short pieces of red ridge crossing the brow: this is a reflection of the small perturbations which break up the whole line of umbilics near the brow.

In a third sequence of figures (7.26) we have drawn red and blue lines of curvature for $a = 60$ and $a = 200$. We simply used a 100 random points on the face and drew the lines of curvature through them for a while. The use of random initial points is why, for instance, the circular lines of curvature around the nose are drawn in quite irregularly, and the left and right sides of the face are not identically sampled. But this certainly gives a startling and dramatic way of seeing a face (reminiscent perhaps of Baskin's drawings). Several points may be

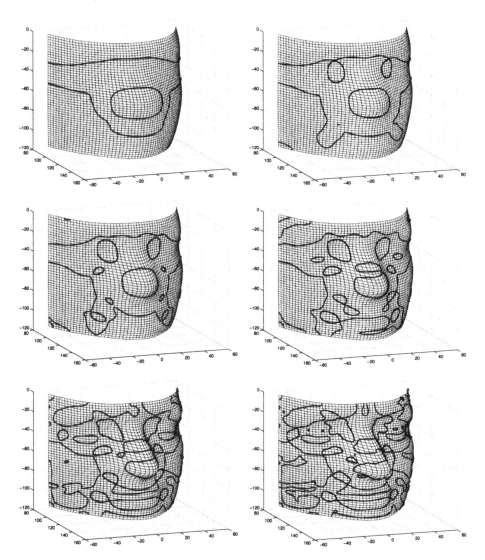

Figure 7.24. Six three-dimensional views of the face with $a = 25, 40, 60, 100, 200$ and 500. The blue parabolic curves are drawn in black and the red parabolic curves are drawn in gray. Note the increasing level of detail, some corresponding to features we expect, such as the lips and eyeballs, and some corresponding to minor features on the cheeks and brow that we normally do not notice.

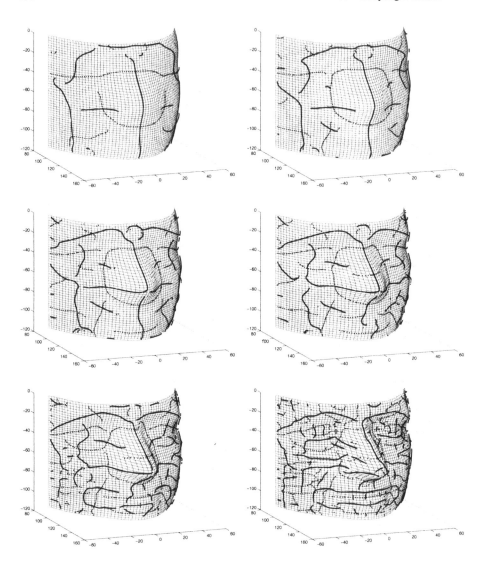

Figure 7.25. Six three-dimensional views of the face with $a = 25, 40, 60, 100, 200$ and 500. The blue elliptic ridges are drawn in black and the red elliptic ridges are drawn in gray. Note again the increasing level of detail, with e.g., the lips and nostrils as well as minor features.

noted: (a) there is an explosion in the number of umbilic points by $a = 200$; (b) there is a tendency of lines of curvature to make sharp bends along a hyperbolic ridge (look, e.g., at the right side of the nose at $a = 200$); (c) the lines of blue

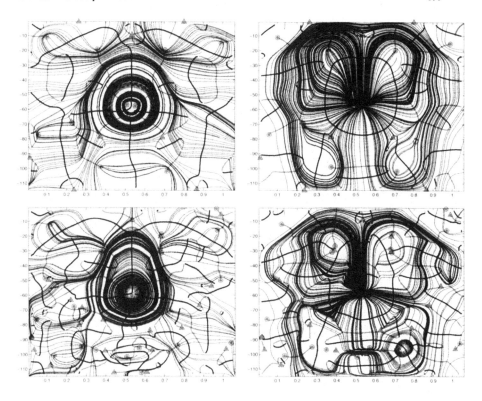

Figure 7.26. A random sample of 100 red and 100 blue lines of curvature for the two values $a = 60$ and $a = 200$.

curvature around the nose are circular while the lines of red curvature around the eye concavities are loops with cusps, which reflects the fact that the nose is a true bell with index $+1$, while the eye concavities are only partial dimples with index $+1/2$. At $a = 200$, we see that this holds even when there are multiple fine structure umbilics in these concavities.

Chapter 8

Finding Facial Features from Range Data

In this chapter we discuss the process of extracting face-specific descriptors from a range data description of a head. The situation is the same as that described in the last section of the previous chapter. The data was acquired by a Cyberware scanner in cylindrical coodinates (r, θ, y) based on a vertical y-axis through the center of the head and consists in measurements $r = f(\theta_i, y_j), 1 \leq i \leq 512, 1 \leq j \leq 256$ including the whole head. We compute the principal curvatures, parabolic and ridge curves as in the previous chapter. The goal now is to extract important scalar features for the purpose of discriminating individual faces. In particular, the following features are extracted:

- nose bridge (nasion)

- nose base (base of septum)

- nose ridge

- eye corner cavities: inner and outer

- convex center of the eye (eyeball/lid region)

- eye socket boundary (surrounding the convex center of the eye)

- boundary surrounding nose

- face region

Typical locations of some of these features are indicated for reference in Figure 8.1.

Each of these face descriptors is defined in terms of a high level set of relationships among depth and curvature features. As such, the feature extraction process is structured as a constrained search in the crowded space of low-level features. As each constraint is enforced, the number of potential locations for the feature

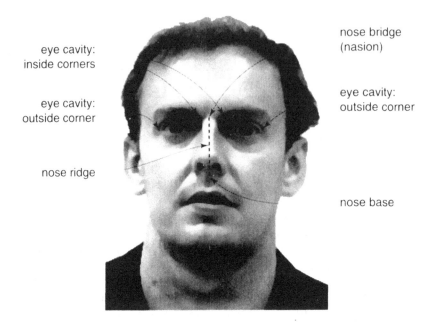

Figure 8.1. Position of some of the features used to describe the face

is reduced. The constraints are designed to reduce the search to a single definition of the feature. At that point, the feature's relationship to other previously extracted features is examined as a verification of its detection. If error conditions are detected during the search or validation, no feature value is recorded. The constraints for one feature are often functions of other related features' values or estimates of these values if a feature is not available. Thus, as the feature detection progresses, these constraints become more well-defined. In some cases, particularly if the previous calculation of a feature produced errors or if the feature value is particularly sensitive in other processes (feature detection or recognition), we extract a feature's description again when more accurate constraints are available. The search process considers constraints on:

- absolute extent of a region on the surface;

- distance of a region or point from the symmetry plane;

- symmetrical pairing of features;

- proximity of a point or region to a target on the surface;

- amount of protrusion of a region from the surrounding surface;

- local configuration of elliptic blue (maximum) ridge lines and elliptic red (minimum) ridge lines (Section 6.4.1 and Section 6.4.2). Here we take the face normal to point inwards. The elliptic red ridge lines will also be called *valley lines*.

We illustrate the use of these constraints in the extraction of the specific features listed above. Several of the features use a similar extraction process, so we group these together.

8.1 Nose Ridge

The most striking aspect of the face in terms of range data is the nose. If the nose can be located reliably, it can be used to put constraints on the location of eyes and other features. There are at least three properties useful in locating the nose. Most obviously, it sticks out from the rest of the face. It also has a characteristic roof-like ridge, which is most often in a vertical orientation. And lastly, this ridge falls approximately on the symmetry plane of the face. In the current implementation we make use of the first two properties as constraints in the location of the nose, which we mark by the location of ridge. The intersection of a surface with a plane of symmetry is always a ridge line in the sense of Chapters 6 and 7 (Section 6.4.1), but this kind of ridge can be extracted to good accuracy in many other

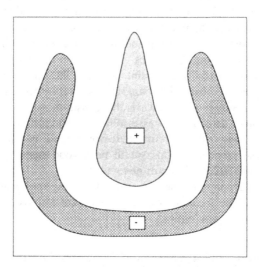

Figure 8.2. Modified center surrounds filter shape used in one of the nose finding stages. It highlights regions in which the average radius in the center is high, relative to the average radius in the surround. White areas do not contribute. High responses therefore indicate protrusion in depth.

ways as well. In fact we can take the level sets of vertical height, $y = $ constant, and determine the points for which $r = f(\theta, y)$ has an extremum: $\partial f/\partial \theta = 0$.

The first step is to locate instances of roughly vertical connected ridges in the depth map. This is done by marking points of positive to negative sign change in $\partial f/\partial \theta$ for which an additional threshold constraint on $|\partial f/\partial \theta|$ on both sides of the nose is met. These requirements are local to the several pixels along the top of the ridge. Connected lines of more than a trivial length are maintained as potential nose ridge sites.

The second constraint we apply is based on degree of protrusion of a region from the surrounding surface. That is, we look for areas of high average radius surrounded on 3 sides by relative low average radius. This test is performed by convolution of the depth data with a modified center surround filter shown in Figure 8.2. Connected regions yielding high responses to this filter are then filtered based on absolute size. Regions which are not within allowable nose dimensions are eliminated. The maximum allowable height is very generous at 75mm; the average nose height of the 58 faces measured was 53mm. The maximum allowable width is 60mm; the average nose width measured in our data base was 42mm.

Final ridge candidates are constrained to overlap one of the regions satisfying the protrusion test. Examples of candidate ridges and protrusion regions are shown for two faces in Figure 8.3. The ridge lines are drawn in black, and the protrusion regions in grey. In one case, the intersection of these two features defines the nose ridge uniquely and in the other, two locations remain. In the few cases where the two constraints do not yield a unique ridge location, additional constraints must be applied. There are many approaches we could take. For instance, we could look for an indication of the symmetry plane of the face and use this information to select among the remaining candidates. However, in the current implementation we use an arbitrary proximity constraint, selecting the ridge closest to the center of the data. For our particular data base, this is a very effective constraint, never producing an erroneous choice. However, the constraint is not very general. Since several other feature detection processes reference the position of the nose ridge, if a bad choice of nose ridge were made, it would result in a high rate of feature detection in these processes. This would be a good signal to restart the face processing with a different choice of nose ridge.

We use the end points of the nose ridge to define the locations of the nose bridge and base. The locations of these points are refined later, based on the position of the nose region outline.

8.2   Eye Features: The Application of Symmetry Constraints

Consistent detection and measurement is a desirable property in selecting features to describe aspects of the face. Among the more consistent curvature features (evident in Figure 8.4) are sets of symmetric concavities (black blobs) which

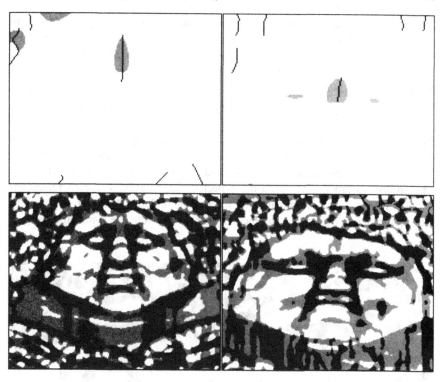

Figure 8.3. Upper row shows examples of candidate nose features: (black)– candidate ridges, (grey)– areas satisfying relative height criteria. Nose ridge must show both features. Lower row shows segmented version of the two faces for which nose features are shown; they are given only as reference for the reader to show the actual location of the nose.

occur at the inside and outside corners of the eyes. Symmetric convex regions (white blobs) are also evident; the pair that is most consistently present defines the location of the eyeballs (or eyelids). Our system finds the location of the eye corners and eyeballs using these features, relying for a large part on symmetry constraints. The search for a given feature can be greatly simplified if the target feature has a characteristic relationship to the symmetry plane, or if it typically has a symmetrical match on the other side of the symmetry plane. We discuss these constraints in the context of extracting these particular eye features; but these processes are general and can be applied in many other cases.

In order to apply these constraints based on symmetry, we must know the parameters of the symmetry plane. The intersection of the symmetry plane with the face surface can be approximated by a straight line in the image (y, θ) plane, which we term the symmetry line of the face — note that the head may not be exactly registered in this coordinate system, so the fit is only approximate. We shall examine constraints based on symmetry in the parameter space across the symmetry line. We shall use the location of the points at the bridge and base of the nose to define the symmetry line. The symmetry line is described by its angle and distance from the origin; most often the symmetry line is close to vertical, so this parameterization is more appropriate than one involving slope.

We use symmetry constraints primarily to match concave and convex regions. The position of each region is defined by its center of mass, a single point. In the case of the search for the eyeballs, which often appear in surface data as convex regions, we begin with the entire space of convex regions. The first step is to eliminate those regions which exceed a width or height limit. This is a straightforward process based on the expected size of eyes. For each remaining region's center of mass, we calculate the perpendicular distance of the point to the symmetry line d_s, and the projection of the point onto the symmetry line p_s.

Figure 8.4. Segmentation of four different faces by sign of Gaussian curvature K and mean curvature H: $K > 0$ concave (black); $K > 0$ convex (white); and two types of hyperbolic ($K < 0$) points: positive mean curvature (light grey) and negative mean curvature (dark grey).

The first type of constraint we apply is to prune, based on the expected range of distances of the target feature from the symmetry line. These distance are defined originally in terms of measurements on the face in mm, then they are transformed into the corresponding distances (in pixels) they describe in the parameter space. Even very generous distance constraints will prune the full set of points considerably.

The second type of constraint is the existence of symmetry pairing among the points remaining. This symmetry matching process is a little less straightforward. We describe it in detail in the following section.

8.2.1 Symmetry Matching

The symmetry match has several stages. We mark each feature with its best symmetry match, then we eliminate nonreciprocal pairings and rematch to find the best available pairing. The first stage is done by matching each feature (as a "target") against all the others (the "candidates"). For each of these matches, we first test if the two features are within the specified symmetry range $(\Delta d_s, \Delta p_s)$ of each other. Then, if the test is positive, we project the target feature across the symmetry line, and measure the distance between this projection and the position of the candidate feature. The label of the candidate feature with closest measured distance specifies the best symmetry match for the target. If no feature is within the symmetry range then a NOMATCH tag is given to the target. Once a NOMATCH tag is given to a feature as a target, it is also no longer considered as a candidate.

We define the allowed error in a given symmetry match by $(\Delta d_s, \Delta p_s)$, where Δd_s is the tolerated difference in distance to the symmetry line for the two matched features, and Δp_s is the tolerated distance between the two features' projections on the symmetry line. If no feature is within this symmetry error window, no match is made. This explicit error in the matching process is necessary because there can be a significant degree of natural asymmetry in a face, as well as error in the identification of the symmetry line parameters. Error in the angle of the symmetry line will have a greater effect on features more distant from the symmetry line. The degree of natural asymmetry will be dependent on the feature we are searching for. For instance, empirically there is a higher degree of asymmetry in features describing the mouth than those describing the eyes.

Once the features have all been tagged with their best symmetry match, we must search for nonreciprocal matches. Because we are allowing for some degree of asymmetry, and because not all the features have symmetry matches in the set, it is common for inappropriate matches to occur. Figure 8.5 shows graphically some examples of how the matching might look at this stage. For each feature which is not tagged NOMATCH, we check the descriptor list of the feature listed as a best symmetry match. If the best symmetry match of this candidate feature is not the same as the label of the target, then we tag the target REMATCH. We then

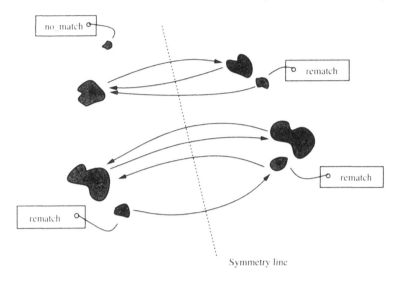

no_match

rematch

rematch

rematch

Symmetry line

Figure 8.5. Example of match state before unreciprocated matches have been rematched

again find the closest symmetry match for all the features tagged REMATCH, using only other REMATCH features as candidates. We must also retest for nonreciprocal matches. Features still without appropriate pairing at this point are assumed to be unpaired and are tagged NOMATCH. All matched features remain part of the search.

8.2.2   Further Details of Eye Feature Extraction

The process of extracting inside and outside corner cavities of the eyes is very similar to the example of the convex regions of the eyeball which we began to describe above.

In each case, we begin with an image of either connected concave or convex regions; the location of each connected region is defined by its center of mass. Geometric constraints based on allowable distances and sizes for eyes are used first to limit the number of points in the search, then symmetry constraints are used to locate candidate pairs. If there are multiple pairs which satisfy both symmetry and geometric constraints, the selection is made among them based on closest distance between the pair's projection onto the symmetry line and a specific target on the symmetry line. If no other eye features have been found, the target is calculated from the nose bridge and base. If other eye features have been identified, the target is the projection of one of those features onto the symmetry line.

Feature	Geometric constraints			Symmetry constraints	
	area	width	height	dist. limits d_s	asymm. $(\Delta d_s, \Delta p_s)$
eyeballs (eb)	0 - 350	0 - 40	0 - 17	35 - 70	12, 15
inside corner eye cavity (iec)	150 - 900	0 - 300	0 - 300	10 - 25	12, 15
outside corner eye cavity (oec)	0 - 900	0 - 300	0 - 300	40 - 70	12, 15

Feature	Proximity Target	Verification Conditions
eyeballs (eb)	$\lvert p_s - p_s(\text{nose center})\rvert < 40$	• p_s above p_s (nose base)
inside corner eye cavity (iec)	$\lvert p_s - p_s(\text{eb})\rvert < 14$ or $\lvert p_s - p_s(\text{nose center})\rvert < 40$	• p_s above p_s (nose base) • d_s (inside corner) $< d_s$ (eyeball)
outside corner eye cavity (oec)	$\lvert p_s - p_s(\text{eb})\rvert < 14$ or $\lvert p_s - p_s(\text{iec})\rvert < 17$ or $\lvert p_s - p_s(\text{nose center})\rvert < 30$	• p_s above p_s (nose base) • d_s(outside corner) $> d_s$ (eyeball) $> d_s$ (inside corner)

Table 8.1. Summary of constraints used in selection of eye descriptors. All values are given in mm (or mm^2 for area). Underlined geometric constraints represent actual limits, whereas other values are currently large enough to represent "don't care" conditions.

The selected location is also tested for validity against other features' relative positions (e.g., outside corners of the eyes must be farther from the symmetry line than the inside corners of the eyes). The verification process continues as additional feature values become defined. Constraints used in the identification of these eye feature points are summarized in Table 8.1. We use d_s, and $(\Delta d_s, \Delta p_s)$ to describe the symmetry constraints, where d_s is the distance from the point to the symmetry line, p_s is the projection of a point onto the symmetry line. Thus, $(\Delta d_s, \Delta p_s)$ gives the the allowable asymmetry between a matching pair.

Three different search examples are summarized graphically for the face depicted in Figure 8.6(a). In (b),(c),and (d), the light grey regions show the initial regions considered in the search (the set of either convex or concave regions). The regions which satisfy constraints on size and distance from the symmetry line are shown in dark grey or black. Symmetry pairs detected are connected by a line, and the final selected pair is marked in black. In the case of the identification of the inside eye corners for this subject, the size and symmetry pairing constraints produced a unique feature identification, so the proximity constraint can be used as additional verification step as opposed to a limiting constraint.

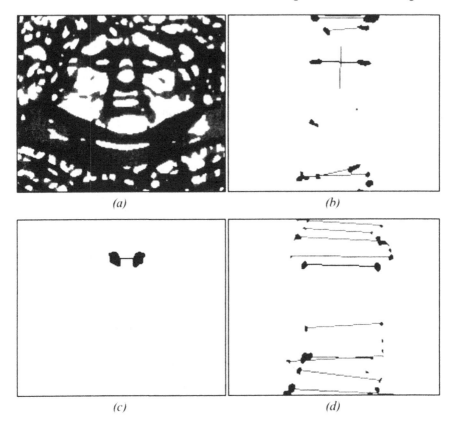

Figure 8.6. (a) Segmentation of original image by sign of principal curvature; (b) selection of the convex region marking the eyelid/eyeball; (c) selection of the concave regions at the inside corner of the eye; and (d) selection of concave regions at the outside corner of the eye.

8.3 Bounding Regions of Convex Structures

Some features are best defined in terms of regions. Hoffman and Richards defined a rule for partitioning a surface into parts in a manner which was supposed to be consistent with the way we naturally mentally segment or organize a shape (Hoffman and Richards 83). Their suggestion is to "divide a surface into parts at loci of negative minima of each principal curvature along its associated family of lines of curvature". In the terminology of Chapter 6, these would be the elliptic red ridges, or valleys, in non-convex regions as well as the hyperbolic blue ridges in concave regions: the former seem to be the curves they had in mind. The applicability of this rule to complex objects has not previously been tested, particularly on real data. One might hope that features which most of us naturally segment as "parts" of the human face such as the nose, mouth, or eyes might be partitioned effectively by this rule. An example of this boundary point criterion is shown in Figure 8.7. It is not clear that the hyperbolic blue ridges in concave regions correspond to anything very perceptual, nor are they continuations of the elliptic red ridges,[1] hence we will not consider them further.

Although close in some cases, it is important to note that this algorithm does not generally yield completely connected boundaries. It is striking that even the nose, which is closest to the Hoffman and Richards' ideal of a convex protrusion added to a lower curvature surface by a smooth join does not appear as a complete part. In Section 7.4, we saw that *after suitable smoothing*, the nose was indeed entirely surrounded by an elliptic red ridge, hence a "part" in their sense, but this only occured at the correct scale. With too little smoothing, this ridge gets lost in finer detail, and with too much smoothing, the whole nose becomes indistinct. In general, part boundaries create curves which can end abruptly with no continuation (unlike the zero crossings of a function). This occurs when a local minimum and a local maximum on one line of curvature coalesce and disappear in nearby lines of curvature, i.e., at turning points in the language of Section 6.4.3 (see also Figure 6.8). Combined with *a priori* knowledge of the face, however, this information is still very useful. If we know what we are looking for, we can use this information to help fill in the gaps and identify significant boundary points using some common morphological operators (for a general reference on morphological image processing, see Serra (82)).

We give as an example, the case of locating bounding areas for the eye socket and nose. For the eye regions, we first use the location of the corner cavities of the eyes (or approximations based on the eyeball location if the cavities weren't located successfully) to establish a bounding area for the search. An example is shown by the rectangle superimposed on Figure 8.8(a). The first of the small images shows the potential boundary points detected in the subimage based on the Hoffman and Richards criterion (Figure 8.8(b)). Without going into details (which can be found in the papers referred to), we perform the following operations: first a morphological dilation in this image using an elementary octagonal structuring element; this will bridge gaps in the boundary (Figure 8.8(c)). Then we compute the skeleton of the enlarged region, using the constraints that: (1) the points in the original boundary image must be included in the skeleton; (2) the homotopy of the region is preserved; and (3) the thickness of any added lines is 1 (Figure 8.8(d)) (Vincent 91, Calabi and Harnett 66). We invert the skeleton and use the convex regions identified as the eyeball or lid as a seed for region-growing (Figure 8.8(e)). In terms of more classical morphology, we are performing a geodesic reconstruction operation, which extracts the connected components marked by

---

[1] We saw in Chapter 6 that the only link between red and blue ridges is at umbilic points, where a hyperbolic red ridge turns into a hyperbolic blue ridge.

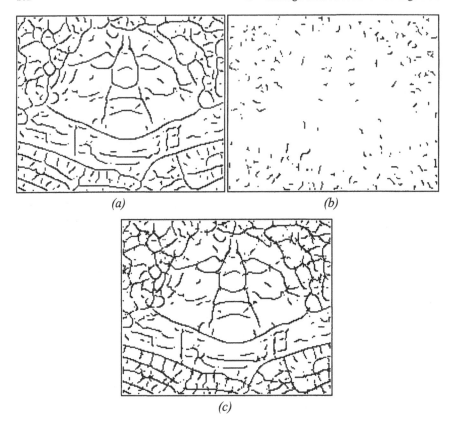

Figure 8.7. Points on part boundaries in (a) $\kappa_2 = \kappa_{min}$, (b) $\kappa_1 = \kappa_{max}$. (c) complete part boundary image

the seed (Lantuéjoul and Maisonneuve 84). This selects the connected region belonging to the eyesocket (Figure 8.8(f)). We can use either the region or its now connected and isolated boundary to describe this area.

Figure 8.9 shows a similar procedure to identify the nose region. The seeds for region-growing are determined by convex regions on the nose ridge. It is common to find more than one such region because there is often at least one "dip" in the profile of the nose ridge. Figure 8.9(b) shows regions selected by both seeds; Figure 8.9(c) shows these regions after a combination of a morphological closing and opening which joins and smoothes the regions.

A graphical summary of these eye and nose feature points and regions as located for several sample faces, is shown in Figure 8.10 as a caricature in parameter space, and in Figure 8.11 as projected onto the surface classified as "face" by the algorithm discussed in the next section.

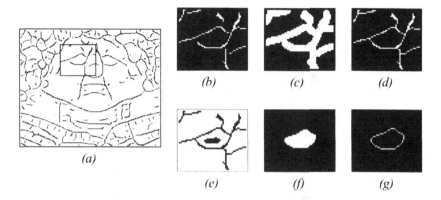

Figure 8.8. Sequence of images illustrating the calculation of the eye region

The position of the nose bridge and base are adjusted if necessary, such that they occur at the intersection of the outline and the nose ridge. This defines the location of the base and bridge point features very specifically as the intersection of the nose ridge ($\partial f/\partial\theta = 0$) and a valley line.

8.4 Face/Non-Face Segmentation

It is important to know what part of the surface actually corresponds to the face. Here we can use the fact that the skin is relatively smooth in comparison with hair or clothing boundaries. On these boundaries and in the hair region itself, we are likely to find relatively high values in one or both of the principal curvatures, whereas on the smooth areas of the skin, such as forehead, cheeks, and neck, both principal curvatures will be low. We began by detecting these smooth areas using the criterion of low Gaussian curvature ($|\kappa_1\kappa_2| <$ thresh). Although this was for the most part effective, an even better criterion is given by the sum of

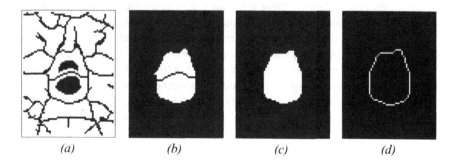

Figure 8.9. Sequence of images illustrating the calculation of the nose region

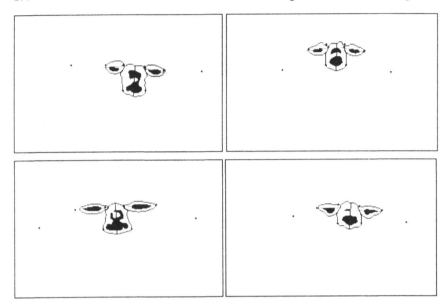

Figure 8.10. Sample results of feature detection. Caricatures show eyesocket and nose region outline with their respective markers. The nose ridge is drawn in black. Eye point features are marked by small crosses. A dotted line shows the principal axis of each eyesocket region.

the squares of the principal curvatures ($\kappa_1^2 + \kappa_2^2 <$ thresh). This function has a steeper slope at boundaries of high curvature, which will produce a smoother, more reliable segmentation. Figure 8.12 shows an example of the difference between these two criteria in practice.

The mask produced by this segmentation will not include several regions in the eyes, nose, or mouth, or other places on the face where interesting curvature events occur. However, since we have already defined enclosing regions for the eyes and nose, we can add them to the mask (we first dilate them for better coverage). This is shown in Figure 8.12(b). We do not attempt to cover holes in the mask due to the mouth and chin, because these areas have a high degree of variation caused by expression and position, and we would like to minimize these differences.

The skin region of the mask must be separated from the rest of the image, which may include small spurious regions of smooth hair or clothing surface. First we perform a morphological closing on the nonsmooth areas of the image (Figure 8.12(c)), then the largest connected component of smooth points is selected as the final mask (Figure 8.12(d)). This mask defining the face region is used in the next chapter to decide over what points valid comparisons can be made between faces.

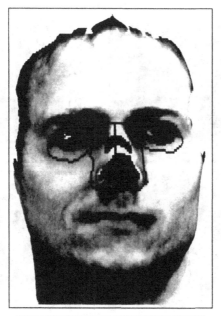

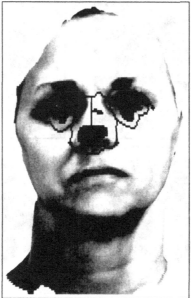

Figure 8.11. Sample results of feature detection. Shown as projected onto the face region in 3-space (surface classified as non-face is not shown).

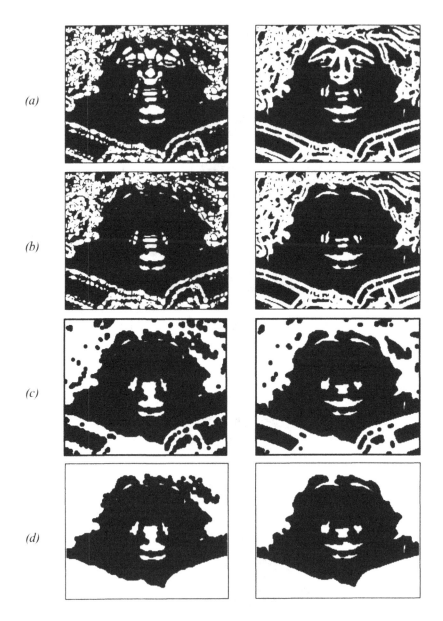

Figure 8.12. (a) Regions satisfying smooth surface criteria; (b) adding the eyes and nose to the mask; (c) after a morphological closing; (d) final mask of face region. Left column uses $|\kappa_1 \kappa_2| <$ thresh as initial criterion, right column uses $\kappa_1^2 + \kappa_2^2 <$ thresh as initial criterion.

Chapter 9

Recognition from Range Data

We can categorize recognition strategies into two general paradigms as in Chapter 2:

- pattern-theoretic methods comparing a template with the data,

- feed-forward methods computing a feature vector from the data and then making comparisons in feature space.

There is an important overlap in the implementations of these two paradigms, the extraction of face specific surface descriptors (hidden variables in the terminology of pattern theory). Methods in the first category do not use these features directly for recognition, but they must use them in order to find the best template match. In the simplest case developed here, they are used in order to choose a good domain for each template, and in order to register the two depth surfaces. Methods in the second category are based directly on the face specific descriptors. We will study both approaches in this chapter.

9.1 Recognition by Depth Template Comparison

We will consider the simplest possible use of templates: we will compare the surfaces of two similar objects by first normalizing the position of both surfaces with respect to a small set of detectable common feature points, and then calculate the volume of the difference region between them. In the case of faces, we hope that the difference between two instances of the same face will be less than that between two different faces. One obvious shortcoming of this method is that it is not tolerant of elastic changes in the surface such as varying facial expression (one of the sources of variation we studied in the 2-D part of this book). For instance, large differences will be found between two face images if the mouth is open in one and closed in the other, even if the two images represent different views of the same person. To reduce these effects we can define regions of the face over which comparisons are most meaningful. For instance, the mouth and chin region are most highly affected by expression change, so we may not wish to consider differences in those regions. Similarly it is important that we be able to differentiate between skin regions and hair regions; not only is the data unreliable and noisy in the hair, but differences in hair style would contribute high values to the difference volume which would outweigh the more subtle but critical differences in the face itself. The following discussion will present the implementation of the feature extraction and template matching process, as well as the experimental results.

9.1.1 Normalization

Our aim is to define a transformation of the face to a normalized position which is consistent for an individual independent of view or expression. We use the location of the bridge of the nose, the base of the nose, and the inside corners of the eyes. The line connecting the two nose feature points is aligned with the vertical or y-axis (determines the rotation about the x- and z-axes), and the line determined by the two inside corners of the eyes is aligned parallel to the x-axis (determines rotation about y-axis). The nose bridge is positioned at a fixed translation along the z-axis from the origin. Figure 9.1 shows a caricature of this normalized view.

Once the transformation to the standard position is calculated, we transform each point on the valid face area of the surface to the new position. There will therefore be holes in the surface which correspond to the hair or other areas which were not included in the mask of points defining the relevant areas for comparison. After the surface mesh is transformed to the standard position, the sample points will be irregularly spaced in θ and y. This makes storage and comparison of the data difficult. The surface is therefore reinterpolated onto the regular cylindrical grid using a cylindrical ray-casting algorithm.

If we could be assured that the ordering of sample points on the grid would be maintained after the transformation, we could simply use bilinear interpolation to "shift" each sample point to the closest point on a new regular grid. However, folds or occlusion can cause the ordering of sample points to change during the transformation.

A more general method of reinterpolating the surface is to find the intersection between the surface and a ray extending parallel to the xz-plane at each regular sample point (θ, y) (see Figure 9.2). Ray-tracing can be very time consuming because it can involve testing each polygon in an object or scene for intersection with each ray. However, in the case of a surface mesh we can take advantage of the locality defined by the grid to limit the number of polygons we must test at each step.

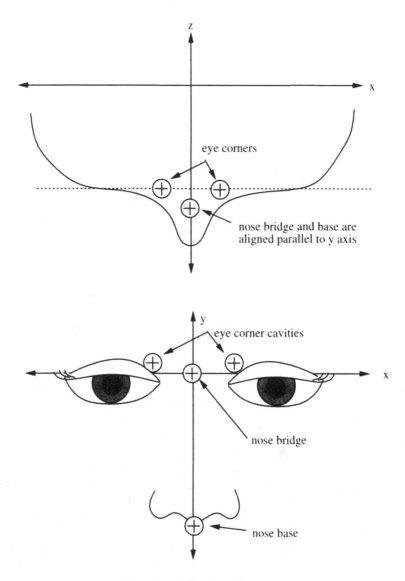

Figure 9.1. Face in normalized position

The most computationally expensive part of the ray-tracing process is the actual test for intersection between a given polygon and ray. This involves finding the plane containing the polygon, calculating the intersection of this plane and the ray, then testing that intersection point for inclusion in the polygon. We divide

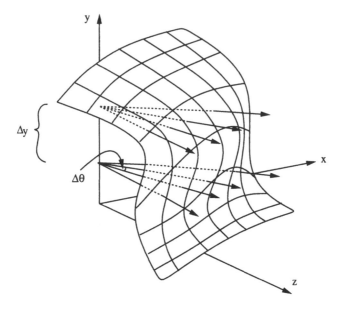

Figure 9.2. Resampling the transformed surface onto a regular cylindrical grid

the surface into triangles to guarantee that the polygon is indeed planar. Because this intersection test is an expensive process, it is wise to first use a few quick comparisons to test whether the ray actually falls within the extent of the polygon in (θ, y). For the large majority of the polygons in the mesh this test will be negative. To further improve the efficiency of the algorithm, we set up a hierarchy of bounds in (θ, y) for subparts of the grid. If the ray falls outside of the bounds of any subpart, none of the polygons contained in that subpart are considered further. Folding of the surface makes it possible that a ray will intersect the surface more than once. So all polygons within range must be tested. If there are multiple intersections, the one farthest from the y-axis is recorded as the surface intersection.

In our implementation, there are 3 levels in this hierarchy. The grid is first divided into a 3×3 grid (9 subparts); then within each ninth, the extents of each "column" in the grid are searched; then beneath that, the extents of each rectangle are considered. If the ray falls within the extents of a grid rectangle, the two triangles contained in that rectangle are tested for intersection. Typical grid sizes are 166×206, or 35,200 grid squares. So each of the nine subparts contains about 70 columns, and each column represents about 56 grid squares. The size of the reinterpolated surface is determined by the extents of the entire surface as transformed, and is thus dependent on the transformation. Typical sizes are 150×320 or less (for a maximum of 48000 rays to trace). However, often as much as a third to a half of the rays will not intersect the surface at all, either because of the holes in the surface or because of the distortion of the transformation itself. Maximum grid squares tested for intersection with any one ray in our experiments was 16; that implies 32 inclusion tests. However the average number of intersection tests for any ray which did intersect with the surface was 2, the minimum possible number.

9.1.2 Template Matching

We then compute the average volume of the space between the two normalized surfaces as a measure of their similarity; small values indicate a high degree of similarity. For two faces, a and b, this volume can be approximated by

$$\text{diff}(a,b) = \frac{1}{\#\text{valid } (\theta,y)} \sum_{\text{valid } (\theta,y)} |R_a^2(\theta,y) - R_b^2(\theta,y)| \qquad (9.1)$$

where $R_a(\theta,y)$ is radius at (θ,y) for surface a, and similarly for surface b. The mask specifying which points are to be considered part of the face is also mapped to the normalized position, and comparisons are only made in the intersection of the two valid regions. This criterion can be used to judge similarity between a test face and each face in a data base. The comparison yielding the smallest difference is identified as the best match to the test face.

9.1.3 Experimental Results

There are two stages involved in performing recognition experiments. First, each face in the data base must undergo feature classification. Then comparisons can be made between all faces for which feature detection was sufficient to allow the construction of the face area mask and normalization of the face to the standard position.

A training set which consisted of 26 individual faces was used to develop and tune the feature detection portion of the system. The faces included 8 women and 18 men; of this group no one wore eyeglasses or beards. The range of ages of the subjects was roughly from early 20's to late 50's. Little information was available about ethnic origin, but at least one subject in the training group was of Asian descent. Feature detection is rated *sufficient* if the verification conditions are satisfied for the outlines of eye and nose regions, the nose bridge and base, and the inside corner eye cavities. Alternatively, if the eye outlines are not successfully identified, they could be approximated if the outside eye corners are identified. So this condition also is considered sufficient. This sufficiency decision is automated

Figure 9.3. Sample of face region masks and difference image comparing two faces in normalized position

and does not guarantee that the feature recognition was accurate. Sufficient feature detection was achieved for 100% of the training set faces.

A *separate* test set was used in recognition experiments. The test set consisted of 8 faces with 3 views each for a total of 24 faces. For each face there are two versions without expression (that is with a neutral expression), and one with an expression. In this group there were 4 women and 4 men. Sufficient feature detection was achieved for 100% of these faces.

The 24 faces in the test set were then subjected to depth template matching. One view of each face was compared against the remaining 23 faces. The faces were ranked in order of increasing average difference. In 8 out of 8 cases, the first ranked image was another view of the same subject. For identification purposes we can consider this a 100% recognition rate. However, there are two faces in the data base matching the identity of each target subject, and in only 5 out of the 8 cases was the second ranked face another view of the target.

To be more specific about these results, let us formalize our recognition hypothesis. For this process to be successful, we would like the difference between two instances of the same face to be smaller than the difference between two faces of different subjects. If we have m subjects, and n instances of each subject, we can divide the total number of faces into two sets:

$$A = \{\alpha_1, \ldots, \alpha_n\} \tag{9.2}$$
$$B = \{\beta_1, \ldots, \beta_{(m-1)n}\} \tag{9.3}$$

Set A contains all instances of the individual, and set B contains all instances of the other subjects. Then we hypothesize that for $i \neq j$

$$\text{diff}(\alpha_i, \alpha_j) < \text{diff}(\alpha_i, \beta_k) \tag{9.4}$$

where $i, j < n$ and $k < (m - 1)n$. Testing how often this relationship holds in the ranking defined by any given target, gives us a more complete idea of the performance of the system. It takes into account how far off the ranking was if a recognition error occurs. For instance, if we are attempting to match two instances of the same face, and 10 faces of different subjects are ranked higher than the other instance of the target face, this will count as 10 incorrect comparisons. For any given target there are $n - 1$ distinct values of $\text{diff}(\alpha_i, \alpha_j)$, which we need to compare relative to $n(m-1)$ values of $\text{diff}(\alpha_i, \beta_k)$. Thus in any experiment there will be $(\# \text{ targets})(n - 1)(m - 1)n$ total comparisons to evaluate with respect to the hypothesis; or in our case, where we used 8 targets and $m = 8$ and $n = 3$, this total comes to 336. We found that in 11 cases out of 336 the hypothesis was not satisfied. So 97% of the comparisons were correct.

Errors in recognition come primarily from two sources. The first source of error is in the extraction of features used for registration of the face surfaces. The second source of error is the comparison between two faces in the area of the neck. Articulation of the head with respect to the neck can cause a large range of depth values over the neck for any given subject in normalized position. This region should be formally eliminated from the comparison process. We are implementing the extraction of a jawline feature, based on the location of the ridge line in the surface which corresponds to the chin; this feature would be useful in the segmentation of the neck.

9.2 Scalar Features from 3-D Data

The second approach to recognition which we will examine is comparison between faces based solely on a set of scalar features calculated from depth and curvature data. The set of features associated with each face can be considered as a vector in feature space. Recognition is reduced to the problem of relating or grouping points within this space on the basis of some similarity measure. This method is practical for large data base applications because comparisons are made on the basis of a small number of feature measures. As a result, less memory is required for storage and comparison is computationally very simple. However, it is more sensitive than the depth template method to the accuracy of the feature detection process. There are strong similarities between this work and Kanade's experiments in face recognition, although the feature calculation is obviously different because we begin with range data instead of intensity data (see Kanade 77).

The most basic set of scalar features describing the face corresponds to measurements of the face. It is straightforward based on the features we developed in Chapter 8 to calculate:

1. left eye width
2. right eye width
3. eye separation
4. total width (span) of eyes
5. nose height
6. nose width
7. nose depth

It is important to note that these measurements will be on an absolute scale (mm), not on a relative scale (pixels). Thus we are not restricted to using ratios of distances as in the case of measurements calculated from intensity images.

The eye measurements are made based on the point features marking inside and outside corner cavities of the eyes. The width of each eye is the difference between the 3-D coordinates of its corners. Similarly, the separation of the eyes is the distance between the two inside corners, and the total width of the eyes is the distance between the two outside corners.

The nose height is the vertical length of the nose and is defined by the distance measured between the bridge and base of the nose. Nose width is the horizontal extent of the nose at the base. It is defined as the distance measured at the symmetrical points with greatest separation in the bottom portion of the nose region outline. The nose depth is a little less straightforward. We first define the tip of the nose as the point with maximal depth in the nose region. Then we measure perpendicular distance between the tip and the line defined by the nose bridge and base.

In addition to the features based on measurement of distance, we also define a set of features which describe the nose ridge and are based on measurement of curvature. They are:

8. maximum Gaussian curvature on the ridge line
9. average minimum curvature $\kappa_{min} = \kappa_2$ on the ridge above the tip of the nose
10. Gaussian curvature at the bridge
11. Gaussian curvature at the base

The calculation of these features is self-explanatory. The maximum Gaussian curvature will occur approximately at the tip of the nose, and provides some description of local shape at that point. The average minimum curvature between the bridge and the tip of the nose is meant to provide a simple measure of the curvature along the ridge. It should describe the spectrum between a "ski slope" nose at the low end, and a "Roman nose" at the high end. Gaussian curvature at the bridge and base of the nose describe the local surface at those points.

9.2.1 Head Width

Ideally, head width should be measured between symmetrical points at the flat portions of the face near the temples or base of the ears. These points are rarely affected by movements of the face, and have a good correspondence with the width of the skull. However, it is difficult to ensure that a particular part of the face, say the temples, will not be obscured by hair in a given depth image. So our approach is to instead look for the maximum width measured at smooth, symmetrical surface points, whose surface normals are perpendicular to the symmetry plane.

More specifically, we again evaluate the points on the face surface by constrained search. The first constraint is that the measurements must be taken over smooth skin, as opposed to hair. We use the same criterion as was used in the determination of the face boundary ($\kappa_{max}^2 + \kappa_{min}^2 <$ thresh, as in Section 8.4) to construct a mask of smooth regions of the surface. However, in this case, we use a lower threshold, corresponding to a more severe smoothness constraint. This smoothness constraint will increase the stability of the calculation of surface normals.

The second constraint is that the measurements be taken at points whose surface normals are approximately perpendicular to the symmetry plane. In fact, we are primarily interested in the components of the surface normals in the plane which slices the face horizontally; so before evaluating the angle of the normal with the symmetry plane, we project the surface normals onto the plane defined by the normal to the symmetry plane and the frontal normal of the face. In the current implementation, we make an assumption about head position which makes this determination trivial. The majority of the time, subjects in our data base were positioned such that the xz-plane was approximately parallel to both the frontal normal of the face and the perpendicular to the symmetry plane. Thus, we can find the angle between the projected normal and the symmetry plane directly from x and z components of the normal (see Figure 9.4). The determination of the frontal normal of the face in this procedure is not very sensitive; the head width calculation resulting from a range of frontal normals will be very close. This is borne out by a very good repeatability of head width within subjects in our experiments.

In addition to the requirements that measurements are made over smooth parts of the surface and at points whose surface normals are approximately perpendicular to the symmetry plane, we also require that measurements are made at symmetrical points. Of all measurements taken satisfying these constraints, we record maximum distance as the head width.

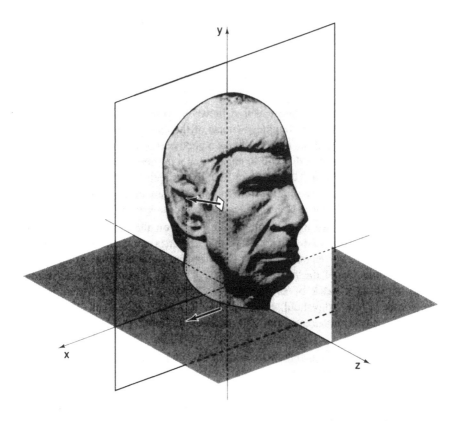

Figure 9.4. Measuring relationship between surface normals and symmetry plane

An example of this process is shown in Figure 9.5. The first image (a) shows the regions of the data satisfying the smoothness constraint. The next image (b) shows the points for which the angle of the projected surface normal is roughly perpendicular to the symmetry plane. The grey and black points in (c) are points which satisfy both of the first two criteria; the subset marked in black also satisfies the symmetry constraint. The line in (c) connects the points at which maximum 3-D distance is found.

9.3   The Algorithm

The vector formed by the set of descriptor values for a given face places the face in the space of all possible faces. To use this representation as an effective basis for recognition, we require that the all the points in feature space which correspond to the same person will cluster with regard to some similarity measure.

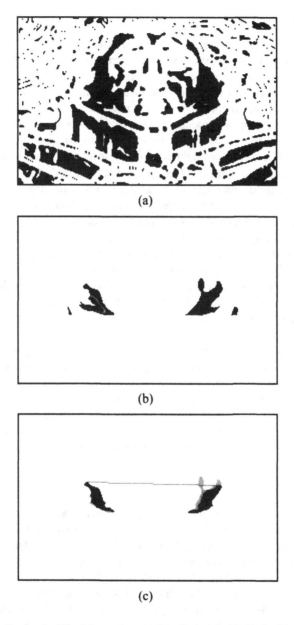

(a)

(b)

(c)

Figure 9.5. Finding head width: (a) smooth parts of surface marked in black; (b) points for which surface normal was roughly perpendicular to the symmetry plane; and (c) grey and black points are intersection of points in (a) and (b), black points also satisfy symmetry pairing. Maximum head width between symmetrical points was found at points connected by line.

9.3.1   Cluster Analysis

A common similarity measure in such classification problems is the distance between samples. If the feature space was sufficiently partitioned such that the points
corresponding to each subject were close to each other, and at a large distance from
other such clusters, classification of best match on the basis of distance would be
an effective criterion. If the distance of a new face were within some distance
limit from a member of a particular cluster, the new face could be considered to
belong to that cluster. If the sample point was not close enough to any existing
cluster, it could be considered unknown with respect to the current data base.

Several critical issues are involved in this analysis: let's first discuss the distance metric in the feature space. A common choice of distance metric is the
Euclidean metric. The Euclidean space is isotropic, however; in most applications, there is no particular reason to expect that the values of one feature would
scale in a similar way as another. If one feature happened to have larger numerical
values than the others it could dominate all distances measured with the Euclidean
metric. If the feature values are assumed to have a normal distribution about the
mean, it is reasonable to scale their values such that across all faces the feature has
zero mean and unit variance. This normalization makes the comparison process
less sensitive to numerical range (in our case choice of measurement scale) of
each feature.

There is prolific literature on statistical methods for clustering analysis (a good
introduction is found in Duda and Hart (73)), which includes a much more thor-
ough examination of similarity measures and cluster segmentation. For the purposes of this investigation, however, Euclidean distance measure in scaled feature
space will be used. The small size of our data base of faces makes it difficult to
adequately evaluate the statistics of feature values. We consider this analysis as a
feasibility study which will provide a good baseline for future work.

9.3.2   System Implementation

As discussed above, after the feature values are calculated for each face we calculate mean and standard deviation for each feature over all faces. Each feature value
is then normalized by subtracting its mean and dividing by its standard deviation.

For a given target face we can then compute the distance between the target's
point in feature space and the other points in the data base. The closest point will
be considered the best match for the target. At this stage we do not address the
possibility of classifying the target as unknown, but simply evaluate the correctness
of the ordered ranking of distances among faces.

A special case we need to address is the problem of missing feature values.
For instance, in the process of detecting the outline of the nose region, an error
is signaled if the region was not completely enclosed. When this error occurs,

no nose outline is recorded. Since the nose width feature depends on the nose
outline, no value of nose width can be calculated in this case. Since quite a bit
of information is contained in the descriptors which were calculated successfully
for such a face, we would still like to be able to compare the incomplete vector
with other points in the data base.

There are several ways we can treat the missing data. We examined three
methods in the following experiments. One is to replace a missing feature with
its mean value across all subjects. This method will tend on average to create
artificially large distances between two data sets from the same face. A second
approach is to consider only components with valid values in both vectors. If
there are n features and k are valid in a given comparison, this means we compute distance in k dimensions instead of n dimensions. This method will cause all
points with incomplete data to be artificially close in comparison with distances
calculated over the full n dimensions. The smaller relative differences will tend
on average to cause "false positives", or matches which look more similar than
they actually are. Another method is to assume that in the comparison of any two
face vectors the differences between individual components will be similar. That
is, we might expect that for different images of the same individual, the component differences would be smaller in general than they would be in comparisons
between unrelated faces. Using this assumption when we compute distance, we
can substitute the average squared component distance over the two vectors in
place of the squared component difference which cannot be calculated because
of incomplete data. This last method seems to offer a compromise between the
first two methods discussed. However, it is not ideal. The component differences
between some vectors will include values which are much larger than average
due to error or distinctive features. If the unknown information describes such
a distinctive feature, substituting an average component difference may lead to
errors in recognition.

All these observations are general, and clearly the effect of missing data will
depend on the feature types involved and the sensitivity of the system in terms of
cluster separation. We should also note that unknown feature values will have the
strongest effect in comparisons based on a small feature set; the larger the feature
set the less effect each feature has in distinguishing among faces. We discuss
these points again in the context of our particular experimental results.

9.4 Experimental Results

Our experimental evaluation of this recognition system uses the same test set of 24
faces discussed in the previous chapter; this includes 8 different subjects, with 3
instances of each. We compute feature vectors for each face, and then compute the
distance between every vector in the feature space. These distances are stored in a
24×24 (symmetric) matrix. To find the best matches for a given target, we sort the

entries in the row of the matrix corresponding to the target by order of increasing distance. Except for the column corresponding to the target itself, which should always have distance 0, the column with the smallest distance corresponds to the best match for the target. Our results are divided into two sections; first is the evaluation of the individual feature descriptors, and second is the evaluation of the recognition system itself.

9.4.1 Evaluating Features

For features to be useful in automatic face recognition, they must ideally satisfy two criteria. First they must be robustly detectable; their measurement must be consistent for the same face over reasonable variations in view position, expression, age, weight, etc. Second, their values must vary distinctly over the range of different individuals. We present a statistical evaluation of our features with respect to both these factors, repeatability and distinctiveness.

Since our data base is relatively small, however, statistical evaluation may not be an accurate characterization of the results in all cases. So we first present for reference the actual data on feature values measured for the faces in our data base. In Figures 9.6, 9.7, 9.8, and 9.9, we show normalized feature values for each of the 12 features discussed in the previous section. In each graph the vertical axis groups the values by subject, and the horizontal axis is the range of values for each feature (zero mean, unit variance). These plots demonstrate graphically how feature values vary for the same face, and among faces. Our comments and statistics in the following paragraphs will be based on this data, and in some cases also on the results of feature detection for the training data base of faces which includes another 25 faces (one view of each subject).

9.4.1.1 REPEATABILITY Two issues are often confounded when considering robustness of feature detection. Variation in a feature value from image to image can occur either because of a change in the underlying physical feature properties, or because of error in the feature detection process. We will look at both issues. We use three images of each subject; two images have very similar facial expressions but vary in "view" or initial position in the scanner, whereas the third shows a different distinct facial expression. In our experiments, the underlying features can change only because of expression, since the data was taken over a short period of time. Variation in feature values across the same subject will be due either to expression change or uncertainty in feature detection, or both. To minimize the first effect, we have selected features which do not vary much with respect to facial expression. For instance, measurements of the mouth are not included.

Table 9.1 shows statistics of the range of feature values measured for the same subject. For each feature, we calculated the maximum range in that feature value for each of the 8 subjects. From among these 8 range values, we list the minimum

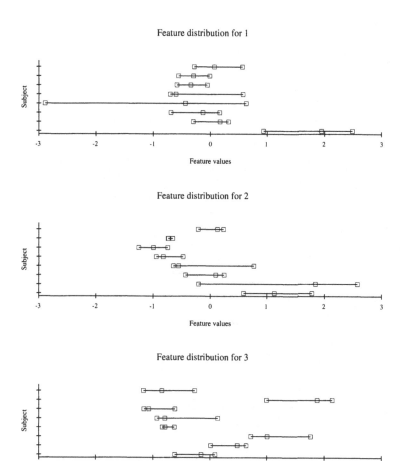

Figure 9.6. Feature values grouped by subject for feature (1) left eye width, (2) right eye width, and (3) eye separation

variation, the maximum variation, the average variation, and the median variation. Examination of the raw data indicates that the median variation statistic is the most representative of the repeatability we can expect from the feature extraction; the maximum within subject variation is often quite high, but this is due to specific problems in one or two individual measurements. We will discuss several of these problem cases below. Over all, however, the median variation within subject ranged from about 1.5 mm to 3 mm, which corresponds to the distance between

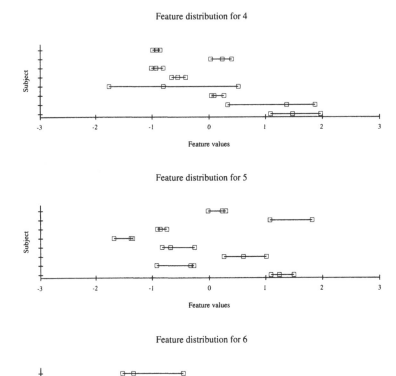

Figure 9.7. Feature values grouped by subject for feature (4) total eye span, (5) nose height, and (6) nose width

1 or 2 grid lines on the surface. Since all of these scalar feature measurements are made between feature points on the surface grid, this correspondence indicates positioning error of $\pm.5 - 1$ pixels. Thus, the feature extraction seems limited primarily by the resolution of the range data. To improve the accuracy, we must consider algorithms with subpixel precision, or use higher resolution data.

The isolated cases with unusually wide variation, within subject are caused either by explicit error in feature detection, or by variation due to expression.

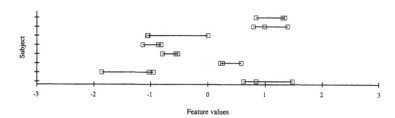

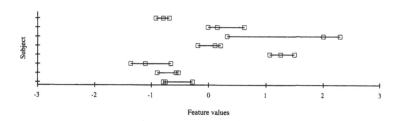

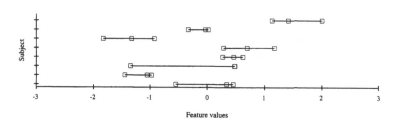

Figure 9.8. Feature values grouped by subject for feature (7) nose depth, (8) maximum Gaussian curvature on nose ridge, and (9) average minimum curvature on the nose ridge

Let us consider several of these specific cases. First, there is a case of feature detection error which causes problems in several measurements of eye width and eye span. The error is directly attributable to improper detection of the outside corner cavities of the eyes. Error in the measurement of one feature point can be responsible for errors in left and right eye width and eye span. An intuitive definition of the outside corner of the eye is the point where the upper and lower eyelids come together. The point we find as the outside corner cavity is just

Feature distribution for 10

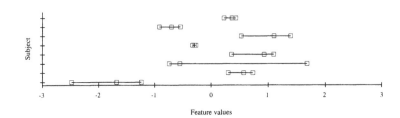

Feature distribution for 11

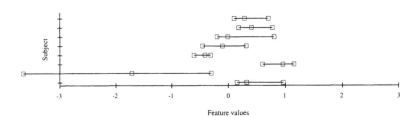

Feature distribution for 12

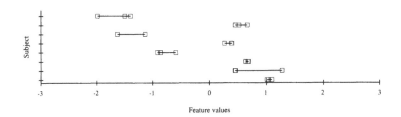

Figure 9.9. Feature values grouped by subject for feature (10) Gaussian curvature at the bridge of the nose, (11) Gaussian curvature at the base of the nose, and (12) head width

outside (away from the center of the face) this junction of the eyelids. It is a much shallower cavity than the inside corner cavity, and is determined in part by the folds of skin leading up to the eyelids. Because of these factors, there is more uncertainty associated with this feature. In 2 out of 49 total cases in our data base, one or both of these cavities were not present. In a few other cases, one of the cavities was mislocated (Figure 9.10 shows the particular case which caused the farthest outlier in the first graph of Figure 9.6). Another way to calculate the

Feature	min. variation	max. variation	ave. variation	median variation
Left eye width	2.03	13.41	4.64	2.79
Right eye width	0.38	12.67	4.31	2.69
Eye separation	0.53	2.87	1.95	2.43
Eye span	0.86	14.69	4.75	1.98
Nose height	0.64	2.95	1.92	2.38
Nose width	1.10	3.70	2.32	2.72
Nose depth	0.68	2.72	1.56	1.41
Head width	0.68	11.18	4.59	5.53

Table 9.1. Variation of measured feature values within subject: statistics over 8 subjects. Values given in mm

location of this feature is to use the extreme corner of the eye socket region, which often corresponds closely to the location of the outside corner cavity even though it is calculated independently. In cases where the two features did not correspond, the eye region feature may actually be the more accurate of the two.

There are two cases where expression played a part in wide feature variation. The anomalous point in the graph of Gaussian curvature at the base of the nose (Figure 9.9, feature (11)) is due to an exaggerated pouting expression present in one view of the subject. It is also interesting to note that this subject has a moustache, which makes the curvature measurements in the two neutral expression images lower than average, and less reliable because of rougher surface over the moustache. This feature also shows relatively high change for subjects with a wide smile. These properties are not very desirable for recognition. There is also an anomalous point in the graph for maximum Gaussian curvature on the nose

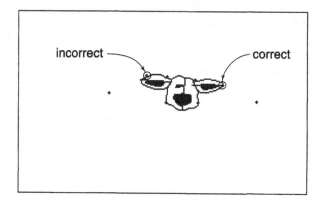

Figure 9.10. Example of error in location of outside corner cavity of eye

(Figure 9.8, feature 8). This point is a measurement made for a subject with a broad smile. However, there are other images in the data base with large smiles for which this measurement is not affected so extremely.

9.4.1.2 DISCRIMINATION   How valuable a feature is when discriminating among subjects, is a function both of repeatability within subject and variation between subjects. We can evaluate this property numerically for our particular data base by using a multiple class version of Fisher's linear discriminant criterion (Duda and Hart 73). This criterion evaluates the discriminating power of a given feature Φ by considering the ratio of between-class variance to within-class variance. We can express this ratio as

$$\frac{\sum\limits_{i=1}^{c} (m_i - m)^2}{\sum\limits_{i=1}^{c} \frac{1}{n_i} \sum\limits_{x \in \Phi_i} (x - m_i)^2}$$

where c is the number of classes (in this case subjects), Φ_i is the set of feature values for class i, n_i is the size of Φ_i, m_i is the mean of Φ_i, and m is the total mean of the feature over all classes. Higher values of this criterion indicate better discriminating power. This is consistent with the intuition that it is desirable for features to be highly repeatable for the same subject (small within class variance) and widely separated for different subjects (large between class variance). Table 9.2 shows the features we have discussed so far, organized from best discrimination to worst. We must note that the usefulness of a feature in discrimination is by nature a function of the particular data base considered.

There is quite a range in the discrimination power of our features. The left and right eye width and the Gaussian curvature at the nose base (features (1), (2), and (11)) showed the poorest performance with respect to this criterion. Examining the raw data for these features, we find that, indeed, the range of values in all subjects for these features is relatively similar, making these features of little use in recognition. We can conclude, based on our earlier observations on repeatability, that the variation in eye width between these subjects is less than the resolution of our measurements. For the case of feature (11), it seems that variation due to expression may be greater than the typical variation within subject. This implies that this feature is also not useful in recognition.

For the reasons discussed above, we do not consider the features measuring eye width or Gaussian curvature at the base of the nose in our recognition experiments.

9.4.2 Evaluating the Comparison Method

As in the previous chapter, we can evaluate the results of this ranking either in terms of raw recognition rates, or by testing how many of the individual relation-

Feature	between/within cluster variance
Head width	24.9
Nose height	16.6
Nose depth	9.6
Nose width	9.2
Eye separation	6.6
K max. on nose ridge	6.2
Ave κ_{min} on nose ridge	4.4
Eye span	4.2
K at nose bridge	3.3
Right eye width	2.4
K at nose base	2.1
Left eye width	1.3

Table 9.2. Ratio of between-cluster variance to within-cluster variance for each feature. Ordered from best discrimination between subjects to worst

ships in each target's similarity ranking satisfy the recognition hypothesis. This hypothesis predicts that instances of the same face should be more similar (closer in feature space) than instances of different faces. For this system we use each member of the test set as a target instead of only one instance of each subject. For the evaluation of ranking, since we have 24 targets instead of 8, the total number of comparisons (recalling the recognition hypothesis, equation (9.4)) in the experiment is 1008.

The comparison process is obviously sensitive to which features we choose initially to represent the face, since this defines the feature space. As we have shown above, there is wide variation in the discriminating power of our features. We tested four different sets of features. The basic set, denoted (I), includes the top 4 features in Table 9.2: head width, nose height, nose depth, and nose width. The other three sets include increasing numbers of features added in order of discriminating power: (II) includes the basic set plus eye separation and maximum Gaussian curvature on nose ridge; (III) includes features from set (II) plus average minimum curvature $\kappa_{min} = \kappa_2$ on the nose ridge and eye span; and (IV) includes features from set (III) plus Gaussian curvature at the nose bridge. We also tested the three different methods discussed for treatment of unknown data: (A) substitution of mean feature value; (B) distance calculated on the basis of valid features only (variable dimensions used at different entries in the distance matrix); and (C) substitution of average component difference in comparison. These results are shown in Table 9.3 in terms of recognition rates, and in Table 9.4 in terms of total number of correct comparisons over the whole ranking.

Feature set	Treatment of unknown data		
considered	A	B	C
I	70.8	66.7	70.8
	54.2	79.2	75.0
II	79.2	91.7	91.7
	75.0	83.3	83.3
III	95.8	100	100
	79.2	79.2	79.2
IV	95.8	95.8	95.8
	83.3	79.2	79.2

Table 9.3. Results in terms of raw recognition rates; each entry gives rates for correct identity of closest match, and correct identity of second-closest match (percentage correct out of 24 targets).

These results show certain trends. Performance improved with additional features (I, II, III) until the discrimination power of the new feature (IV) was too low to contribute positively to recognition. It is interesting to note that in the case of feature set IV, that the performance actually decreased. As is the case in each of the three features at the low end of the discrimination rating, the feature values are all very similar, *except for the cases with large feature detection error, or variation due to expression.* Thus, the only discrimination of the new feature is on the basis other than identity. Our results also show that in all cases using the mean feature value to replace unknown data, (A) showed poorer performance than the other test conditions related to unknown data (B, C).

The raw recognition results were qualitatively fairly similar over several sets of test conditions, including categories (II), (III), (IV), and (B), (C). There were only one or two identification errors out of 24 cases based on the closest match condition. This clearly indicates that clustering with respect to the Euclidean

Feature set	Treatment of unknown data		
considered	A	B	C
I	92.8	95.9	96.1
II	96.3	98.1	98.1
III	97.4	99.4	99.4
IV	97.1	98.2	98.2

Table 9.4. Results in terms of percentage of total correct comparisons in matching each of the 24 separate targets against remaining data base of 23 faces. Calculated based on a total of 1008 possible comparisons

distance measure is occurring. However, there were more errors in identifying the second instance of the target face in the data base. Under these conditions, the second-closest match was correct in 19 or 20 cases out of 24. This is indicative that the clusters are not completely separated in any of the different feature spaces with this similarity measure. We should also note that these results are comparable, and in most cases a little better, than the results of the depth template based system in the previous chapter.

The evaluation of the relative ranking of the data base with respect to each target gives us a better picture of performance. The best performance of the system, which occurs in cases (III)/(B) and (III)/(C), gave only 6 ordering errors out of 1008 comparisons in the ranking. Even though recognition results are fairly similar in the various test conditions, we can see that under some of the conditions the correct matches are closer to the top of the ranking – which means the clustering is better. As mentioned before, however, the distances between unrelated faces is still very similar to the distances between related faces, so there is not a distinct separation between the clusters. As we might expect, the two subjects for which the ranking errors occurred most often were subjects which had especially wide variation (due either to error or expression) in one or more of their feature values.

How we choose to treat missing feature values has an effect on the performance of the system. The use of mean feature values in these cases is not a good choice. For the smallest feature set, method (C) showed a small advantage over method (B). There was no difference in performance between methods (B) and (C) with any of the larger feature sets. This may either be because the assumption of similar component differences holds better with a larger feature base, or because the larger feature base makes the treatment of unknown data less critical in recognition.

One further test we performed is to add the 25 faces from our training set to our data base to see how it affects our results. We use feature set (III) and the same set of targets as in previous experiments. We evaluate the relative ranking of the full data base (48 faces) with respect to all the targets and find that 98.6% of the rank comparisons were correct. Recognition rates showed 22/24 (91.7%) correct identifications in the closest match, and 20/24 (83.3%) in the case of second-closest match. Although the performance was not quite as good as in the smaller set test case, the results were not seriously affected by the addition of the 25 unrelated faces.

As long as the features illustrate some distinction among subjects, we would expect that using more features should increase the performance of the system. This trend is already noticeable in our experiments, as long as the features are above some threshold in the discrimination rating. We can predict continued improvement for larger feature sets. Another improvement concerns clustering: there are many more statistically robust clustering methods which should produce better segmentation. Among other issues, we have assumed that our features were independent. This is not true in general. For instance, error in detection of eye corner points caused correlated error in at least two measurements used in our feature set. The covariance of the features warrants further examination. Also, the choice of which combination of features is most useful in distinguishing among faces is clearly important in the performance of the system. We offered intuitive observations on this issue based on separation among faces in the individual feature values, and known error in the feature detection process. However, there are more formal methods to establish a relative weighting of the features which can be found in the statistical literature (e.g., Breiman et al. 84).

9.4.3 Comments

This chapter has shown the possibility of computing geometric descriptors provided *range data* is supplied, and that these descriptors convey much visual information which can be used for face recognition. But what are the prospects for obtaining this type of information from *intensity images*? It has been known for some time (Koenderink and van Doorn 80, Yuille 89) that there are direct relationships between some of these geometric descriptors and intensity images (assuming Lambertian reflectance models). The analyses in these papers, however, were purely theoretical. More recently, work by Haddon and Forsyth (98) on finding folds and grooves suggests that it may indeed be possible to extract certain geometric features from intensity images. If multiple intensity images are available, there are many approaches to estimating the 3-D structure. The classic method if multiple views with varying geometry are available is to match visible surface points between two views and use trigonometry – so-called stereographic reconstruction of 3-D structure. Alternately, we discussed in Section 3.5 computing 3-D structure from multiple intensity images with varying illumination and fixed geometry. Using any of these methods in combination with a 3-D recognition scheme has not yet been carefully investigated.

Chapter 10

What's Next?

The state of face recognition has advanced greatly in the last ten years. There has also been an explosion of papers on these topics, but often with considerable overlap and re-invention of techniques. Much of this work has been motivated by short-term goals and the myriad of exciting possibilities for building systems for such tasks as identification, human computer interaction, and even reconstruction of the faces of burn victims. In contrast, we have emphasized the importance of basic research and the mathematical challenges involved in putting many of these theories on a firm footing. Our belief is that the analysis of how and why ad hoc algorithms work is an essential step to building more complex and more successful systems.

We have attempted to isolate some of the basic problems that need to be solved and, we hope, pointed the way toward further progress. In particular, we have emphasized the pattern-theoretic approach of analysis by synthesis and the importance of modeling geometrical changes and illumination effects. We hope that this book encourages further work on the development of stochastic models of shapes and images. In this chapter, we give a very brief sketch of some of the directions in which we hope research will be fruitful and where we think exciting models may be found. We divide this into issues relating to modeling the 2D image and to issues involving modeling shape.

10.1 Modeling the 2D Image

The intensity model, based on superposition of faces lit from a single light source, seems to us to be in fairly good shape. It would certainly be useful to extract from data a better model of common lighting conditions, i.e., a prior on the shading coefficients. This might include the fact that there is usually a large extended light source overhead (either from the sky or from light reflected off the ceiling) that would greatly assist in finding faces in cluttered scenes.

The deformation model is much more ad hoc.   We considered a 'generic' elasticity-based model and some simple experiments with principal components to refine this model. Clearly these models and experiments can be extended. Here are some ideas for doing this:

1. Elasticity models with a non-homogeneous strain-energy tensor $e(J, \vec{x})$ depending on $\vec{x}$ and not satisfying the isotropy assumption $e(JR, \vec{x}) = e(J, \vec{x})$ should be able to do a much better job of modeling the deformations of the face. For example, the eyes should be allowed to move easily toward and away from the nose bridge but should move as a relatively rigid unit: this can be achieved by a suitable e.

2. The approximate bilateral symmetry of the face is a global constraint that is not modeled by local approaches such as the use of strain-energy. This is rather a grammatical constraint, like the agreement in number between the subject and the verb in a sentence, and could be incorporated using a context-sensitive grammar of the type discussed in the next section.

3. Deformation models should have separate terms for warpings caused by expression change and by differences between individuals. We should factor the warping ϕ into subwarps created by expressions and by individuals. There have recently been several starts at modeling standard expressions (driven by applications to animation).

4. In our work above, we considered turning the head as yet another occurrence in the world leading to warping of visual images. The advantage of this approach (as opposed to using a full 3D model) is that it leads to a model dealing directly with the nature of the visual signal and not with a huge number of estimated hidden variables describing the 3D shape. If the face were planar, this would work very well: pose changes would simply cause affine warps of the facial image. The largest divergence from planarity is, of course, the nose. Models could perhaps use the nose, especially its divergence from symmetry and its shadows to estimate pose and thus incorporate systematic corrections.

5. In the theory of stereo vision and of motion tracking, warpings are used to match up two or more views of a single scene, either from two viewpoints or at multiple times. In these cases, it has proved very important to label unmatched pixels explicitly and to use warpings that are not necessarily diffeomorphisms but might be "diffeomorphisms with tears" (where one image is ripped open and extra pixels are added or pixels are discarded before matching). These unmatched pixels are surface points that are visible in one image but not in another due to occlusion by a foreground

object. Psychophysics has shown that our perception is exquisitely sensitive to them. The same philosophy should be used in matching a face to a template. When the pose is not purely frontal, there will be pixels in the template that disappear in the observed image, and vice versa. Identifying these is another route to determining pose.

We believe that all these aspects can and must be modeled stochastically in order to have a complete and sound theory of 2D facial images that can match human performance in recognition tasks.

10.2 Stochastic Models for Shape

By a stochastic model for shape, we mean putting a probability measure on the infinite-dimensional space of objects $S \subset \mathbf{R}^n$, where S is something reasonably nice like the closure of an open set with piecewise smooth boundary. This is related to the problem we have studied of creating stochastic models for warpings, i.e., putting probability measures on the infinite-dimensional space of diffeomorphisms from some domain to itself (or some variant of this). For instance, we can define a mapping from the space of diffeomorphisms ϕ to the space of shapes S by mapping ϕ to $S = \phi(D)$, D being the unit ball in n-space. Then a probability measure on the space of ϕ's defines one on the space of S's, namely its direct image. However, putting the emphasis on the shape leads one in different directions. For instance, one can look at the differential geometric properties of the boundary ∂S of S and use these to define the probability of the shape S. This would be a natural development of the theory of 3D facial geometry presented in the last four chapters. Another approach is to imagine the most compact codes for some types of shapes that one often encounters (like alpha-numeric characters or the silhouettes of animals) and define the probability by $p(S) = 2^{-\text{codelength}(S)}$.

It is only in two dimensions, i.e., $S \subset \mathbf{R}^2$, that stochastic theories of shape have been worked on to date. But the three-dimensional case is the one needed to transform the theory presented in the last four chapters into a part of pattern theory. In this section, we will sketch some of this work in the 2D case and then outline some of the problems in making this into a 3D theory.

10.2.1 Two-dimensional shape

We believe it is natural to build a stochastic theory of shape in three stages. These stages seem very natural if we think of the coding perspective and pass to the equivalent problem of encoding a shape in the smallest possible number of bits. Then the first stage encodes the shape through its boundary, which is constructed in terms of its curvature. The second stage uses the interior of the shape and encodes a) ribbon-like pieces of the shape as matched pairs of curves on the two sides of the ribbon and b) crudely circular pieces of the shape via a big circle. This is done via constructions such as the medial axis. The third stage brings in the whole language of grammars and encodes the shape by a parse tree of parts.

10.2.1.1 MODELS BASED ON THE CURVATURE OF THE BOUNDARY ∂S OF S The basic idea goes by the name of 'snakes' (Kass, Witkin and Terzopoulos, 87) and considers this boundary as a parametrized curve, i.e., the image of a map $\phi : [0, 1] \to \mathbf{R}^2$, which is assumed 1:1 and, for the case of closed curves, periodic. One assigns to such a curve the energy

$$E(\phi) = \int_0^1 c_1 \parallel \dot{\phi}(t) \parallel^2 + c_2 \parallel \ddot{\phi}(t) \parallel^2 dt.$$

One can then define a probability measure of the space of ϕ's by $p(\phi) = \frac{1}{Z} e^{-E(\phi)}$. This makes sense in the case where ϕ is approximated by a finite set of samples and the space becomes finite-dimensional. It is not hard to make a rigorous mathematical version for arbitrary ϕ using the theory of stochastic differential equations (Hoel, Port and Stone 71). For models of the boundary of the shape without any parameterization, one can consider instead the energy functional of $C = \partial S$ first studied by Euler:

$$E(C) = \int_C \kappa(p)^2 ds(p),$$

where p is a point of C, s is arclength and $\kappa(p)$ denotes the curvature of C at p. The stochastic version of this was studied in (Mumford 93). To reproduce empirical shapes even better, (Zhu 99a) introduced energies such as:

$$E(C) = \int_C (\psi(\kappa(p)) + \dot{\kappa}(p))^2 ds(p),$$

where an unknown function ψ is learnt from training data. More precisely, ψ is chosen so that, when random curves are sampled from this model, their curvatures will have the same histogram as those in a database of true contours, see Figure 10.1.

10.2.1.2 USING THE INTERIOR OF THE SHAPE   The basic idea is to describe the full shape S by its medial axis Γ_S and the distance function $r_S : \Gamma_S \to \mathbf{R}_+$ from the axis to the boundary of S. We then seek to put a probability measure on the set of pairs (Γ, r) that come from shapes S. This approach has also been studied by Zhu (99a,b). The big difference with the previous approach is that it introduces explicit hidden variables given by the axis for generating protrusions and ribbon-like structures in the shape: one part of the contour has knowledge

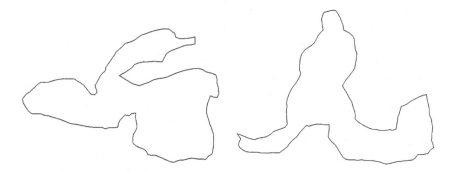

Figure 10.1. Sample contours generated by the theory of Zhu (99a) where the model is learned from training data. (Figure courtesy of S.C. Zhu.)

of other nearby parts and on opposite sides of the contour (with respect to the symmetry axis). The resulting models therefore are much better at describing and generating shapes with limb-like protrusions, see Figure 10.2 for details, we refer the reader to the papers of Zhu (99a,b).

10.2.1.3 A PARSE TREE OF PARTS The basic idea is to make explicit the decomposition of a shape into parts and of its parts into subparts, etc. These parts make up a parse tree, as discussed in Section 1.2. This approach is under active development by S. Geman and his co-workers (Bienenstock, Geman, and Potter 1997, Potter 1998). They choose the domain of alpha-numeric characters on which

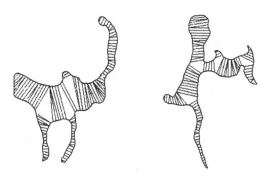

Figure 10.2. Regions generated by Zhu's theory (99a,b) where there is a hidden variable representing the symmetry axis, which induces couplings, illustrated by straight lines, between points on opposite sides of the contour. (Figure courtesy of S.C. Zhu.)

to test their theory because such shapes naturally break up into various types of strokes. The biggest difficulty is that, although this leads clearly to a grammar, the grammar is not context-free. For example, the letter 'N' is made up of three strokes, but the first and third strokes must be roughly parallel. This is a non-local dependency that creates context-sensitivity in the grammatical rules. There are ways around this, e.g., by augmenting the set of symbols in the grammar with all sorts of properties, but this seems to explode in your face when dealing with the complexities of shapes. Only for context-free grammars is there a well-developed stochastic theory (Booth and Thompson 1973).

Geman, et al., have introduced a new class of probability measures, which they call compositional probabilities, that arise very naturally from the code-length perspective. Their basic definition is this: assume that the parse tree has labels, and consider a node of a parse tree with label ℓ and subtrees $\alpha_1, \cdots, \alpha_n$ below it. They denote the subtree with root ℓ as $< \ell, \alpha_1, \cdots, \alpha_n >$. Their basic assumption is that how well the constituents satisfy the constraints (such as line endpoints matching up, lines being parallel or perpendicular, etc.) is computable from a 'binding function' $B_\ell(\alpha_1, \cdots, \alpha_n) \in S_\ell$ and that there is a function $f : S_\ell \to \mathbf{R}$ such that

$$\mathrm{Prob}(< \ell, \alpha_1, \cdots, \alpha_n >) = f_\ell(\alpha_1, \cdots, \alpha_n) \prod_i \mathrm{Prob}(\alpha_i).$$

The context-free case is simply the special case where f_ℓ is a function only of the labels of the roots of the trees $\alpha_1, \cdots, \alpha_n$. To date, however, only a small number of examples of these grammars have been studied.

10.2.2   Three-dimensional shape

This is what we really need to make a stochastic theory of facial shapes. Here is a list of problems which have to be addressed:

1. For parametrized surfaces, analogs of snakes can certainly be defined using energy integrals motivated by continuum mechanics. One can use these in variational problems or to define probabilities in finite-dimensional discrete approximations. Presumably, the theory of Gaussian random fields can be used to make these into probability models in the continuum limit.

2. For unparameterized surfaces, however, it seems harder to carry out this construction. One would like a probability model of the form $p(S) = \frac{1}{Z}e^{-E(S)}$, $E(S) = \int \int (\kappa_1^2 + \kappa_2^2)dA_S$, where κ_i are the principal curvatures, and dA_S is the surface area of S. Unlike the case of curves, there is no simple analog of arc-length parameterization for surfaces.

3. What does the medial 'axis' of the face look like, and how well does it reflect the perceptual structures in the face? There should be prominent sheets in the symmetry plane of the nose and protruding toward the brow, but this has not been computed to our knowledge.

4. The medial 'axis' for 3D shapes is itself a surface, as mentioned above. This seems well suited to a compact description of sheet-like parts of a shape. But for generalized cylinders (cylinders whose axis is allowed to twist and turn, and whose cross-section may vary slowly), it gives a complex set of internal plates rather than a simple space curve tracing the core of the cylinder. How should such a curve be found? The issue is: is there is a mathematical way of saying that a cow has four legs?[1]

5. The 'grammar' by which shapes in three dimensions are assembled into more complex shapes is *much* more complicated than in two dimensions. The mess that one finds in CAD/CAM programs for 3D testifies to this complexity. This is a reflection of the fact that the topology of 3D is much more complicated than that of 2D. The grammar of the face should include all the named parts of the face. We expect that this decomposition should lead to a much more realistic synthesis of faces and to the best 3D stochastic model.

6. If we use a lighting model as discussed above, e.g., with Lambertian and specular terms, one can generate 2D images from these 3D shapes. An interesting issue is how to compute the 3D descriptor from the 2D image. For example, it often happens that the image intensity has a large gradient near the ridges of the 3D shape because of the rapid variation of the normal plane. How robust such algorithms are does not seen to have been studied on realistic images or in a stochastic context.

---

[1] We quote M. Gromov.

References

Y. Amit 1994, "A non-linear variational problem for image matching," *SIAM J. Sci. Comp.,* vol. 15, 207–224.

Y. Amit, U. Grenander and M. Piccioni, 1991, "Structural image restoration through deformable templates," *J. Amer. Stat. Assoc.,* vol. 86, 376–387.

Y. Amit, D. Geman and B. Jedynak, 1998, " Efficient focusing and face detection," in *Face Recognition: From Theory to Applications,* H. Wechsler and J. Phillips, eds., Springer-Verlag

Y. Amit and D. Geman, 1999, "A computational model for visual selection, neural computation," to appear in *Neural Computation.*

J. Atick, P. Griffin and N. Redlich, 1996, "Statistical approach to shape from shading," *Neural Computation,* vol. 8, 1321–1340.

F. Attneave, 1954, "Some informational aspects of visual perception," *Psychophys. Rev.,* vol. 61, 183–193.

R. Bajcsy and S. Kovacic, 1989, "Multiresolution elastic matching," in *Comp Vision: Graphics Image Proc.,* vol. 46, 1–21.

R. Bajcsy, R. Lieberson and M. Reivich, 1983, "A computerized system for elastic matching of deformed radiographic images to idealized atlas images," *J. Comp. Assisted Tomography,* vol. 5, 618–625.

H. Barlow, 1961, "Possible principles underlying the transformation of sensory messages," in *Sensory Communication,* W. Rosenblith, ed., MIT Press.

P. Belhumeur, J. Hespanha, and D. Kriegman, 1996, "Eigenfaces vs. fisher-faces: recognition using class specific linear projection," *IEEE Trans. Pattern Anal. Mach. Intell.,* 711–720.

P. Belhumeur, D. Kriegman and A. Yuille, 1997 and 1998, "The generalized bas relief ambiguity," in *Proc. of Comp. Vis. and Patt. Recog. (CVPR '97)*, Puerto-Rico, 1060–1066; expanded version in *Int. J. of Comp. Vis.*, to appear.

D. Beymer and T. Poggio, 1996, "Image representations for visual learning," *Science*, vol. 272, 1905–1909.

I. Biederman, 1987, "Recognition by components: a theory of human image understanding," *Psychol. Rev.*, vol. 94, 115–147.

I. Biederman and P.C. Gerhadstein, 1993, "Recognizing depth-rotated objects: evidence and conditions for three-dimensional viewpoint invariance," *J. Exp. Psychol: Human Percep. Perform.*, vol. 19, 1162–1182.

E. Bienenstock and R. Doursat, 1989, "Elastic matching and pattern recognition," in *Neural Networks*, L. Personnaz and G. Dreyfus, eds., IDSET Press, 472–482.

E. Bienenstock and R. Doursat, 1991, "Issues of representation in neural networks," in *Representations of Vision*, A. Gorea, ed., Cambridge University Press, 47–67.

E. Bienenstock and R. Doursat, 1994, "A shape-recognition model using dynamical links," *Network*, vol. 5, 241–258.

E. Bienenstock, S. Geman and D. Potter, 1997, "Compositionality, MDL priors and object recognition," in *Advances in Neural Information Processing Systems*, M. Mozer, M. Jordan and T. Petschel, eds., MIT Press, 838.

M. Black and Y. Yacoob, 1995, "Tracking and recognizing rigid and non-rigid facial motions using local parametric models of image motion," in *Proc. Int. Conf. on Comp. Vis.*, 374–381.

T. Booth and R. Thompson, 1973, "Applying probability measures to abstract languages," *IEEE Trans. Comp.*, vol. C-22, 442–450.

C. Bregler and S. Omohundro, 1995, "Nonlinear manifold learning for visual speech recognition," in *Proc. IEEE Int. Conf. on Comp. Vis.*, 494–499.

L. Breiman, J. Freidman, R. Olshen and C. Stone, 1984, *Classification and Regression Trees*, Wadsworth Int. Group, Belmont, CA.

C. Broit, 1981, "Optimal Registration of Deformed Images," PhD thesis, University of Pennsylvania.

J. W. Bruce and P. J. Giblin, 1992, *Curves and Singularities*, Cambridge University Press, 2nd edition.

J. W. Bruce, P. J. Giblin and C. G. Gibson, 1985, "Symmetry sets," in *Proc. Royal Soc. Edinburgh*, 101A, 163–186.

J. W. Bruce, P. J. Giblin and F. Tari, 1995, "Families of surfaces: height functions, Gauss maps and duals," in *Real and Complex Singularities,* W. L. Marar, ed., Pitman Research Notes in Mathematics, vol. 333, 148–178.

J. W. Bruce, P. J. Giblin and F. Tari, 1996a, "Parabolic curves of evolving surfaces," *Int. J. Comp. Vis.,* vol. 17, 291–306.

J. W. Bruce, P. J. Giblin and F. Tari, 1996b, "Ridges, crests and sub-parabolic lines of evolving surfaces," *Int. J. Comp. Vis.,* vol. 18, 195–210.

J. W. Bruce, P. J. Giblin and F. Tari, 1999, "Families of surfaces: focal sets, ridges and umbilics," *Math. Proc. Camb. Phil. Soc.,* vol. 125, 243–268.

H. Buelthoff and S. Edelman, 1992, "Psychophysical support for a 2-D view interpolation theory of object recognition," in *Proc. Nat'l. Acad. Sci. USA,* vol. 1992, 60–64.

J. Buhmann, J. Lange and C. von der Malsburg, 1989, "Distortion invariant object recognition by matching hierarchical components," *Int. Joint Conf. on Neural Networks,* IEEE, 155–159.

D. J. Burr, 1981, "A dynamic model of image registration," *Comp. Graph. Image Proc.,* vol. 15, 102–112.

L. Calabi and W. E. Harnett, 1966, "Shape recognition, prairie fires, convex deficiencies and skeletons." Parke Mathematical Laboratories, Inc., Scientific Report #1, Carlisle, MA.

P. Cavanagh, 1991, "What's up in top-down processing," in *Representations of Vision,* A. Gorea, Y. Fregnac, Z. Kapoula, and J. Findlay, eds., Cambridge University Press.

R. Chellappa, C. Wilson and S. Sirohey, 1995, "Human and machine recognition of faces: A survey," in *Proc. IEEE,* vol. 83, 705–741.

C. S. Choi, T. Okazaki, H. Harashima and T. Takebe, 1990, "Basis generation and facial images using principal component analysis," Tech report IPSJ: Graphics and CAD, vol. 46, 43–50.

N. Chomsky, 1965, *Aspects of the Theory of Syntax,* MIT Press.

R. Cipolla and A. Blake, 1992, "Surface orientation and time to contact from image divergence and deformation," in *Proc. Eur. Conf. on Comp. Vis.,* 187–202.

R. Cipolla and P. Giblin, 1999, *Dynamic Shape of Curves and Surfaces,* Cambridge University Press, to appear.

T. Cootes, C. Taylor, A. Lanitis, D. Cooper and J. Graham, 1993, "Building and using flexible models incorporating grey level information," in *Proc. 4th ICCV.*

T. Cootes and C. Taylor, 1992, "Active shape models—smart snakes," in *Proc. Brit. Mach. Vis. Conf.*

G. Cottrell and M. Fleming, 1990, "Categorization of faces using unsupervised feature extraction," in *Proc. Int. Joint Conf. Neural Networks,* vol. 2, 65–70.

T. Cover and J. Thomas, 1991, *Elements of Information Theory,* Wiley.

I. Craw and P. Cameron, 1991, "Parameterising images for recognition and reconstruction," in *Proc. Brit. Mach. Vis. Conf.,* P. Mowforth, ed., Springer-Verlag, 489–507.

I. Craw and P. Cameron, 1992, "Face Recognition by Computer," in *Proc. Brit. Mach. Vis. Conf.,* D. Hogg and R. Boyle, eds., Springer-Verlag.

R. Duda and P. Hart, 1973, *Pattern Classification and Scene Analysis,* Wiley.

P. Dupuis, U. Grenander and M. Miller, 1998, "Variational problems on flows of diffeomorphisms for image matching," *Q. Appl. Math.,* vol. 56, 587–600.

R. Durbin, R. Szeliski and A. Yuille, 1989, "An analysis of the elastic net approach to the travelling salesman problem," in *Neural Comp.,* vol. 1, 348–358.

David Eberly, 1996, *Ridges in Image and Data Analysis,* Kluwer, Boston, MA.

S. Edelman and H. Buelthoff, 1992, "Orientation dependence in the recognition of familiar and novel views of 3-D objects," *Vis. Res.,* vol. 32, 2385–2400.

P. Ekman, 1972, *Emotion in the Human Face,* Cambridge University Press.

R. Epstein, P. Hallinan and A. Yuille, 1995, "5 eigenimages suffice: an empirical investigation of low-dimensional lighting," in *Proc. IEEE Wkshop. on Physics-based Mod. in Comp. Vis.,* 108–116.

R. Epstein, A. Yuille and P. Belhumeur, 1996, "Learning and recognizing objects using illumination," in *Obj. Repr. Wkshop, Eur. Conf. Comp. Vis.,* Cambridge, England, J. Ponce, A. Zisserman, and Mitterbert, eds., Springer-Verlag, 179–200.

I. Essa, 1995, "Analysis, Interpretation, and Synthesis of Facial Expressions," PhD thesis, Media Arts and Science, School of Architecture, MIT.

K. Etemad and R. Chellappa, 1997, "Discriminant analysis for recognition of human faces," *J. Opt. Soc. of Amer.,* vol. 14, 1724–1733.

M. Fischler and R. Elschlager, 1973, "The representation and matching of pictorial structures," in *IEEE Trans. Comp.,* vol. C-22, 67–92.

R. A. Fisher, 1936, "The use of multiple measures in taxonomic problems," *Annals of Eugenics,* vol. 7, 179–188.

C.-S. Fuh, 1992, "Visual motion analysis: estimating and interpreting displacement fields," PhD thesis, Division of Applied Sciences, Harvard University.

I. Gauthier and M. J. Tarr, 1997, "Becoming a Greeble expert: exploring mechanisms for face recognition," *Vis. Res.* vol. 37, 1673–1682.

D. Geman, 1990, *Random Fields and Inverse Problems in Imaging,* Lecture Notes in Mathematics 1427, Springer-Verlag.

A. Georghiades, D. Kriegman and P. Belhumeur, 1998, "Illumination cones for recognition under variable lighting: faces," in *Proc. IEEE Conf. on Comp. Vis. and Patt. Recog.,* 52–58.

P. J. Giblin and S. A. Brassett, 1985, "Local symmetry of plane curves," *Amer. Math. Monthly* vol. 92, 689–707.

A. J. Goldstein, L. D. Harmon and A. B. Lesk, 1971, "Identification of human faces," *Proc. IEEE,* vol. 59, 748–760.

M. Golubitsky and V. Guillemin, 1973, *Stable Mappings and Their Singularities,* Graduate Texts in Mathematics, Springer-Verlag.

G. Gordon, 1991, "Face recognition from depth and curvature," PhD thesis, Division of Applied Math., Harvard University.

U. Grenander, 1976–1981, *Lectures in Pattern Theory* (3 volumes), Springer-Verlag.

U. Grenander, Y. S. Chow and D. Keenan, 1991, *HANDS: A pattern-theoretic study of biological shapes,* Springer-Verlag.

U. Grenander, 1993, *General Pattern Theory,* Oxford University Press.

W. E. Grimson, 1990, *Object Recognition by Computer,* MIT Press.

M. Gurtin, 1981, *An Introduction to Continuum Mechanics,* Academic Press.

J. Haddon and D. Forsyth, 1998, "Shading primitives: finding folds and Shallow grooves," in *Proc. Int. Conf. on Comp. Vis.,* Bombay, India, 236–241.

G. Hager and P. Belhumeur, 1996, "Real-time tracking of image regions with changes in geometry and illumination," in *Proc. IEEE Conf. on Comp. Vis. and Patt. Recog.,* 403–410.

N. Haig, 1984, "The effect of feature displacement on face recognition," *Perception,* vol. 13, 505–512.

P. Hallinan, 1991, "Recognizing human eyes," in *SPIE Proc. on Geom Methods in Comp. Vis.,* vol. 1570, 214–226.

P. Hallinan, 1994, "A low-dimensional lighting representation of human faces under arbitrary lighting conditions," in *Proc. IEEE Conf. on Comp. Vis. and Patt. Recog.,* IEEE Press, 995–999.

P. Hallinan, 1995, "A deformable model for the recognition of human faces under arbitrary illumination," PhD thesis, Division of Applied Sciences, Harvard University.

K. Hayakawa, 1994, "Photometric stereo under a light source with arbitrary motion," *J. Opt. Soc. Amer. A,* vol. 11, 3079–3089.

J. Hertz, A. Krogh and R. Palmer, 1991, *Introduction to the Theory of Neural Computation,* Addison-Wesley.

P. Hoel, S. Port and C. Stone, 1971, *Introduction to Stochastic Processes,* Houghton-Mifflin.

D. Hoffman and W. Richards, 1983, "Parts of recognition." MIT Artificial Intelligence Laboratory Memo #732.

B. Horn and M. Brooks, 1989, editors, *Shape from Shading,* MIT Press.

B. Horn and M. Brooks, 1981, "Determining optical flow," *Art. Int.,* vol. 17, 185–203.

P. Huber, 1981, *Robust Statistics,* Wiley and Sons.

M. Isard and A. Blake, 1996, "Contour tracking by stochastic propagation of conditional density," in *Proc. Eur. Conf. Comp. Vis.,* 343–356.

L. Iverson and S. Zucker, 1995, "Logical/linear operators for image curves," *IEEE Trans. Patt. Anal. and Mach. Intell.,* vol. 17, 982–996.

M. Jones and T. Poggio, 1998, "Multidimensional morphable models," in *Proc. Int. Conf. Comp. Vis.,* Bombay, India, 683–688.

T. Kanade, 1973, "Picture processing system by computer and recognition of human faces," PhD thesis, Dept. of Information Science, Kyoto University, Kyoto, Japan.

T. Kanade, 1977, *Computer Recognition of Human Faces,* Birkhäuser.

M. Kass, A. Witkin and D. Terzopoulos, 1987, "Snakes: active contour models," *Int. J. Comp. Vis.,* vol. 1, 321–331.

M. Kirby and L. Sirovich, 1990, "Application of Karhunen-Loeve procedure for the characterization of human faces," *IEEE Trans. Patt. Anal. and Mach. Intell.,* vol. 12, 103–108.

J. Koenderink, 1990, *Solid Shape,* MIT Press.

J. Koenderink and A. van Doorn, 1980, "Photometric invariants related to Solid shape," *Opt. Acta,* vol. 27, 981-1006.

J. Koenderink and A. van Doorn, 1982, "The shape of smooth objects and the way contours end," *Perception,* vol. 11, 129–137. D. Kriegman and P. Belhumeur, 1998, "What shadows reveal about object structure," in *Eur. Conf. on Comp. Vis.,* Springer-Verlag, 399–414.

M. Lades, 1994, "Invariant object recognition with dynamical links, robust to variations in illumination," PhD thesis, Univ. Bochum, Germany.

M. Lades, J. Vorbruggen, J. Buhmann, J. Lange, C. V. D. Malsburg and R. Wurtz, 1993, "Distortion invariant object recognition in dynamic link architecture," *IEEE Trans. Comp.,* vol. 42, 300–311.

Ch. Lantuéjoul and F. Maisonneuve, 1984, "Geodesic methods in image analysis," *Pattern Recognition,* vol. 17, 117–187.

M. Leyton, 1987, "Symmetry-curvature duality," *Comp. Vis., Graphics and Image Processing,* vol. 38, 327–341.

Z. Liu and D. Kersten, 1998, "2D observers for human 3D object recognition," *Vis. Res.,* vol. 38, 2507–2519.

D. Lowe, 1985, *Perceptual Organization and Visual Recognition,* Kluwer.

C. von der Malsburg, 1981 and 1994, "The correlation theory of brain function," internal report; reprinted in *Models of Neural Networks II,* Domany, van Hemmen, Schulten, eds., Springer-Verlag.

J. E. Marsden and T. J. Hughes, 1983, *Mathematical Foundations of Elasticity Theory,* Dover.

D. Marr and K. Nishihara, 1978, "Representation and recognition of the Spatial organization of three-dimensional shapes," in *Proc. Royal Soc.,* London, vol. 200, 269–294.

L. Matejic, 1997, "Group cascades for representing biological variability," PhD thesis, Division of Applied Mathematics, Brown University.

R. Manmatha, 1994, "A Framework for recovering affine transforms using points, lines, or image brightness," in *Proc. Comp. Vis. and Patt. Recog.,* IEEE Press, 141–146.

M. Miller, A. Banerjee, G. Christensen, S. Joshi, N. Kaneja, U. Grenander and L. Matejic, 1997, "Statistical methods in computational anatomy," *Stat. Meth. in Med. Res.,* vol. 6, 267–299.

C. Moore and P. Cavanagh, 1998, "Recovery of 3D volume from 2-tone images of novel objects," *Cognition,* vol. 67, 45–71.

Y. Moses, Y. Adini and S. Ullman, 1994, "Face recognition: the problem of compensating for illumination changes," in *Proc. Eur. Conf. Comp. Vis.,* 286–296.

D. Mumford, 1991a, "On the computational architecture of the neocortex, I: The role of the thalamo-cortical loop," *Biol. Cybernetics,* vol. 65, 135–145 and "On the computational architecture of the neocortex, II: The role of cortico-cortical loops," *Biol. Cybernetics,* vol. 66, 241–251.

D. Mumford, 1991b, "Parametrizing exemplars of categories," *J. Cog. Neurosci.,* vol. 3, 87–88.

D. Mumford, 1992, "Pattern theory: a unifying perspective," in *Proc. 1st Eur. Cong. of Math.,* Birkhäuser; revised version in *Perception as Bayesian Inference,* D. Knill and W. Richards, eds., Cambridge University Press, 1996, 25–62.

D. Mumford, 1993, "Elastica and computer vision," in *Algebraic Geometry and Its Applications,* C. Bajaj, ed., Springer-Verlag, 507–518.

J. Mundy and A. Zisserman, 1992, *Geometric Invariants in Computer Vision,* MIT Press.

H. Murase and S. Nayar, 1995, "Visual learning and recognition of 3-D objects from appearance," *Int. J. Comp. Vis.,* vol. 14, 5–24.

S. Nayar, K. Ikeuchi and T. Kanade, 1991, "Surface reflections: physical and geometric perspectives," in *IEEE Trans. on Patt. Anal. and Mach. Intell.,* vol. 13, 611–634.

B. O'Neill, 1966, 1997, *Elementary Differential Geometry,* Academic Press 1966, 2nd edition 1997.

D. Osherson and S. Weinstein, 1984, "Formal learning theory," in *Handbook of Cognitive Psychology,* M. Gazzaniga, ed., Plenum Press, 275–292.

J. Pearl, 1988, *Probabilistic Reasoning in Intelligent Systems,* Morgan-Kaufman.

A. Pentland, 1992, "Finding the illuminant direction," *J. Opt. Soc. Amer. A,* vol. 4, 448–455.

T. Poggio and S. Edelman, 1990, "A network that learns to recognize 3-D objects," *Nature,* vol. 343, 263–266.

I. R. Porteous, 1994, *Geometric Differentiation,* Cambridge University Press.

D. Potter, 1998, "Compositional pattern recognition," PhD thesis, Division of

Applied Mathematics, Brown University.

L. Rabiner, 1990, "A tutorial on hidden Markov models and selected applications to speech processing," in *Readings in Speech Recognition,* A. Waibel and K.-F. Lee, eds., Morgan-Kaufmann.

L. Rabiner and B. Huang, 1993, *Fundamentals of Speech Processing,* Prentice-Hall.

B. Ripley and N. Hjort, 1995, *Pattern Recognition and Neural Networks,* Cambridge University Press.

J. Rissanen, 1989, *Stochastic Complexity in Statistical Inquiry,* World Scientific.

S. Schwartz and R. Bajcsy, 1985, "Three-dimensional elastic matching of ventricles," in *Comp. Graph. and Image Proc.*

J. Serra, 1982, *Image Analysis and Mathematical Morphology,* Academic Press.

A. Shashua, 1992, "Geometry and photometry in 3D visual recognition," PhD thesis, Department of Psychology, MIT.

W. Silver, 1980, "Determining shape and reflectance using multiple images," MA thesis, Department of Electrical Engineering and Computer Science, MIT.

L. Sirovich and M. Kirby, 1987, "Low-dimensional procedure for the characterization of human faces," *J. Opt. Soc. Amer. A,* vol. 4, 519–524.

M. Tarr and S. Pinker, 1989, "Mental rotation and orientation dependence in shape recognition," *Cogn. Psych.,* vol. 21, 233–282.

B. S. Tjan and G. E. Legge, 1998, "The viewpoint complexity of an object-recognition task," *Vis. Res.,* vol. 38, 2335–2350.

A. Trouve, 1999, "Diffeomorphism groups and pattern matching," *Q. J. Appl. Math.,* to appear.

M. Turk and A. Pentland, 1991, "Eigenfaces for recognition," *J. Cog. Neurosci.,* vol. 3, 71–86.

S. Ullman, 1996, *High Level Vision,* MIT Press.

S. Ullman and R. Basri, 1991, "Recognition by linear combination of models," in *IEEE Trans. Patt. Anal. Mach. Intell.,* vol. 13, 992–1006.

L. Vincent, 1991, "Efficient computation of various types of skeletons," in *Proc. SPIE Conf., Medical Imaging V,* San Jose, California.

K. Waters and D. Terzopoulos, 1990, "A physical model of facial tissue and muscle articulation," in *Proc. 1st Conf. Vis. Biom. Comp.,* Atlanta, Georgia.

K. Waters and D. Terzopoulos, 1992, "The computer synthesis of expressive faces," *Phil. Trans. R. Soc. Lond. B,* vol. 335, 87–93.

B. Widrow, 1973, "The rubber mask technique," *Patt. Recog.,* vol. 5, 175–211.

L. Wiskott and C. von der Malsburg, 1993, "A neural system for the Recognition of partially occluded objects in cluttered scenes," *Int. J. Patt. Recog. and Art. Intell.,* vol. 7, 935–948.

L. Wiskott, 1995, "Labelled Graphs and Dynamic Link Matching for Face Recognition and Scene Analysis," PhD thesis, Univ. of Frankfurt.

R. Woodham, 1981, "Analysing images of curved surfaces," *Art. Intell.,* vol. 17, 117–140.

A. L. Yuille, 1988. "The creation of structure in dynamic shape," in *Proc. 2nd Int. Conf. Comp. Vis.* Tampa, Florida, 685–689.

A. L. Yuille, 1989, "Zero crossings on lines of curvature," *Comp. Vis., Graph. and Im. Proc.,* vol. 45, 68–87.

A. L. Yuille and M. Leyton, 1987, "Symmetry duality theorems for 3-D objects," in *Proc. Int. Conf. Comp. Vis.,* London, England.

A. L. Yuille and M. Leyton, 1990, "Symmetry duality theorems for 3-D objects," *Comp. Vis., Graph. and Im. Proc.,* vol. 52, 124–140.

A. L. Yuille, D. Cohen and P. Hallinan, 1989 and 1992, "Feature extraction from faces using deformable templates," in *Proc. Comp. Vis. and Patt. Recog.,* 104–109, IEEE Press; complete version in *Int. J. Comp. Vis.,* vol. 8, 99–111, 1992.

A. L. Yuille and P. Hallinan, 1992, "Deformable templates," in *Active Vision,* A. Blake and A. Yuille, eds., MIT Press.

A. L. Yuille, M. Ferraro, T. Zhang, 1998, *Image Warping for Shape Recovery and Recognition: Computer Vision and Image Understanding,* vol. 72, no. 3, 351–359.

A. L. Yuille and D. Snow, 1997, "Shape and albedo from multiple images using integrability," in *Proc. Comp. Vis. and Patt. Recog.,* Puerto-Rico, IEEE Press, 158–164.

J. Zhang, Y. Yan and M. Lades, 1997, "Face recognition: eigenface, elastic matching, and neural nets," in *Proc. IEEE,* vol. 85, 1423–1435.

Q. Zheng and R. Chellapa, 1991, "Estimation of illumination direction, albedo and shape from shading," in *Proc. Conf. Comp. Vis. and Patt. Recog.,* IEEE Press, 540–545.

S. C. Zhu, Y. Wu and D. Mumford, 1997, "Minimax entropy principle and its applications to texture modeling," *Neural Comp.,* vol. 9.

S. C. Zhu, 1999a, "Stochastic jump-diffusion process for computing medial axes in Markov random fields, in *Proc. Conf. Comp. Vis. and Patt. Recog.,* Santa Barbara CA, June 1998, IEEE Press and *IEEE Trans. Patt. Anal. and Mach. Intell.,* to appear in 1999.

S. C. Zhu, 1999b, "Embedding gestalt laws in Markov random fields," in *Wkshop on Percep. Organiz. in Comp. Vis.,* Santa Barbara CA, IEEE Press and *IEEE Trans. Patt. Anal. and Mach. Intell.,* to appear in 1999.

Index

Printed in the United States
by Baker & Taylor Publisher Services